"IF TODAY YOU HEAR HIS VOICE"

If Today You Hear His Voice
Reflections on the Sunday Second Readings

Fr. Albert Cylwicki, CSB

ALBA · HOUSE NEW · YORK

SOCIETY OF ST. PAUL, 2187 VICTORY BLVD., STATEN ISLAND, NEW YORK 10314

The majority of Scripture texts used in this work are taken from the *New American Bible*, copyright © 1970, by the Confraternity of Christian Doctrine, Washington, D.C., and are used by license of copyright owner. All rights reserved.

Some quotations are used from *The Jerome Biblical Commentary*, ed., by Brown, Fitzmyer, Murphy, © 1968. Reprinted by permission of Prentice-Hall, Inc., Englewood Cliffs, N.J.

The use of the words from "Remember Me" is with permission by the songwriter, Joe Wise.

Library of Congress Cataloging in Publication Data

Cylwicki, Albert.
  If today you hear His voice.

  Includes index.
  1. Church year meditations. I. Title.
BX2170.C55C93   242'.3   81-10966
ISBN 0-8189-0418-6   AACR2

Nihil Obstat:
M.C. Notzon
Censor deputatus

Imprimi potest:
†John L. Morkovsky
Bishop of Galveston-Houston
April 14, 1981

The Nihil Obstat and Imprimatur are
a declaration that a book or pamphlet is considered
to be free from doctrinal or moral error. It is not implied
that those who have granted the Nihil Obstat and
Imprimatur agree with the contents,
opinions or statements expressed.

Designed, printed and bound in the United States of
America by the Fathers and Brothers of the
Society of St. Paul, 2187 Victory Boulevard,
Staten Island, New York 10314, as part of their
communications apostolate.

---

1 2 3 4 5 6 7 8 9 (Current Printing: first digit).

© *Copyright 1981 by the Society of St. Paul*

CONTENTS

Section One

Procrastination	Page 3
Profiles in Scripture	5
Patience	7
Superman	9
Scrooge	11
Family Life	13
The Best	15
Universality	17
Amazing Grace	19
Bite the Bullet	21
Love Poured Out	23
Light In The Lord	25
Brought Back	27
He Emptied Himself	29
Death To Life	31
New Birth	33
Beyond All Price	35
Stray Sheep	37
Your Own Best Friend	39
Ever Ready	41
The Great Hope	43
Rejoicing	45
In The Holy Spirit	47
Fellowship	49
One Bread, One Body	51
Dedication	53
Called	55
The Kansas Model	57
Jane Addams	59
Power of Persuasion	61
Heaven	63

All Things Are Yours	65
Judgment	67
Pioneers and Settlers	69
Abraham's Faith	71
Lawrence of Arabia	73
Operation SAMM	75
New Life	77
Life by the Spirit	79
Creation's Destiny	81
Praying in the Spirit	83
Eugene O'Neill	85
Vietnam War Vet	87
Revitalization Corps	89
Irrevocable	91
Butterflies	93
Offer Your Bodies	95
The Tramp	97
We are the Lord's	99
Bicentennial Saint	101
Unity In Space	103
Transcendental Meditation	105
Coping	107
Something Beautiful	109
Beverly Sills	111
Stevie Wonder	113
Death and Beyond	115
Sudden Death	117
King Faisal	119

Section Two

Richly Endowed	123
New Heavens	125
Rejoice Always	127
Believing and Obeying	129

Christmas with Mame	131
Water	133
Top Priorities	135
Christ Crucified	137
God's Handiwork	139
Obedience	141
Raised up with Christ	143
Faith Conquers	145
Forgiveness	147
Becoming	149
Show Me	151
God Is Love	153
Seeing God	155
Adoption	157
Blood	159
The Body	161
Time Is Short	163
Marriage and Celibacy	165
All Things	167
The Glory of God	169
Yes	171
Recommendations	173
Struck Down, But Not Destroyed	175
Courage	177
We Walk By Faith	179
Love Impels Us	181
Enriching Others	183
Thorns in the Flesh	185
Our Deepest Needs	187
Brought Near	189
Bearing Lovingly	191
A Fresh Way	193
The Way of Love	195
Present Opportunities	197

Married Love	199
God's Word	201
Discrimination	203
Faith and Works	205
Sowing	207
Riches	209
Leadership and Suffering	211
Influential Books	213
He's Been There	215
Priests	217
Jesus Saves	219
Die Once	221
Masterpiece	223
Liberator	225

Section Three

Crisis	229
Things That Really Matter	231
The Circus	233
The Hunchback	235
Reflection of the Father's Glory	237
Jesus Is Lord	239
Restoration	241
One Step Away	243
A New Creature	245
Reaching the Goal	247
New Unleavened Bread	249
Aslan The Lion	251
You're a Good Man, Jesus Christ	253
Winners	255
Renaissance Center	257
City Lights	259
Come	261
Oh, God	263

Handing Over	265
Variety of Gifts	267
One Body	269
Gandhi and Paul on Love	271
Roots	273
First Fruits	275
The Renaissance Man	277
Victory	279
Values	281
He Set Me Apart	283
Alexander the Great	285
Unity	287
Freedom Festival	289
The Marks of Jesus	291
Image of the Invisible	293
Joy in Suffering	295
Baptism of the Holy Spirit	297
Things Above	299
Faith in the Unseen	301
Perseverance	303
Discipline	305
Honor Society	307
Amnesty	309
Sin Remembered	311
All Men	313
Fight the Good Fight	315
Enthusiasm	317
No Chaining the Word	319
Uses of Scripture	321
Fighting and Finishing	323
Doomsday	325
Steadfast Endurance	327
Work	329
What He Has Done	331

THE LITURGICAL YEAR

	A	B	C
ADVENT 1	Rm 13:11-14 Procrastination, p. 3	1 Cor 1:3-9 Richly Endowed, p. 123	1 Th 3:12-4:2 Crisis, p. 229
ADVENT 2	Rm 15:4-9 Profiles in Scripture, p. 5	2 P 3:8-14 New Heavens, p. 125	Ph 1:4-6, 8-11 Things That Really Matter, p. 231
ADVENT 3	Jm 5:7-10 Patience, p. 7	1 Th 5:16-24 Rejoice Always, p. 127	Ph 4:4-7 The Circus, p. 233
ADVENT 4	Rm 1:1-7 Superman, p. 9	Rm 16:25-27 Believing and Obeying, p. 129	Heb 10:5-10 The Hunchback, p. 235
CHRISTMAS	Tt 2:11-14 Scrooge, p. 11	Tt 3:4-7 Christmas With Mame p. 131	Heb 1:1-6 Reflection of the Father's Glory, p. 237
HOLY FAMILY	Col 3:12-21 Family Life, p. 13		
JAN 1	Gal 4:4-7 The Best, p. 15		
EPIPHANY	Ep 3:2-6 Universality, p. 17		
LENT 1	Rm 5:12-19 Amazing Grace, p. 19	1 P 3:18-22 Water, p. 133	Rm 10:8-13 Jesus is Lord, p. 239
LENT 2	2 Tm 1:8-10 Bite the Bullet, p. 21	Rm 8:31-34 Top Priorities, p. 135	Ph 3:17-4:1 Restoration, p. 241
LENT 3	Rm 5:1-8 Love Poured Out, p. 23	1 Cor 1:22-25 Christ Crucified, p. 137	1 Cor 10:1-12 One Step Away, p. 243
LENT 4	Ep 5:8-14 Light in the Lord, p. 25	Ep 2:4-10 God's Handiwork, p. 139	2 Cor 5:17-21 A New Creation, p. 245
LENT 5	Rm 8:8-11 Brought Back, p. 27	Heb 5:7-9 Obedience, p. 141	Ph 3:8-14 Reaching the Goal, p. 247
PASSION SUN	Ph 2:6-11 He Emptied Himself, p. 29		
EASTER 1	Rm 6:3-11 Death to Life, p. 31	Col 3:1-4 Raised Up With Christ, p. 143	1 Cor 5:6-8 New Unleavened Bread, p. 249
EASTER 2	1 P 1:3-9 New Birth, p. 33	1 Jn 5:1-6 Faith Conquers, p. 145	Rv 1:9-19 Aslan the Lion, p. 251
EASTER 3	1 P 1:17-21 Beyond All Price, p. 35	1 Jn 2:1-5 Forgiveness, p. 147	Rv 5:11-14 You're a Good Man, Jesus Christ, p. 253
EASTER 4	1 P 2:20-25 Stray Sheep, p. 37	1 Jn 3:1-2 Becoming, p. 149	Rv 7:9, 14-17 Winners, p. 255

EASTER 5	1 P 2:4-9 Your Own Best Friend, p. 39	1 Jn 3:18-24 Show Me, p. 151	Rv 21:1-5 Renaissance Center, p. 257
EASTER 6	1 P 3:15-18 Ever Ready, p. 41	1 Jn 4:7-10 God is Love, p. 153	Rv 21:10-14, 22-23 City Lights, p. 259
ASCENSION	Ep 1:17-23 The Great Hope, p. 43		
EASTER 7	1 P 4:13-16 Rejoicing, p. 45	1 Jn 4:11-16 Seeing God, p. 155	Rv 22:12-20 Come, p. 261
PENTECOST	1 Cor 12:3-13 In the Holy Spirit, 47		
TRINITY	2 Cor 13:11-13 Fellowship, p. 49	Rm 8:14-17 Adoption, p. 157	Rm 5:1-5 Oh God, p. 263
CORPUS CHRISTI	1 Cor 10:16-17 One Bread, One Body, p. 51	Heb 9:11-15 Blood, p. 159	1 Cor 11:23-26 Handing Over, p. 265
SUNDAY 1 (BAPTISM)	Ac 10:34-38 Dedication, p. 53		
SUNDAY 2	1 Cor 1:1-3 Called, p. 55	1 Cor 6:13-15, 17-20 The Body, p. 161	1 Cor 12:4-11 Variety of Gifts, p. 267
SUNDAY 3	1 Cor 1:10-13, 17 The Kansas Model, p. 57	1 Cor 7:29-31 Time is Short, p. 163	1 Cor 12:12-30 One Body, p. 269
SUNDAY 4	1 Cor 1:26-31 Jane Addams, p. 59	1 Cor 7:32-35 Marriage and Celibacy, p. 165	1 Cor 12:31-13:13 Gandhi and Paul on Love, p. 271
SUNDAY 5	1 Cor 2:1-5 Power of Persuasion, p. 61	1 Cor 9:16-23 All Things, p. 167	1 Cor 15:1-11 Roots, p. 273
SUNDAY 6	1 Cor 2:6-10 Heaven, p. 63	1 Cor 10:31-11:1 The Glory of God, p. 169	1 Cor 15:12-20 First Fruits, p. 275
SUNDAY 7	1 Cor 3:16-23 All Things Are Yours, p. 65	2 Cor 1:18-22 Yes, p. 171	1 Cor 15:45-49 Renaissance Man, p. 277
SUNDAY 8	1 Cor 4:1-5 Judgment, p. 67	2 Cor 3:1-6 Recommendations, p. 173	1 Cor 15:54-58 Victory, p. 279
SUNDAY 9	Rm 3:21-28 Pioneers and Settlers, p. 69	2 Cor 4:6-11 Struck Down But Not Destroyed, p. 175	Gal 1:1-10 Values, p. 281
SUNDAY 10	Rm 4:18-25 Abraham's Faith, p. 71	2 Cor 4:13-5:1 Courage, p. 177	Gal 1:11-19 He Set Me Apart, p. 283
SUNDAY 11	Rm 5:6-11 Lawrence of Arabia, p. 73	2 Cor 5:6-10 We Walk by Faith, p. 179	Gal 2:16-21 Alexander the Great, p. 285
SUNDAY 12	Rm 5:12-15 Operation SAMM, p. 75	2 Cor 5:14-17 Love Impels Us, p. 181	Gal 3:26-29 Unity, p. 287
SUNDAY 13	Rm 6:3-11 New Life, p. 77	2 Cor 8:7-15 Enriching Others, p. 183	Gal 5:1, 13-18 Freedom Festival, p. 289

SUNDAY 14	Rm 8:9-13 Life by the Spirit, p. 79	2 Cor 12:7-10 Thorns in the Flesh, p. 185	Gal 6:14-18 Marks of Jesus, p. 291
SUNDAY 15	Rm 8:18-23 Creation's Destiny, p. 81	Ep 1:3-10 Our Deepest Needs, p. 187	Col 1:15-20 Image of the Invisible, p. 293
SUNDAY 16	Rm 8:26-27 Praying in the Spirit, p. 83	Ep 2:13-18 Brought Near, p. 189	Col 1:24-28 Joy in Suffering, p. 295
SUNDAY 17	Rm 8:28-30 Eugene O'Neill, p. 85	Ep 4:1-6 Bearing Lovingly, p. 191	Col 2:12-14 Baptism of the Holy Spirit, p. 297
SUNDAY 18	Rm 8:35-39 Vietnam War Vet, p. 87	Ep 4:17-24 A Fresh Way, p. 193	Col 3:1-5, 9-11 Things Above, p. 299
SUNDAY 19	Rm 9:1-5 Revitalization Corp, p. 89	Ep 4:30-5:2 The Way of Love, p. 195	Heb 11:1-2, 8-19 Faith in the Unseen, p. 301
SUNDAY 20	Rm 11:13-15, 29-32 Irrevocable, p. 91	Ep 5:15-20 Present Opportunities, p. 197	Heb 12:1-4 Perseverance, p. 303
SUNDAY 21	Rm 11:33-36 Butterflies, p. 93	Ep 5:21-32 Married Love, p. 199	Heb 12:5-13 Discipline, p. 305
SUNDAY 22	Rm 12:1-2 Offer Your Bodies, p. 95	Jm 1:17-27 God's Word, p. 201	Heb 12:18-24 Honor Society, p. 307
SUNDAY 23	Rm 13:8-10 The Tramp, p. 97	Jm 2:1-5 Discrimination, p. 203	Phm 9-10, 12-17 Amnesty, p. 309
SUNDAY 24	Rm 14:7-9 We Are the Lord's, p. 99	Jm 2:14-18 Faith and Works, p. 205	1 Tm 1:12-17 Sin Remembered, p. 311
SUNDAY 25	Ph 1:20-27 Bicentennial Saint, p. 101	Jm 3:16-4:3 Sowing, p. 207	1 Tm 2:1-8 All Men, p. 313
SUNDAY 26	Ph 2:1-11 Unity in Space, p. 103	Jm 5:1-6 Riches, p. 209	1 Tm 6:11-16 Fight the Good Fight, p. 315
SUNDAY 27	Ph 4:6-9 Transcendental Meditation, p. 105	Heb 2:9-11 Leadership and Suffering, p. 211	2 Tm 1:6-14 Enthusiasm, p. 317
SUNDAY 28	Ph 4:12-20 Coping, p. 107	Heb 4:12-13 Influential Books, p. 213	2 Tm 2:8-13 No Chaining the Word, p. 319
SUNDAY 29	1 Th 1:1-5 Something Beautiful, p. 109	Heb 4:14-16 He's Been There, p. 215	2 Tm 3:14-4:2 Uses of Scripture, p. 321
SUNDAY 30	1 Th 1:5-10 Beverly Sills, p. 111	Heb 5:1-6 Priests, p. 217	2 Tm 4:6-8, 16-18 Fighting and Finishing, p. 323
SUNDAY 31	1 Th 2:7-13 Stevie Wonder, p. 113	Heb 7:23-28 Jesus Saves, p. 219	2 Th 1:11-2:2 Doomsday, p. 325

SUNDAY 32	1 Th 4:13-18 Death and Beyond, p. 115	Heb 9:24-28 Die Once, p. 221	2 Th 2:16-3:5 Steadfast Endurance, p. 327
SUNDAY 33	1 Th 5:1-6 Sudden Death, p. 117	Heb 10:11-18 Masterpiece, p. 223	2 Th 3:7-12 Work, p. 329
SUNDAY 34	1 Cor 15:20-28 King Faisal, p. 119	Rv 1:5-8 Liberator, p. 225	Col 1:12-20 What He Has Done, p. 331

INTRODUCTION

For almost one hundred years, the Church has been blessed by a magnificent resurgence in scripture studies. From the end of the 19th century until today, there has been a steady flow between the abstract research of the scholars and the popular writing which applies that scholarship to the concrete circumstances of contemporary life of the average Christian. There will always be a need to connect scholarly exegesis with the moment-to-moment struggle of the average Christian. In his book, *If Today You Hear His Voice*, Father Al Cylwicki has endeavored to build another bridge between abstract research and the concrete circumstances in contemporary living of the average Christian. In my opinion, this collection of one hundred and sixty-three reflections on Sacred Scripture achieves that end.

Each introductory example immediately draws the attention of the reader: these examples, which show how events in the lives of today's Christians have scriptural relevance, are taken from newspapers, books, movies and even television scripts. Some of the people are real, others are fictitious; and whether or not the authors of the original pieces designed them to be evidences of the Divine in the human, all are real signs that in our times God's Word is proclaimed in our midst and reveals His Activity among us.

Our Lord Himself told stories and parables, using the happenings and surroundings of His time and place to illustrate the dynamics of the Kingdom of God. Following this great model, Father Cylwicki employs this most successful means to make an impact on the modern mind, using fresh parables drawn from the world of today to illustrate the new, the thrilling reality of the coming of the Kingdom of God. His reflections are like vignettes setting off the Word of God in the concrete surroundings of today.

Whenever we recognize a quest for excellence, witness a conversion or experience a noble gesture, we can hear God saying something to us about our lives, challenging us to greatness, calling us to repentence, or inviting us to generosity. Father Al Cylwicki's book is a fresh and valuable aid in bringing about this recognition. I urge the reader to approach this book with the same freshness and seriousness with which Father Cylwicki brings it to us.

†John McCarthy
Auxiliary Bishop
Diocese of Galveston-Houston

SECTION ONE

Cycle A

First Sunday of Advent
Rm 13:11-14

Procrastination

In one of her articles, newspaper reporter Barbara McIntosh discusses the habit of putting things off, the habit of saying, "I'm going to do that, just as soon as . . . ," yet never actually doing what we promise. All of us procrastinate from time to time about certain things like waiting until the deadline before doing our income tax. But some of us are hard core procrastinators who put off just about everything.

To kick the habit of putting things off, Barbara McIntosh quotes recommendations from behavior psychologists, organization experts and time management analysts. Some of their suggestions include: setting realistic goals, ranking our tasks according to importance, dividing our tasks into smaller parts, and doing the most difficult tasks first.

St. Paul, too, has some suggestions to make about putting things off in our spiritual life. He says to the Romans: "It is now the hour for you to wake from sleep. The night is far spent; the day draws near."

It seems that Paul is seized with a sense of urgency. "It is NOW the hour," he says. Not tomorrow or next week, but NOW. Not next month or next year, but NOW. What is it that is so pressing upon him and cannot be put off? "Wake from sleep," he cries. "Cast off deeds of darkness and put on the armor of light. Live honorably as in the day."

There is no time for procrastination in the Christian life in Paul's view. Time is too precious and Christ is coming. This is the meaning of the word "Advent"—coming. Jesus is coming at the end of our life, he is coming at Christmas and he is coming now in sacrament.

We might be able to put off some of our Christmas shopping until a week before Christmas, but we cannot put off Christ's coming in the present moment. We cannot say, "Come, Lord Jesus, but not just now." "I'll stop irritating others or being a nuisance to them, just as soon as . . ." "I'll be more cheerful around the home or do my share of the work, just as soon as . . ."

The opportunity is in the here and now. Either we waste it by postponing our waking from sleep and making some conversion, or we use it by living honorably and doing some good that is asked of us. We cannot sit back and procrastinate by making excuses. "I'll quit smoking or overeating so much when my tensions ease." "I'll visit my aging parents or give my children more attention when I have more time."

The power to act is in the present moment, rich in possibilities. Either we forfeit it by attempting nothing and offering feeble excuses, or we capitalize on it by trying something and trusting in the Lord. Christ comes at Christmas when we commemorate his birth. But he also comes at every moment of time in the challenges we face, the work we do and the people we meet. It is now the hour to welcome him in these comings and not put it off until Christmas. It is now the hour to be reconciled with someone we've hurt, thank someone we've forgotten, love someone we've neglected.

As we prepare for Christ's coming in the Eucharist we might think about this quotation from *The Sanskrit*: "Yesterday is already a dream, and tomorrow is only a vision; but today, well lived, makes yesterday a dream of happiness, and every tomorrow a vision of hope."

Second Sunday of Advent
Rm 15:4-9

Profiles In Scripture

In 1957, when he was still a senator, John F. Kennedy won a Pulitzer Prize for his book *Profiles in Courage*. The book consisted of a series of biographies of noted American legislators who displayed political courage. Among these profiles we find such political figures as Daniel Webster, John Adams, Edmund Ross and Senator Taft. These and others dared to dissent from popular opinion and assert their independence in the face of opposition. Kennedy's book not only helped to free himself from the tyranny of public opinion, but also inspired many of his colleagues to be more willing to fight for the sake of moral principle, and even to face defeat in doing so.

The aim and impact of Kennedy's book gives us some inkling of the purpose and power of the Bible. St. Paul calls our attention to this in his epistle to the Romans: "Everything written before our time was written for our instruction, that we might derive hope from the lessons of patience and the words of encouragement in the Scriptures."

When we look at the Bible the way Paul does, it is anything but an old, boring book. Instead the pages dance with stories and episodes that are just as inspiring today as when they were first written down. The Scriptures record God's dealings with his people in salvation history. When we realize this we can't help but be moved by the way people responded to him.

Who cannot be aroused by the initial weakness and subsequent strength of Moses as a leader; the loyalty and valor of the ninety-year-old Eleazar when he was martyred; the courage and daring of women like Esther and Judith in the face of peril? Who cannot be influenced by the patience and perseverance of Job after he lost everything; the love and spirit of forgiveness of Joseph even after being sold into slavery by his brothers; the faith and trust of Abraham when he was asked to sacrifice his only son Isaac?

The Scriptures are filled with profiles of heroism in the midst of dangers, endurance through all sorts of trials, and tenderness in so many human relationships. These profiles were written for our instruction, as Paul says, that we too might derive courage to meet our own crises, acquire patience to cope with our own difficulties, and manifest love in our own human relationships.

But the most important profile in the Bible, the supreme source of our hope and encouragement, is none other than the story of Jesus Christ. Jesus is the one whom all the others prefigure and point to. Jesus is the one who sums up and surpasses all their qualities.

The period of Advent is our own time of hopeful expectation for the coming of Christ. Like Isaiah we eagerly wait for the root of Jesse to make his appearance, to bring us wisdom and understanding, justice and peace, forgiveness and healing. Like John the Baptist we anticipate the Lord's coming by preparing the way before him, by confessing our sins and reforming our lives.

Jesus is the one who saves. Jesus is the one for whom the whole Bible was written. Jesus is the one who gives meaning to Christmas and to our life. His profile is the one we must study and imitate. His life is the one we must share. His love is the one we must show to each other.

Everything about the Advent liturgies we celebrate is for our advantage—the word of Scripture is spoken to instruct us; the bread of the Eucharist is broken to feed us; the community of God's people is present to encourage us. Praise the Father for giving us Jesus as the source of our hope. Thank the Father for the words of life he speaks to us through his Son Jesus.

Third Sunday of Advent
Jm 5:7-10

Patience

One of the more palatable commercials on TV is the one featuring Orson Welles for Paul Masson Wines. It begins with a Beethoven symphony, which Orson Welles points out took five years to compose. The commercial compares good wine with good music and then concludes with a quotation from Paul Masson himself: "We'll sell no wine before its time."

It is most important to wait patiently for grapes to ferment before good wine can be enjoyed. In the chalky vineyards of Champagne France, where the genuine bubbly champagne is produced, it takes at least five years to get an exquisite sparkling wine.

Patient waiting is one of the lessons St. James teaches through his letter when he writes: "Be patient, therefore, my brothers, until the coming of the Lord. See how the farmer awaits the precious yield of the soil. He looks forward to it patiently while the soil receives the winter and spring rains. You, too, must be patient."

What is this patience which we must practice as we wait for the Lord to come? Theologian Donald Gray has some insights that might help us answer this question. On the one hand, consider what patience is not. The virtue of patience is not apathy. It cannot be associated with indifference as regards change and improvement.

On the other hand, consider what patience is. First, it involves a certain kind of passivity. We undergo many things in life that are outside our own choosing—the sex we were born with, the conditions of the weather, the increasing price of oil. Patience enables us to respond to these in a mature way.

Second, patience implies an openness in getting to know someone or something. We cannot force the self-revelation of the other either on the interpersonal or on the aesthetic level. In the presence of the mystery of another person or of a work of art we have to be patient and wait for the other to speak to us.

Third, patience includes letting others be, not in the sense of standing off from someone, but in the positive sense of allowing someone enough space to come to the full realization of his potentialities. The prodigal father in the gospels exemplifies such patient letting-be.

Fourth, patience has a sense of timing. There is a time to act and a time to withhold from acting. Patience is the art of discerning the difference between the two. The mark of a successful leader or businessman is to know when to wait and when to act decisively.

Fifth, patience takes a long view of life. It enables us to bear with the ambiguities of an unfinished reality and to steadily pursue our goals. A patient law student has his heart set on being a lawyer, but he is content for now with the struggle of study to get there. The end seems far off, but he attends to what is close at hand.

Also, patience imitates the way God deals with us. In his love for us God does not desire in a short time what can only be realized over a long period. He allows ample time for our failures and he refuses to intervene when we make mistakes. By waiting until we turn to him God reveals as much in what he does not, as in what he does.

Waiting patiently for the coming of the Lord is not something we do just during Advent, like little children who must wait until Christmas Day to open their gifts. Practicing patience is much wider and much more profound than that. If we want to taste the champagne of life, then we have to be patient with the way the Lord comes to us in all the circumstances of life, patient with others who live and work with us, and patient with ourselves so that we have enough space and time to grow.

Fourth Sunday of Advent
Rm 1:1-7

Superman

The film *Superman, the Movie* is a modern messianic myth. Superman, played by Christopher Reeve, is a new messiah sent by his father, played by Marlon Brando. He says to his son Superman, "Earthlings can be a great people, they lack only the light. For this reason I've sent them you, my only son."

The rocket ship from the planet Krypton becomes a star of Bethlehem announcing Superman's arrival on earth. As a teenager he leads a hidden life, for only his foster parents, the Kents, know about his supernatural origin and powers. After a twelve year educational journey through the cosmos, Superman begins to reveal himself to the public at the age of thirty. Some of his messianic feats include saving the world from Lex Luthor's nuclear missiles and resurrecting Lois Lane by reversing the flow of time.

What the film script says about the human and superhuman natures of Superman is something like what Scripture says about Jesus Christ. St. Paul begins his letter to the Romans by saying: "Greetings from Paul, called to be an apostle and set apart to proclaim the gospel of God—the gospel concerning his Son, who was descended from David according to the flesh, but was made Son of God in power according to the spirit of holiness, by his resurrection from the dead: Jesus Christ our Lord."

In a few sentences Paul summarizes the significance of the Incarnation and the Feast of Christmas. He contrasts the earthly and human side of Jesus' person with his transcendent and divine characteristics: descended from David, made Son of God; according to the flesh, according to the Spirit. This is the whole mystery of Christmas—God becoming man, the divine taking on the human, the invisible made visible.

To appreciate this mystery better it might help if we continue with the Superman example. We have already seen some of the striking similarities between the movie and the gospels. Rev. Ken Reichley of New York points out some of the all-important differences.

Superman is born as a man of steel; Jesus is born as the Word made flesh. Superman comes as a strong hero; Jesus comes as a Suffering Servant. Superman becomes invulnerable and dons a special costume; Jesus becomes vulnerable and looks like the rest of men. Superman can't die from ordinary causes; Jesus dies the same death that comes to all of us. Superman manipulates fate and history as he reverses time to undo an earthquake fatality; Jesus works within history, conforms to time and respects human freedom. Superman can save us only if we fall out of a tall building; Jesus saves us by faith, he has the words of eternal life.

From this list of differences we can see that our celebration at Christmas is not like watching a Superman movie. The Christmas story is not superficial, popcorn theology. It is much more profound than that. The Christmas story is the tremendous mystery of God so loving the world that he sent this only Son, a divine Son who became human like us in the flesh so that we might become divine like him in the spirit.

A movie like Superman can serve a good purpose by reawakening our religious sensibilities. But only the liturgy of Christmas can make Christ present in our midst to share his gift of love with us.

Christmas
Tt 2:11-14

Scrooge

After the story of the birth of Christ, what is the next most popular Christmas story? Some would say the poem about Santa Claus in *'Twas the Night Before Christmas*. Others would say the movie *White Christmas* starring Bing Crosby. Still others would choose the classic novel written by Charles Dickens, *A Christmas Carol*.

According to Prof. Robert Patten of Rice University, Dickens adapted a biblical theme to write a parable for his own time. Dickens lived in the first half of the 19th century, a period marked by the rise of materialism among England's industrial society. It was also a time when Prince Albert introduced England to the Christmas tree custom.

So Dickens used the biblical theme decrying materialism and combined it with the redemption story of Christ's birth. That's why he contrasts the material wealth and spiritual poverty of Scrooge with the actual poverty and richness of spirit of Bob Cratchit. That's why he employs the three spirits of Christmas to show Scrooge the possibility and the path to redemption.

Scrooge and Bob Cratchit exemplify the effects of Christ's birth as man, effects described by St. Paul in his letter to Titus: "The grace of God has appeared, offering salvation to all men. It trains us to reject godless ways and worldly desires, and live temperately, justly, and devoutly in this age as we await our blessed hope, the appearing of the glory of our savior, Christ Jesus."

Times have changed much since Dickens' day, but not materialism. We still have our Scrooges. There is something of the materialistic Scrooge in our society every time we promote pornography instead of culture, waste natural resources instead of developing them, or abort the unborn instead of protecting them.

There is something of the Scrooge inside us every time we set aside spiritual values to seek material ones, neglect our personal life and health in the pursuit of pleasure, or hurt our family relationships to gain financial success. The miser Scrooge in Dickens' story has become a symbol for all who are spiritually impoverished, realize their emptiness, and reach out for redemption in Christ Jesus.

When we read *A Christmas Carol* or see it dramatized on TV, we see in Scrooge our own spiritual poverty and the possibilities for change. We feel that like him, we too can reject our godless ways and worldly desires and live more the way Bob Cratchit did—temperately, justly and devoutly. We feel that like Scrooge, we too can quit stepping over people or exploiting them, and start doing more things to make them happy.

Pope Paul VI once said: "No one can truly enjoy Christmas without making happy, at least a little, someone who in these blessed days might need bread, or work, or a home, or care, or friendship, or comfort, or faith." In the same way, we cannot truly enjoy life unless, like Scrooge, we triumph over our greed and selfishness and try to make others happy with our generosity and love; unless we allow the grace and glory of God to appear again through us by becoming more Christ-like.

Holy Family ABC
Col 3:12-21

Family Life

A special film shown on TV which received considerable attention was *Who Are the DeBolts—And Where Did They Get 19 Kids?* It was the story of Robert and Dorothy DeBolt and their family of 19 children—13 of whom they adopted. Some of these adopted children are severely handicapped, mentally and physically. For example, there is Sunee who had an American father and a Korean mother. Sunee was dropped off at an orphanage, a polio victim paralyzed from the waist down. Then there is Karen, an American Black who has stumps for arms and uses hooks for hands. Karen was also born without legs and has to use false legs to get around. Another child is J.R., an American Caucasian who is both blind and a paraplegic. Doctors said he would never walk, even with crutches, yet for his mother's birthday J.R. inched his way across the living room.

The DeBolts insist that each child do everything he or she can do without help. Each has chores to do, no matter how trivial. Those who disobey are scolded or punished. The DeBolt household is a picture of what St. Paul had in mind when he wrote to the Colossians: "Clothe yourselves with heartfelt mercy, kindness and patience. Bear with one another; forgive whatever grievances you have against one another. Over all these virtues put on love."

During Christmas we remember another holy family, the family of Joseph, Mary and Jesus. Sometimes we tend to make their life too ideal, a life of perfect peace and unity. But when we look into the Scriptures we see that tension and conflict were a part of their family life as they are of ours.

Mary was pregnant before she married Joseph. This caused considerable anxiety for Joseph until he was finally told about the special origin of her child. Later Joseph was instructed by an angel in a dream to flee into Egypt to save the child Jesus. This must have caused Mary to wonder about Joseph since this time she had no special revelation. Then there was the time Jesus went back to the temple without telling his parents. This made both Joseph and Mary worry since they thought their son was lost. These incidents show that life in the Holy Family was not always peaceful and harmonious. There were the inevitable tensions and unavoidable conflicts that are part of every family life.

The DeBolts and the Holy Family are two models of family living. What can we do in a practical way to make our family life, too, an authentic expression of Paul's ideals mentioned above? We can comfort and support one another in times of sorrow and suffering. We can deepen and share our faith by praying together, both at home and in church. We can help each other develop our personality and grow in maturity. We can strengthen one another in times of difficulty by words of encouragement and inspiration. We can give recognition to each other's accomplishments and celebrate notable events like birthdays and anniversaries, and we can be more sensitive to one another's needs and make unselfish sacrifices for one another's well-being.

In the liturgy the Eucharist is a family meal which symbolizes our mutual love and care in the home. But it only becomes an effective sign when we do some of the practical things we've just outlined, when we do what Paul says, "bear one another's burdens and put on love."

January 1 ABC
Gal 4:4-7

The Best

Near the end of every year we get bombarded with announcements about what was the best during the past twelve months—the best songs, the best books, the best dressed woman or man, the best athlete, and so on. As the new year progresses we will hear more about the best actor or actress, the best movie, the best TV show, and so on. Our tendency to single out the best can be a good thing because it gives us someone to emulate or some work of excellence to imitate. This is why the Church singles out Mary from all other Christians.

Mary is "Number One," she is the best because she has a unique record—only she is the Mother of God. If the Guinness Book of World Records were to say something about who is the best Christian, it would probably say: "Mary, only woman to be the Mother of God."

To find out more about why Mary is the best we have to turn to another book—the Bible. For example, St. Paul writes to the Galatians: "When the designated time had come, God sent forth his Son born of a woman, born under the law, to deliver from the law those who were subjected to it, so that we might receive our status as adopted sons."

The gospels around Christmas time go on to describe how the shepherds and later the Magi found Mary and Joseph and the baby lying in the manger, and how Mary had the child circumcised and given the name Jesus. Later on the gospels tell us how Mary worried when her son was lost, how she was concerned about others at Cana, and how she stood by the cross of Jesus when his disciples abandoned him.

Mary, then, is the best Christian because of her faith in the power of God's word to make her the Mother of God, her hope when others would have despaired, her love for family and neighbor, and her loyalty in times of crisis.

The Church singles out Mary as the best not to make her appear as some sort of superwoman, but to present her as what being fully human should mean—a person with deep faith in God, a strong hope in times of trouble and a tender love for other people.

But it is not only Mary who has been given special gifts. As Paul pointed out above, all of us have a privileged position—we are no longer slaves but sons, and because of our new status as God's children we are also heirs with Christ.

The beginning of a new year is a good time to take stock of ourselves, to realize what we have going for us as Christians. We may not be the best of all people to be singled out as *Time* magazine's "Man of the Year," but we do have the best of opportunities to practice faith when all seems dark; to have hope where others would get discouraged; and to love those who are most despised or least cared for.

We may not be the best like Mary, but why not make this the best year of our lives? A year of overcoming adversities instead of being defeated by them; a year of growing in character because of our difficulties instead of being diminished by them; a year of avoiding people less and sharing with them more.

At the beginning of the new year the Church singles out Mary as the best example of what a fully human Christian life should be. Why not single out this year and make it the best one of our lives?

Epiphany ABC
Ep 3:2-6

Universality

In May of 1980, nearly 100,000 Cuban refugees entered the U.S. through Florida. They left behind family, homeland and material acquisitions. They risked traveling over dangerous waters in small boats that were overcrowded and unsafe. They gambled their futures on the American dream of freedom and opportunity.

On the one hand, their settlement underlined some of the principal problems troubling the U.S.—rivalry for jobs, rising inflation, housing shortages and racial tensions. On the other hand, their entrance into the U.S. pointed out some of our advantages, especially our rich resources because we are multi-ethnic, multi-racial and multi-cultural.

Imperfect though it is, the U.S., in this sense, is a model of what Christ's church is, namely, a place where men and women of every nation, language and culture can unite to form one people, share the same dream and work for a common purpose. This is the kind of vision St. Paul had when he wrote: "God's secret plan was revealed to me. It is no less than this: in Christ Jesus the Gentiles are now coheirs with the Jews, members of the same body and sharers of the promise through the preaching of the gospel."

The universality of the church is the focus of the Feast of the Epiphany. The coming of the Magi to the Christ child signifies the entrance of the Gentiles into the community of God's chosen people. At first the word "universal" seems to make the church remote and distant. But if we take a second look we see that the universality of the church touches our lives in close quarters and nearby.

In a negative way it prevents us from becoming exclusive and possessive. Having been members of the church for so long we tend to consider it an elite society and as something belonging to us. We can become so familiar and comfortable with the church that we resent any intrusion by new members who might upset the *status quo*. This is especially true if they speak a different language, have a different color and live by different customs.

We need to be reminded that all peoples—regardless of how much different they are from us—are called to be coheirs with us. Otherwise we become selfish and insecure about those with whom we live, work and worship. Otherwise we become narrow minded and feel threatened by anyone who wants to belong to our group.

In a positive way universality makes us humble and grateful. Once we remember that we, too, entered the church at some time like the Cubans and Magi—as strangers and foreigners—we can't help but realize that our membership is a gift and that we are only guests.

So it shouldn't matter whether we're black or white, Polish or Irish, Cuban or Mexican—we are all members of the same body of Christ. It shouldn't make any difference whether we're rich or poor, educated or uneducated, old or young—we are all fellow travelers and sharers of the same promise.

Because we belong to a universal church we can risk reaching out to come to know each other. Because we are called to the same faith we can support one another as we follow a star and a dream in search of Christ.

First Sunday of Lent
Rm 5:12-19

Amazing Grace

Most of us know the story of Fr. Damien the Leper, but few of us know about Brother Joseph Dutton who worked with Fr. Damien. Brother Joe was a First Lieutenant in the Civil War, got married and divorced after the war, and then became an alcoholic for nearly a decade. Drinking nearly ruined his life until he finally took the pledge and turned his back on alcohol for the rest of his life. Joe Dutton then became a Catholic at the age of forty.

Three years later he volunteered to work for Fr. Damien among the lepers on Molokai Island. There he served for forty-five years before dying at the age of eighty-eight. During that time Brother Joe built homes for the lepers and nursed the sick. He was friendly to everyone and brought peace wherever he went.

Brother Joseph Dutton can claim as his own, St. Paul's words to the Romans: "If by the offense of one man all died, much more did the grace of God through Jesus abound for all. If death began its reign through one man because of sin, much more shall those who receive the overflowing grace live through one man, Jesus Christ."

For almost ten years Brother Joe was a slave to alcohol, but how much more God's grace abounded during the last forty-five years of his life. The impact of God's grace in our lives can be just as powerful.

If we depend too much on drinks or tranquilizers, or if we are subject to chain smoking or compulsive eating, then our human freedom is gradually being destroyed. Yet, the grace of God can deliver us from this kind of domination and make us abound in good works. Instead of pursuing pleasure and gratification for ourselves all the time, we can become more like Brother Joe and seek happiness and satisfaction for others.

If we are habitually dishonest in our dealings with others, or prejudiced in our outlook on others, then our vision of reality is becoming increasingly distorted and we run the risk of spiritual blindness. Yet, the grace of God can remove this blindness and open our eyes to see and respect the rights of others, especially the rights of those who are disadvantaged, handicapped or belong to a minority. Instead of seeing others as rivals or competitors, we can become more like Brother Joe and see the face of Christ on them.

No matter how serious our sins may be—theft, adultery, hypocrisy—with God's boundless grace we can surmount them. No matter how far we stray from the Lord into agnosticism or the occult, his limitless grace can bring us back. No matter how often we fall—once a month, once a week or every day—God's all-powerful grace can lift us up again.

With St. Paul and Brother Joe, we too can renounce our sins and renew our friendship with the Lord; we too have access to God's overflowing grace to reverse our direction from darkness towards light and from death towards life.

There is no better time than during Lent to let our Lord's amazing grace abound and expand in our lives; to let the Lord rescue us from the ruin caused by sin; to restore us to the divine image in which we were created.

There is no better time than during Lent to sing praise about God's boundless and overflowing goodness towards us: "Amazing grace! how sweet the sound that saved and set me free! I once was lost but now am found, was blind but now I see. 'Twas grace that taught my heart to fear, and grace my fears relieved. How precious did that grace appear the hour I first believed."

Second Sunday of Lent
2 Tm 1:8-10

Bite the Bullet

At home, America is currently confronted by at least two crises, namely, the energy crisis caused by the shortage of oil and the economic crisis caused by spiraling inflation. At the advent of these two crises, when he was President, Gerald Ford addressed the American public and urged us to bear our share of the burdens brought on by them. To use the catch phrase of the day, we were asked to "bite the bullet" by conserving fuel and by cutting back on our spending and borrowing.

When he wrote to Timothy his co-worker St. Paul made a similar request, but for different reasons: "Bear your share of the hardship which the gospel entails." In other words, accept your responsibilities as an apostle of Christ and live up to the commitments you have made as a Christian.

Ford's words or Paul's words can serve as a slogan to shake us out of our lethargy during Lent: "Bite the bullet." "Bear your share of the hardship." As citizens of the U.S. we can contribute our part to ease the energy crisis and reduce inflation. As dwellers on the Planet Earth we can give some of our resources to alleviate the world hunger problem. As members of the human family we can lend our support to protect the unborn and rehabilitate prisoners.

None of these social obligations are easy to fulfill, yet we must bear our share of the burdens. None of these involvements may show any immediate, visible results, yet we must proclaim the gospel message.

It is no different in the more personal affairs of our life. Like Christ when he became man, we have to accept the human condition; we have to put up with misunderstanding, criticism and discouragement; we have to experience pain, weariness and loneliness.

Becoming a Christian does not mean that we can escape from these human conditions. Rather, it means that we can bear these burdens with steadfastness, dignity and even joy. We can do this because we have faith in Christ.

The transfiguration stories of the gospels give us both a preview of Christ's passion and a glimpse of his glory. Unless we want to be disciples in name only, we will have to participate in Christ's passion. Unless we want to be card-carrying Christians only, we will have to bear our share of the hardship which the gospel entails: taking care of a senile relative; getting laid off from our job with bills still to be paid; looking after the children when we'd rather go out bowling or see a movie.

But if we do these things with patience and cheerfulness, then we too will one day be transfigured into glory and appear as dazzling as the sun and as radiant as light. If we bear our burdens of the gospel with generosity and joy, then we too will one day hear the Father say to us as he said to Christ: "You are my beloved son who bore your share of hardship. On you my glory rests."

Third Sunday of Lent
Rm 5:1-8

Love Poured Out

An interesting book to read is *My Life for my Friends: The Guerrilla Journal of Nestor Paz, Christian*. It is the story of a young man who left his wife and children to join the Bolivian National Liberation Army in 1970. Nestor Paz joined the guerrillas because he was convinced that armed revolution was the only path left to gain justice. He writes: "We are taking up arms to defend the poor from exploitation and to win back dignity for a dehumanized people."

In July of 1970 Nestor Paz wrote to his parents: "At this moment I am happy, for I realize that I am achieving my goal in life—to do something meaningful for others and to put into concrete actions my desire to love." In August he wrote to his wife: "I miss you and love you totally. Even if I die I know that I'm one with you, because we are fulfilling the ideal of our lives—to make this a better world for our children to live in." In September Nestor Paz and the guerrillas suffered a series of severe losses in battle. In October Nestor Paz died of starvation one day before his twenty-fifth birthday.

Indeed, Nestor Paz is a man who might be described by St. Paul's letter to the Romans when he talks about the Christian and about Christ: "And this hope will not leave us disappointed, because the love of God has been poured out in our hearts through the Holy Spirit who has been given to us. At the appointed time, when we were still powerless, Christ died for us godless men. It is rare that anyone should lay down his life for a just man, though it is barely possible that for a good man someone may have the courage

23

to die. It is precisely in this that God proves his love for us: that while we were still sinners, Christ died for us.''

This is the kind of love all disciples of Christ should have: on the one hand, a love that *fills* our hearts because it is poured out into them by the Holy Spirit; on the other hand, a love that *flows* out of our hearts to others as we lay down our lives for them.

The first aspect of love stresses the fact that its source is the Holy Spirit, it is a gift from God. We cannot earn it or do anything to deserve it. All we can do is open our hearts to receive it.

It is a love that enables us to find deep personal satisfaction and fulfillment, and to feel good about ourselves as loveable and beautiful. Through this kind of love we become more sensitive to God's presence in creation, more eager to hear him speak to us in Scripture, and more enthused about proclaiming his praise.

The second aspect of love stresses the fact that it cannot be contained, it must burst out and overflow into the lives of others. Once we are overwhelmed with the force of God's love, we want others to experience it too.

It is a love that impels us to reach out with mercy to the sick, listen to someone who is lonely, and understand someone who is depressed. It is a love that compels us to feel hunger with the poor, show respect for the outcast, and seek justice for the oppressed.

Consequently, when the love of God is poured out into our hearts by the Holy Spirit it not only abounds with the peace and joy of Christ in our own lives, it also overflows like water into the lives of others. Like it did for Nestor Paz, the love of God leads us to find our own fulfillment and to transcend our own interests so as to lay down our lives for others in some form of ministry or service.

Fourth Sunday of Lent
Ep 5:8-14

Light in the Lord

The book *Now I See* tells the story of Charley Boswell. Charley is totally blind and yet shoots golf in the low 80's. He lost his sight in World War II when his tank exploded after being hit by an enemy shell. During his rehabilitation period he was very discouraged and disinterested.

Then one day a young corporal prodded him into trying the game of golf. Charley not only learned how to play, but to play very well. He can drive a golf ball 250 yards straight down the fairway. He has won more than 20 national golf tournaments for the blind, and he was selected one year by the Philadelphia Sportswriter Association as "The Most Courageous Athlete of the Year."

Charley Boswell must be thrilled every time he hears St. Paul's words in his letter to the Ephesians: "There was a time when you were darkness, but now you are light in the Lord. Well, then, live as children of light. Light produces every kind of goodness and justice and truth."

There was a time when Charley Boswell almost despaired because he was doomed to a life of blindness. But *Now I See* is both the title of his book and his way of life. As he himself says, "As long as I can shake a leg I'll go like the wild goose—in golf, in business, in social life. Is there any other way?"

We may not be blind like Charley Boswell, but we have experienced the darkness of sin. "Vain and shameful deeds" are part of every human history. But thanks to Jesus we have been delivered from darkness and brought into the light. No longer do we have to walk in the darkness of selfishness, injustice and deceit. Instead, we can produce every kind of goodness, justice and truth.

We may not have been born blind like the man in John's gospel, but we have been touched by Christ in the sacraments and come back able to see. Because of Christ we're able to move out of the darkness harboring hate, greed and suspicion into the light showing love, generosity and trust.

It doesn't matter whether we are great sinners in need of a dramatic conversion, or lesser sinners in need of more dedication. All of us are called during Lent to "awake from sleep, arise from the dead, and let Christ give us light." If we are alcoholics, crooked politicians or unfaithful spouses, we are being called out of our darkness to live as children of light. If we are average Christians or ordinary disciples, we are being called to come out of the shadows and let the spirit of the Lord lead us into the brightness of greater works in his service.

The following lines by Sr. Roberta Reynolds, OSS express this call in poetic terms: "Arise! Reflect your light filling mankind with a burst of glory. Manifest happiness to lives consumed by sadness. Share bread with those who hunger next door. Visit the less fortunate bringing human dignity into hopelessness. Reveal warmth, thereby unfolding Christ to others. Shine forth to dispel darkness and allow the shadows to become like noon."

Before we come to church for Sunday services our vision is dimmed by the difficulties and disappointments of the week. When we leave the church after the services our sight is restored so that we can see our difficulties and disappointments in a clearer light. These difficulties and disappointments will not necessarily disappear, and, like Charley Boswell, we may still have to walk in the darkness of the valley, but we will no longer have to be afraid because we have Christ at our side to be our light.

Fifth Sunday of Lent
Rm 8:8-11

Brought Back

Miss America 1980, Cheryl Prewitt of Mississippi, is a born-again beauty who talks about her faith in Jesus every day and vowed to give to him 10 percent of all her earnings. She used her year as Miss America as a ministry for the Lord, not only by witnessing at revivals and crusades, but also by giving testimony to non-church audiences.

Cheryl Prewitt's profound faith goes back to 1968 when her left leg was crushed in an automobile accident. The injury left her in a body cast and wheelchair for eight months. Although doctors said she would never walk again, she was healed completely at a revival meeting in 1974.

She attributes her miraculous cure and subsequent success to the power of the Holy Spirit. Because of what happened in her life she has a special insight into the meaning of St. Paul's words to the Romans: "If the Spirit of him who raised Jesus from the dead dwells in you, then he who raised Christ from the dead will bring your mortal bodies to life also through the Spirit dwelling in you."

Cheryl's left leg was dead for all practical purposes. But the Spirit dwelling within her healed that leg and gave it new life. She was unable to walk because she was crippled. But the Spirit dwelling within her brought back her ability to walk and raised her from a wheelchair.

If we had faith, resurrection experiences would be a common occurrence among us. We don't have to wait until we're put in the grave like Lazarus before we know what it is to be raised from the dead in some way. Every conversion from sin to grace is a sort of resurrection. Every turning away from selfishness to service, from greed to generosity and from hatred to love is a raising up to new life.

If we really believed that the Spirit of the Lord is dwelling within us, occurrences of being brought back to life would be happening more frequently for us. We might be destroying our life because of some bad habit like drinking or drugs or gambling. But we don't have to continue that way. The Spirit can raise us up to a new life of self-control and temperance.

We might be putting our family relationships to death by a neurotic quest for a bigger income or by an ego-trip in pursuit of a higher promotion. But we don't have to let divorce be the death sentence of our marriage. The Spirit can restore our family life of mutual love, sharing and support.

As a society we might be burying minority groups, the handicapped, criminals or undesirables by our prejudice, indifference, hostility or ignorance. But we don't have to stand by and pretend not to see their sufferings. The Spirit can bring us back to our nation's ideals of justice, equal opportunity, tolerance and understanding.

If we have faith we can hear the Lord call us: "Lazarus, come out. Come out of your tomb of self-centeredness, insecurity and fear. Let me remove from you the wrappings of worry, depression and self-pity so that you can go free and live by the Spirit dwelling within you, the Spirit of light and wisdom, the Spirit of courage and fortitude, the Spirit of peace and joy. Go free and proclaim what I have done for you and people like Cheryl Prewitt. Let the whole world see how you were once dead because of sin, and how you have been brought back to life because of the Spirit dwelling within you."

Passion Sunday ABC

He Emptied Himself

The Human Factor is a movie based on a book written by Graham Greene. It is a spy story about a British Intelligence agent named Maurice Castle who worked in South Africa. Castle lives with his black African wife, Sara, and her son whom he has adopted. Because of his gratitude to a Soviet spy who had helped Sara escape from South Africa, Castle has become a double agent.

Determined to terminate his double-agent role, Castle nevertheless decides to pass one more secret because he believes he may be able to save the lives of many people by this act. This leads to his downfall as an agent and isolation in Moscow, but at the same time to his salvation as a person because of his love for people.

What Castle did resembles what Jesus did on a more magnificent scale. St. Paul describes it in his letter to the Philippians: "He emptied himself and took the form of a slave, being born in the likeness of man. It was thus that he humbled himself, obediently accepting even death, death on a cross! Because of this, God highly exalted him and bestowed on him the name above every other name."

In becoming man Jesus did not empty himself of his divinity, but of the glory and privileges to which he had a right. Not only did he become a real man, but like all other men was given no preferential treatment.

Like Castle in the movie, Jesus sacrificed himself in order to save the lives of others—not just to the point of losing his status and being forced to live in exile as in the case of Castle, but even to the point of losing his life on the cross and being buried in a tomb.

Moreover, just as Castle did, Jesus valued the lives of people he loved, more than his condition as Lord—not only people like his mother and the twelve apostles, but also outcasts like the ten lepers, the handicapped like the man born blind, and sinners like the woman caught in adultery.

There is a sense in which we too must empty ourselves in order to serve others and save ourselves. We can fill up our lives with so many good things—television, cars, work, money—that we don't leave much room for God and others.

In an article in *Sojourners* Joyce Hollyday writes: "God calls us to empty ourselves of our pride, our agendas for success, our greed for comforts. He calls us to proclaim a kingdom of peace, reconciliation and justice, and that proclamation calls for sacrifice and servanthood, a continual pouring out of our love, our compassion, and our lives for each other."

When we empty ourselves in this way it becomes possible for the Lord to use us as instruments to save others, and lead us to our own personal fulfillment. Graham Greene's story *The Human Factor* illustrates this to some extent. The gospel stories about Jesus Christ stress this. Our own story concerning this is yet to be written.

First Sunday of Easter
Rm 6:3-11

Death to Life

When she was seventeen years old, Joni Eareckson broke her neck diving into Chesapeake Bay. Since that accident in 1967 she has been a quadriplegic living in a wheelchair and depending on others to bathe and dress her.

For a long time Joni was depressed, angry and bitter. But with the help of God she gradually worked through much of this. She has become an excellent artist by learning how to paint with a brush between her teeth; has acted as a counselor for other paraplegics; and has learned to drive a van.

Joni understands well the following words of St. Paul to the Romans: "Are you not aware that we who have been baptized into Christ Jesus were baptized into his death? Through baptism into his death we were buried with him, so that, just as Christ was raised from the dead by the glory of the Father, we too might live a new life. If we have been united with him through likeness to his death, so shall we be through a like resurrection."

Paul, of course, is speaking about dying to sin and selfishness in order to live for God in Christ Jesus—a kind of resurrection we can experience here and now. He is also speaking about our union with Christ in actual death and our likeness to him through the resurrection of our bodies.

But between our baptism and death we go through a variety of dyings and risings—little ones like dying to the things of childhood in order to rise to the new life of an adolescent, and major ones like Joni Eareckson's experience.

When Joni was crippled it meant the death of her former way of life. No longer could she go diving and swimming in Chesapeake Bay; no longer could she walk or run where she wanted; no longer could she even bathe or dress herself.

To cope with her handicapped condition, Joni had to learn a new lifestyle, acquire new skills and seek new goals. To rise above her initial despair she had to deepen her faith in God and discover some purpose in her wheelchair existence.

Not every dying-rising episode is as dramatic as Joni's was, but it should be part of a regular pattern in our lives. In his book *The Resurrection* F.X. Durwell writes: "Our passage from the world of sin and death to the order of resurrection and glory is not achieved at once. Our Christian life is an advance towards its full accomplishment."

In his work on St. Paul, *Christ's Resurrection in Pauline Soteriology*, David Stanley says: "For Paul, the dialectic of human history consists in a series of crises, of dyings and risings, involving the individual, the nation, the universe, because such was the form in which the salvation of all men has been accomplished by him 'who died and was raised for them.' "

By our baptism, then, we are committed to a dying-rising way of life; we begin a journey of repeated passovers from death-to-sin to life-for-God. We set out on a series of adventures that never end until the day we die.

Every day we are called anew to live as Easter people by putting aside our selfishness and greed to opt for loving concern and sharing. Every hour we are challenged to destroy hatred and injustice so as to build up a community of peace and opportunity for all. All our lives—like Joni Eareckson in her wheelchair—we can unite ourselves with the death and resurrection of Christ in order to live anew for the glory of the Father.

Second Sunday of Easter
1 P 1:3-9

New Birth

1975 marked the centennial of the birth of Dr. Albert Schweitzer, the world famous missionary, doctor, theologian, and musician. Dr. Schweitzer influenced many people during his lifetime. One such person is actor Hugh O'Brian. In 1957 Hugh O'Brian visited Dr. Schweitzer for a week in Africa. That week with Dr. Schweitzer changed Hugh's whole life.

Before that he was a typical Hollywood success. Girl friends, parties and expensive cars ranked highest on his list of values. But after meeting Dr. Schweitzer, actor Hugh O'Brian moved by the presence of God, changed his lifestyle from luxury to simplicity, and got interested in helping people. For example, every year now Hugh O'Brian sponsors at his own expense, a Jaycees leadership seminar for young people.

The impact of Dr. Schweitzer on the life of Hugh O'Brian is similar to the impact Jesus had on the early Christians. They were changed people. They had a new sense of self-awareness, a new set of values and a new purpose in life. If they were wealthy, they no longer had to pursue pleasure with a passion or be afraid of losing everything at death. They had found Jesus and he gave life an ultimate purpose.

If they were slaves, they no longer had to be ashamed of themselves or feel inferior because of their poverty. They had become brothers of Jesus and through him they found freedom and nobility. No matter what level of society one came from, when he became a Christian he became a new creature. His whole life was transformed because of Jesus.

This change in a Christian's life was so radical that it was compared to a new birth. This is the theme of one of St. Peter's letters when he quotes an early Christian hymn for baptism: "Praise God—who in his great mercy gave us new birth; a birth unto hope which draws its life from the resurrection of Jesus Christ from the dead; a birth to an imperishable inheritance incapable of fading or defilement . . . a birth to a salvation which stands ready to be revealed in the last days."

In a few lines this hymn digests a whole theology of baptism. First, baptism is described as a new birth. Just as none of us brings about his own physical birth, so too none of us can bring about his own spiritual birth. It is a gift from our Father in heaven.

Second, baptism is a birth unto hope and draws its life from Christ's resurrection. Our civilization can produce magnificent works of art and technology, but without the event of Christ's resurrection from the dead we would still be without hope.

Third, baptism is a birth to an imperishable inheritance incapable of fading or defilement. Fortunes are gained and lost, friends come into our lives and leave, and our youth blossoms and fades, but the life of grace we share in Christ will last forever.

Also, baptism is a birth to a salvation which stands ready to be revealed in the last days. Our salvation is both already here and yet to come. It is already here in principle, but its perfection is yet to be unveiled. Its victory is already won, but its battle is yet to be fought.

This, then, is what Christ's resurrection and each person's baptism meant to the early Christians—an experience so radical that it changed their lives—an event so profound that it was likened to a new birth. Is the same true of us? If Dr. Schweitzer could change Hugh O'Brian's life in a significant way, how much more might Jesus change our lives—from doubt to faith, from despair to hope, from selfishness to love. Praise the Father for giving us a new birth through his risen Son, Jesus.

Third Sunday of Easter
1 P 1:17-21

Beyond All Price

In 1976 the U.S. celebrated the bicentennial of its Declaration of Independence. We relived some of the events of the American Revolution, like the incident in 1770 known as the "Boston Massacre." It started with the issue of excessive taxation. There had been some skirmishes between the British redcoats and the angry Boston citizens.

At the front line of a band of protesters at the Customs House was a sailor and former runaway slave by the name of Crispus Attucks. When the redcoats fired at these demonstrators he was the first man to get killed. Crispus Attucks and four other men who were killed were given a massive public funeral. One hundred years later they were elevated to the status of national heroes with a monument erected in their honor in Boston Common.

Crispus Attucks is honored and held as a hero because he was the first man to shed his blood in the American Revolution. For a greater reason we honor and worship the Lord Jesus. As St. Peter writes: "Realize that you were delivered from a futile way of life, not by any perishable sum of silver and gold, but by Christ's blood beyond all price, the blood of a spotless and unblemished lamb."

There are two Old Testament images Peter is using. The first is the symbol of the Passover Lamb from the Book of Exodus. The Jews used the blood of that lamb to mark their doorposts so that the angel of death would pass over their houses and not slay their first-born sons. The second image is from Isaias 53. There the Suffering Servant is described as a lamb led to the slaughter—

harshly treated and submissive, silent and not opening his mouth. Yet, because he surrendered himself to death, he shall take away the sins of many.

Both images stress the notion of sacrifice through the shedding of the lamb's blood so that we might be released from slavery and delivered from death. Jesus didn't ransom us from slavery by paying off silver and gold. He shed his blood for us. He didn't free us by giving a speech or signing a contract. He shed his blood for us. He didn't rescue us by changing laws or sending an army. He shed his blood for us.

No wonder we worship him as Lord and Savior. No longer are we doomed to a futile way of life, a life of lost hopes and quiet desparation. Instead we look with joyous expectation to the glory that is to be revealed in us. No longer are we bound by ignorance like the Jews who crucified Jesus. Instead we can acknowledge and proclaim that Jesus is the Son of God. No longer are we handicapped by spiritual blindness like those two disciples going to Emmaus. Instead we have been given sight to recognize the presence of the Lord in creation, in history and in other people.

During the liturgy of the Eucharist Jesus speaks through the priest: "This is the cup of my blood which will be shed for you. Do this in memory of me." In other words, Jesus is telling us *to do* what he has *done* for us—shed our blood for one another.

In a sense, Jesus is saying: "Be a Crispus Attucks and fight for the cause of freedom, whether for the unborn or the orphan. Be a Crispus Attucks and defend your brother's dignity, whether he is a migrant worker or an aging relative. Be a Crispus Attucks and pour out your blood in service, whether as husband or wife, parent or teacher, doctor or nurse, priest or sister. My blood was shed for you. Do the same thing for one another in memory of me."

Fourth Sunday of Easter
1 P 2:20-25

Stray Sheep

In 1967 a twenty-four year old black man by the name of Vaughn Booker was convicted of killing his wife. He was sentenced to serve from fifteen years to life imprisonment for this crime. Eight years later he was ordained at the Pennsylvania State Prison as an Episcopalian deacon. Even though he is not eligible for parole until 1982, Vaughn Booker wants to make his stay in prison meaningful for himself and a ministry to his inmates.

Imagine what an impact St. Peter's words must have on Booker whenever he reads or hears them: "At one time you were straying like sheep, but now you have returned to the shepherd and guardian of your soul." At one time in his life Vaughn Booker had strayed like a lost sheep into hatred, anger and violence. But now he has returned to the Lord, his shepherd and guardian. Moreover, by being ordained a deacon he himself has become a shepherd to his fellow prisoners.

When Peter wrote his letter he was writing from his own personal experience. He himself had strayed from our Lord like a lost sheep. In fact, he ran away from our Lord like a scared sheep. But thanks to the Lord's forgiveness and gentleness, Peter came back to start all over again. He returned to become himself the chief shepherd of the Lord's disciples.

The lives of both Peter and Booker point out the pattern of Christian discipleship. On the one hand, whenever we stray from the Lord like lost sheep, he calls us by name to repent and return to him so that we might have life and have it to the full. On the other hand, he appoints us in turn to be shepherds to other people, so that through us they, too, might come to know the Lord, enter his fold and have life to the full.

Sometimes we turn away from our Lord and get involved in serious sin, like Booker's murder, Peter's betrayal or David's adultery. Yet the Lord goes out to search for us. Finding us wounded and disillusioned he carries us gently back with him in order to heal us.

At other times we turn away from our Lord in less serious ways, such as a lack of response to his call to be more considerate towards our family, more generous toward the needy or more prayerful with him. Yet he calls us by name to trust him more completely, to follow him more closely and to live his life more fully.

Moreover, just as Christ is a Good Shepherd towards us, we in turn must be good shepherds towards others. As Peter remarks: "Christ left you an example to have you follow in his footsteps." Like Vaughn Booker, then, we have to reach out to others, especially if they are outcasts of society like criminals. Like Jesus we have to protect the unwanted, from the youngest child left as an orphan to the oldest senior citizen cast aside by neglect.

Fr. Henry Fehren has some comments about this responsibility. After reminding us that sheep are repulsive because they have a bad odor, he says: "We who are members of Christ must be shepherds to others. This involves not just seeing people at a distance, but getting close no matter how badly their odor might seem because of their personality, habits, customs or homes."

Glorify the Lord for being our Good Shepherd. He calls us back when we go astray and restores or deepens our friendship with him. Thank the Lord by being his good shepherd for others. Be at their side when they have to walk in darkness and support them when they are weary.

Fifth Sunday of Easter
1 P 2:4-9

Your Own Best Friend

A book that was a best seller for a long time was *How To Be Your Own Best Friend*. Its authors are Mildred Newman and Bernard Berkowitz. It is a book about self-psychotherapy. As its title indicates, the chief purpose of this book is to help us learn to like ourselves, appreciate better the positive aspects of our personality, and improve our self-image.

The authors assert that if we have a strong sense of self-esteem, then we won't ever need the professional help of a psychoanalyst. If we make a healthy affirmation of our own uniqueness, then we can become the person it is in our power to be.

Essentially this is the same message in St. Peter's letter to the early Christians. He reminds them that they are something very special in the eyes of God. "You, however, are a chosen race, a royal priesthood, a holy nation, a people he claims for his own to proclaim his glorious works."

If what St. Peter says is true, then there is no excuse for us to downgrade ourselves. Instead we should always consider ourselves as very special individuals. If indeed we are everything St. Peter claims we are, then there is no reason for every considering ourselves rejected or unloved. Rather we should realized how precious we are to the Lord and continue becoming the person we have it in our power to be.

What is it in our power to be? First, we are chosen. *The Jerome Biblical Commentary* says that this phrase "expresses our corporate destiny as Christians stemming from our divine election." In other words, we have a new unity in Christ, a unity transcending all barriers and distinctions.

Second, we are a royal priesthood. This means that we have access to God ourselves; we have a responsibility to bring others to God; we make offerings of our work and leisure to God.

Third, we are a holy nation. The root meaning of the word holy is, to be set apart and consecrated to the service of God. As disciples of Christ we are different from the world because our values are those of the gospel. Nonetheless, we are dedicated to transforming the world and restoring it in Christ.

Also, we are a people God claims as his own. The literal meaning is that we are God's private property, a people for God's own special possession. Many things in a museum are valuable because they belonged at one time to a famous person. Similarly, we may be a very ordinary person in the world, perhaps even inferior, useless or unwanted. But because we belong to the Lord, we acquire a new and priceless value.

No wonder then that we should be our own best friend. Considering what the Lord has done, we have so many good things going for us that we should like ourselves. Because of our special relationships to the Lord, we have dignity and nobility. As authors Newman and Berkowitz point out, we should have a strong sense of self-esteem.

When we appreciate our own very special individuality because of God's love for us, we can't help but proclaim his glorious works. We will not hate or downgrade ourselves when we fail or make a mistake. Instead, the steadfast pursuit of our ideals will proclaim that we are God's chosen ones and of his royal priesthood. We will not consider ourselves rejected or unloved when others hurt or disappoint us. Instead, our inner peace and security will proclaim that we are a holy nation and God's own people.

Sixth Sunday of Easter
1 P 3:15-18

Ever Ready

One of the most fascinating stories of Christian witness is that of Charles de Foucald. Born as a viscount in a wealthy French family, Charles was spoiled and selfish as a young man. When he was a military officer he threw wild parties, was a connoisseur of fine wines and fancy food, gambled excessively, and had a blonde mistress.

At the age of twenty-three he left the army and became an explorer for several years of the Sahara Desert. Then he began to pray, turned over his fortune to his sister, and became a Trappist monk. After he was ordained a priest in 1901 he went to live as a hermit in the African desert.

Charles de Foucald knew that he would never convert the Arab Moslems in that area, but he could make Christ present among them by the peace he found in prayer and by the kindness of his service. Although he died alone when he was murdered by an Arab thief, a religious community known as The Little Brothers of Jesus has been formed to continue his witness.

The witness Charles de Foucald gave among the Arab Moslems illustrates St. Peter's words: "Should anyone ask you the reason for this hope of yours, be ever ready to reply, but speak gently and respectfully."

Charles didn't move among the Moslems like some high pressured salesman. He announced the good news of Jesus through the peace and joy that was manifested in his own life and through the kindness and generosity he showed towards others. Then if an Arab asked him why he prayed, fasted and served others, Charles could answer that it was because of Jesus. Then if a Moslem inquired how he could live like a hermit in a desert and still be so happy, Charles could say that it was because of Jesus.

From Charles de Foucald we learn that the first key to Christian witness is prayer. We don't announce the good news of Jesus by stopping people in a hurry on the streets, or by holding press conferences on TV. Instead, the power of our persuasion must come through prayer.

Through prayer we become so possessed by the peace of Christ that its presence will be felt by others. Through prayer we become so overwhelmed by the joy of experiencing Christ that we will make others wonder. They will especially wonder how we can rejoice like the apostles when we have to suffer for the name of Jesus.

G.K. Chesterton's remark comes to mind: "Joy, which was the publicity of the pagan, is the gigantic secret of the Christian." This, then, is the first key to Christian witness—having such a close personal relationship with Christ through prayer that we will be filled to overflowing with peace and joy.

The second key to Christian witness is the love we show to others. "By this shall all men know you are my disciples," says the Lord, "if you have love for one another." The only authentic way to proclaim that Jesus is Lord is to practice what he did. "I give you a new commandment," he adds, "love one another as I have loved you."

Like Jesus we should be forgiving when we are hurt by others, and sensitive when others have been hurt. Like Jesus we should be responsive to the needs of others, and generous in our help.

If we don't attract people to Christianity, the fault may be in our failure to love. Again, as G.K. Chesterton once said: "Christianity has not been tried and found lacking; it has been found difficult and not tried."

We may not live in the Sahara Desert like Charles de Foucald did. Yet we can pray and fast as he did to become more Christ-like. We may not live among the Arab Moslems like Charles did, yet we can love one another as Christ loved us. Then if anyone should ask us about our peace, our joy and our love we will be ready to reply: "It is because of Jesus."

Ascension ABC
Ep 1:17-23

The Great Hope

There is a new stage play in London entitled *Mary Barnes*. It is a true story about the recovery of Mary Barnes from severe schizophrenia to normal sanity. Under the direction of Dr. Laing an unconventional psychiatric commune was set up to treat patients like Mary Barnes. Instead of applying the usual treatments given to the mentally ill—drugs, electric shock, lobotomies—Laing and his associates used supportive care.

No matter how disruptive the patients became or what kind of tantrums they went through, they were given loving acceptance and supportive care instead of being forced or coerced to comply. In the play we see Mary Barnes struggle to be reborn and thus wipe out her unhappy childhood. We watch her go back to the womb under the guidance of a psychiatrist to relive the whole process of growing up. Today Mary Barnes leads a normal life.

The secret of this success was to get Mary Barnes to realize how great and wonderful a person she could become. This parallels what St. Paul is trying to get us to do regarding ourselves, namely to know how lovable we are right now and how glorious is our destiny in the future. He says: "May the Father of glory grant you a spirit of wisdom and insight to know him clearly. May he enlighten your innermost vision that you may know the great hope to which he has called you."

How fortunate we are even now because we are children of God who know him as our Father. How blessed we are because we have a glorious heritage awaiting us in the future—life on high with Jesus who sits at the right hand of the Father.

This is one of the main messages about the Feast of the Ascension—have a strong hope in our own call to the glory of heaven. It is summed up in the words of the Preface used in the liturgy for this celebration: "Christ has passed beyond our sight, not to abandon us but to be our hope. Christ is the beginning, the head of the Church. Where he has gone, we hope to follow."

There is a striking contrast here. The revelation of our glorious human destiny stands in opposition to our human misery. In a sense, we are all somewhat like Mary Barnes when she was schizophrenic—we need healing. To a certain degree, we all suffer from fear and anxiety, hostility and anger, selfishness and greed. Moreover, as we look around us we see how society, too, needs healing. Hunger and poverty, injustice and prejudice, violence and crime are only some of the ills afflicting society.

We need a strong faith in what Christ has already done for us before healing can take place. His dying and rising have, in fact, won the victory for us. His ascension has already begun his cosmic kingship. All we have to do is accept this victory and submit to his kingship. This is simple, but not easy.

It is simple because we can know and experience the risen Lord here and now. The Bible, sacraments, prayer, work, leisure and service are all ways in which we can glorify the exalted Christ in the present moment. It is not easy because we are still in the process of being healed. We still have to struggle with out own neuroses, physical ailments and emotional hurts.

The Ascension inspires great hope of winning this struggle by giving us a glimpse of the glory that awaits us. The Ascension gives us courage by setting before us a vision of our own heavenly destiny.

Seventh Sunday of Easter
1 P 4:13-16

Rejoicing

In 1975 Art Carney won the Academy Award for Best Actor in recognition of his performance in the film *Harry and Tonto*. For more than forty years, since the time he was eighteen, Art Carney had been an actor on stage, radio, TV and film. During those forty years he had enjoyed some success, especially in the TV series called *The Honeymooners*. But *Harry and Tonto* was his first role as a star in a movie.

Like most actors in show business, Art Carney's career had a large share of disappointments and failures. Consequently, when he received the Academy's Oscar he must have felt very proud and overjoyed. All the sufferings and struggles of those forty years were worth the supreme success he had now achieved.

This relationship between suffering and rejoicing is reflected in St. Peter's letter: "Rejoice insofar as you share in Christ's sufferings. When his glory is revealed you will rejoice exultantly." This same theme is found in the Last Supper scene of John's gospel just before Christ goes to suffer on the cross: "Father, the hour has come. Give glory to your Son that your Son may give glory to you."

How is it that the hour of Christ's passion is also the hour of his glorification? How is it that our sharing in Christ's sufferings is a cause for rejoicing, not only when his glory is revealed later, but even now? In his book *Joy* author Louis Evely tries to answer these questions.

First, he says that Christian joy is not an easy contentment. It is a sadness overcome. Christian joy is the denial by Peter overcome by the Lord's forgiveness; the disbelief of Thomas dispelled by the touch of the Lord; the fear of all the apostles overpowered by the Lord's greeting of "Peace." Our religion is not a religion of death on the cross, but of resurrection from the tomb. It is not a religion of absence symbolized by the empty tomb, but of the real presence of the risen Lord.

Second, Evely says that Christian joy is not necessarily a feeling of exuberance. It is a joy in faith. Many times we feel good and express our joy in song and celebration: on Thanksgiving Day and Christmas Day, on weddings and anniversaries, at graduations and alumni reunions. Then there are other times when we feel sad, burdened with sorrow perhaps; times when we don't even want to hear a "Good Morning," or sing a happy song. But these are precisely the times when we can rejoice in faith, because the source of our joy is deeper than the level of our feelings. It is on the level of faith in the Lord's promise to be always with us; faith in our own inner capacity to create joy where none exists.

Third, Evely says that Christian joy is not a naive optimism. It is confidence in a victory already won by Christ. This is why Jesus could pray at the Last Supper the way he did. He had confidence that his Father had already given him the victory; he trusted that the sufferings of Good Friday would only be a prelude to the glory of Easter Sunday. By baptism this victory is ours, too. All we have to do is claim it. All we have to do is trust in the Lord that somehow, somewhere darkness will be displaced by light and sadness will yield to joy.

Consequently, even though our glorification has not yet been revealed, we can still rejoice over our share in the sufferings of Christ. We can rejoice because we have faith that just as death was overcome by the resurrection of Christ, so, too, will our sufferings be conquered by the power of that resurrection.

Pentecost ABC
1 Cor 12:3-13

In the Holy Spirit

On one of its voyages to Bermuda the luxury liner Queen Elizabeth II was disabled by boiler problems. For several days the world's second largest passenger ship drifted helplessly in the sea. Without any power to operate its engines the huge ship could do nothing but float on the water and roll with the waves until repairs were made.

This is something like our own situation without the presence and the power of the Holy Spirit. We become spiritually disabled, drifting helplessly through the sea of life. Without the Holy Spirit we can do nothing but move in the direction the waves of chance push us.

St. Paul had something like this in mind when he wrote to the Corinthians: "No one can say Jesus is Lord, except in the Holy Spirit." Paul was speaking from experience. Without the Holy Spirit he persecuted Christ's Church; but once he received the Holy Spirit he became one of Christ's apostles.

Others have had similar experiences. Without the Holy Spirit actress Betty Hutton never really knew the Lord. In her book *Judge Me Not* she tells about her life which was a succession of broken marriages and emotional breakdowns until she attempted suicide. Then she accepted the Holy Spirit, proclaimed Jesus, and transformed her entire life.

In a similar way, singer Johnny Cash tried to live without the Lord. In his book *Man in Black* he tells how he went to jail seven times, had a bad drug habit and almost killed himself once. Then, under the influence of the Holy Spirit, he turned himself over to the Lord and changed his whole lifestyle.

Although we may not sink to the same depths as Betty Hutton and Johnny Cash did, still all of us, in some way or another, know what it is to be without the help of the Holy Spirit. We find ourselves helpless in the face of temptations to selfishness, materialism and dishonesty. Our efforts become futile when we try to pray, fast or share with people in need.

None of us can overcome difficulties, handle disappointments or make new beginnings except in the Holy Spirit. None of us can say, "Jesus is Lord"; see him in others or serve him among the poor except in the Holy Spirit.

Before the descent of the Holy Spirit on Pentecost, the disciples were afraid to proclaim Jesus as Lord outside their own little group. But once they received the Holy Spirit they went out boldly to preach to the crowds about Jesus, perform miracles in his name, and suffer joyfully for his sake.

Pentecost is perennial—it happens every year for us if only we are expectant enough. Without the Holy Spirit we are as helpless as the Queen Elizabeth II without its engines. But with the Holy Spirit we can make a new voyage, write a new story like Betty Hutton, or sing a new song like Johnny Cash.

Trinity Sunday
2 Cor 13:11-13

Fellowship

Shortly after his arrival in the U.S. to take up residence, exiled Soviet author Alexander Solzhenitsyn was named by Stanford University as an honorary fellow. Under this title Solzhenitsyn did research for a book at the university's Hoover Institution on War, Revolution and Peace.

In academic circles such a fellowship is one of the highest marks of distinction. It confers dignity and honor upon the member by recognizing his outstanding work or talent, and it gives to the member a sense of intimate belonging to a select society of scholars.

This twofold meaning of fellowship is found somewhat in St. Paul's farewell to the Corinthians: "The grace of our Lord Jesus Christ, the love of God, and the fellowship of the Holy Spirit be with you." This text reflects not only Paul's belief in the Trinity, but also his understanding of its meaning.

Through the fellowship of the Holy Spirit we become members of a community of believers, the Church. Through this fellowship we are endowed with dignity and honor as God's chosen people, and we experience a sense of intimate belonging as children in God's own family.

How can we become one with the Trinity? Unlike the fellowships of learned societies, we don't have to possess a superior intelligence. All we need is the simplicity of faith. We don't have to accomplish outstanding works. All we need to do is one essential thing—love one another.

The doctrine of the Trinity, then, is not some sort of supreme test of our faith. It is the revelation of our fellowship with God. The Trinity is not a statement about some mysterious Triad that transcends our comprehension. It is a living experience of God's love and grace which has been lavished upon us.

Because of our fellowship with the Trinity we are endowed with a nobility which no one can take from us. Sometimes our own sins may humiliate us and our own failures embarass us. But we can always rise and go to our loving Father who will make all things new. Sometimes other people will ridicule us or laugh at us. But we should not get discouraged because we have a strong sense of identity; we know who we are—disciples of Jesus Christ sent in the power of the Holy Spirit.

Because of our fellowship with the Trinity we also have a strong sense of belonging. We are never isolated, never left alone, although loneliness may overwhelm us at times when no one seems to care or understand. But this is never the case. The Trinity is always with us supporting us in our struggles and strengthening us in our efforts. Sometimes it seems as if we are ignored or even rejected by everyone and no one seems interested in us. But this is not so. The Trinity is always with us comforting us with a great presence and assuring us of loving acceptance.

It is interesting to note that Paul's blessing contains his final words to the Church in Corinth, the conclusion of his letter to them. These same words are now used as a greeting to the congregation at the beginning of the liturgy of the Eucharist. The love Paul felt for his fellow Christians at Corinth is the same love we should feel for one another. The bread we break together celebrates our common fellowship with the Trinity, proclaims our dignity as God's chosen people, and renews our sense of belonging to the same family of God.

Corpus Christi
1 Cor 10:16-17

One Bread, One Body

Whenever the play-offs in the National Basketball Association reach the championship series, the TV commentators point out that one of the keys to the success of the winning team is their teamwork, their unity. In the history of the NBA no team that depended on the efforts of one prolific scorer has ever won a championship. It takes solid team defense and getting everyone on the floor involved in the offensive movement to win championships in the NBA.

Moreover, superstars like Julius Irving and Dave Bird play on teams that are championship contenders because they excell not only in scoring but also in rebounding. In other words, they are team players and are not just individual stars; they are more concerned about unifying the team effort than improving their own personal statistics.

Unity is one of the themes of St. Paul's understanding of the Eucharist: "Is not the bread we break a sharing in the body of Christ? Because the loaf of bread is one, we, many though we are, are one body for we all partake of the one loaf."

To understand Paul's words better we have to realize that the Christian community at Corinth was noted for its dissension and quarrelling. They were split into rival factions each interested in themselves to the exclusion of others. Paul, therefore, makes an appeal to their most basic bond of unity—the Eucharist. Because of their communion in the Eucharist the Corinthians should settle their arguments and live in unity.

The link between the Eucharist and unity is no less essential for us. According to the documents of Vatican II, as often as the Eucharist is celebrated the unity of all believers who form one body in Christ is both expressed and brought about. In other words, the Eucharist is both the sign and the source of two kinds of unity—our unity with Christ and our unity with each other.

If only we could grasp this truth, how different our life would be. Fed by this living bread we can survive even in a desert like the Jews did because we are united to Jesus. No matter what kind of desert experience we may have, we can endure its privations and emptiness because Jesus is with us. No matter what kind of frustrations and losses we may suffer, we can accept them because the Lord is with us.

Fed by the Eucharist we can overcome any differences between us because we are united to each other. All our differences of time and place, culture and color, politics and philosophies become irrelevant when we realize that we are one with each other because we eat together from the same loaf of bread.

The Eucharist compels us to reach out with concern to that alienated member of our family, show compassion for that unemployed neighbor down the street, and sympathize with the sick or grieving friend. The Eucharist makes us conscious of how we should care about the angry ghetto dwellers and the oppressed minorities, feel compassion for the handicapped and the imprisoned, and share our bread with the poor and the hungry.

Unity is so important for us. Without it we end up like the Corinthians—split into factions and rivalries. The effects range from discontent to divorce and from quarrels to wars. But with unity there is no end to what we can accomplish: basketball teams can win championships; rescue missions can be organized; homes and jobs can be found for refugees; disaster areas can be rebuilt. May the unity we celebrate in liturgy become a unity we experience in reality.

First Sunday of the Year ABC
Ac 10:34-38

Dedication

Sarah Caldwell was the first woman ever to conduct an opera at the New York Metropolitan Opera House. In a profession where few women have succeeded to date, Sarah Caldwell has had to build her reputation by hard work as well as by brilliance.

In an interview Sarah Caldwell said she asks 200% of herself and those who work with her, often working close to twenty-four hours a day when deadlines for performances are approaching.

Dedication to a profession and commitment to a cause is one of the dimensions of our Lord's baptism. His baptism marked the beginning of his public mission as Messiah. From that point on he is no longer a carpenter of Nazareth, but the Lord's chosen servant, the one who proclaims the "good news of peace."

As St. Peter says in the Acts: "I take it you know what has been reported all over Judea about Jesus of Nazareth; of the way God anointed him with the Holy Spirit and power. He went about doing good works and healing all who were in the grip of the devil, and God was with him."

Through his baptism Christ dedicated himself to the work of the Kingdom of God. He made a public commitment to carry out all that his Father commanded. Thus he was empowered to transform the lives of people around him. Matthew the tax collector became Matthew the evangelist. Magdalen possessed by seven devils became Mary in love with the Lord.

Because of his dedication and commitment, Christ made a difference in the world. The spell of sin was broken by his life of grace; the dominion of death was destroyed by his resurrection.

If our own life is going to make any difference in the lives of others, we have to be dedicated to something worthwhile. Parents have to dedicate themselves to the good of their children to raise a fine family. A politician like a president has to dedicate himself to the best interests of his citizens to guarantee their justice and freedom.

If we're going to make any difference in the world, we have to commit ourselves to some cause. A doctor has to be committed to healing to help people recover their health. A teacher has to be committed to education to shape the future through his students.

Moreover, like Christ, by our baptism we dedicate ourselves not only to some particular work like nursing or accounting, but especially to the work of the Kingdom of God. Our Christianity is not supposed to be a part-time engagement, but a full-time one. We should always be proclaiming the good news of Jesus Christ in our lives, not so much by word of mouth, as by our readiness to feed the hungry and free the oppressed; to befriend the lonely and defend the weak.

By our baptism we make a commitment to the cause of Christ. We stand up to be counted among those who take seriously the teachings of Christ: those who are compassionate with the handicapped and patient with the ignorant; who are kind to outcasts and comfort the sorrowful.

To be a success as a woman conductor, Sarah Caldwell has to be totally dedicated to her musical profession. To find any personal satisfaction for ourselves and to do any good for the world, we have to be completely committed to the cause of Christ. We made this commitment at baptism. We renew this commitment every time we assemble for the Eucharist. But we have to practice it everyday of our lives.

Second Sunday of the Year
1 Cor 1:1-3

Called

A book entitled *Playboy to Priest* tells the story of how Fr. Ken Roberts was called by the Lord to leave the jet set and enter the seminary. During the years he worked as an air steward for BOAC and as an interpreter on the Queen Elizabeth liner, Ken Roberts enjoyed the lifestyle of a playboy—money, sports cars, a London penthouse and female companions. Yet the Lord called Ken Roberts to abandon his pleasures as a playboy to become a priest at the age of thirty-five.

Ken Roberts can identify with St. Paul when he says to the Corinthians: "Paul, called by God's will to be an apostle of Christ Jesus, and Sosthenes our brother, send greetings to the Church of God which is in Corinth."

History is full of people who have been called by the Lord to be his servants and apostles in some capacity. From the time of Abraham and Moses in the Old Testament to the time of Martin Luther King and Cesar Chavez in the 20th century; from the time of Judith and Esther in the ancient past to the time of Dorothy Day and Teresa of Calcutta in the modern era, the Lord continually calls men and women to be his servants and apostles.

Moreover, the Lord's call is not restricted to a select few like St. Paul or Ken Roberts. All of us are called by the Lord to be his servants somehow, somewhere. As St. Paul adds, "We have been consecrated in Christ Jesus and called to be a holy people."

Our call from the Lord may not be as dramatic as it was for Paul but it is still just as radical. It means that we must experience a conversion from self-indulgence to selflessness, a turning from self-centeredness to Christ-centeredness.

Our call may not bring publicity as it does for Cesar Chavez or Teresa of Calcutta, nevertheless it is just as profound. It means that the glory of the Lord must shine through us as we forgive instead of sulk, help instead of hurt and give instead of take.

Our call from the Lord may not be as clear as it was for John the Baptist or Joan of Arc. Nonetheless it is just as compelling. It means that sometimes we have to make hard decisions like taking care of a sick neighbor when we would rather not get involved, or acting honestly when theft would be so easy.

There is a song entitled *I Heard the Lord Call My Name*. It continues with the words: "Listen close, you'll hear the same. Place your hand in his, he will show you where to go. Take his hand, and we are glory bound."

When the Lord calls us by name to be his servants and apostles all we have to do is respond to that call with faith, take his hand with trust, and let him lead us to glory. If we do these things, then the Lord will accomplish in us what he did in Ken Roberts' life—he will put "a new song in our mouth" and "show us how to delight in doing his will."

If we have a deep conviction about our call from the Lord, then he himself will strengthen us to become all we are meant to be, to fulfill our special work in life, and to bring his grace and peace into the lives of others.

Third Sunday of the Year
1 Cor 1:10-13, 17

The Kansas Model

In looking over the newspaper sometimes one is struck by contrasting articles. For example, one day there was an editorial about the war which has been going on in Northern Ireland for several years. The violence there between the British and the Irish illustrates the destruction that can be caused when people are divided.

In that same newspaper there was also an article about a small town in Kansas called Geneseo with a population of five hundred. Once a thriving town it is now threatened with extinction because its oil wells have dried up and many of its farmers have moved out. But when the School Board tried to close their high school the people rallied. They launched what they called Operation Success, a program to save both their school and their town.

The people of Geneseo pulled together to build a new American Legion Hall, to enlarge a machine shop and to start their own newspaper. It was common to see the townspeople gather after supper to do things together like mowing the lawn in their cemetery. The town of Geneseo, Kansas is a model of what people can do constructively when they unite.

Unity is one of St. Paul's subjects when he writes to the Corinthians: "I beg you, brothers, to agree in what you say. Let there be no factions or quarreling among you. Rather, be united in mind and judgment."

Unity is so important in our lives. Without it we cause divisions and dissension: on the religious level as between the British Protestants and Irish Catholics; on the political level as between the Jews and Arabs; on the economic level as between the farm workers and farm owners. Without unity we cause suspicion and unreasonable competition, as, for example, between the sexes, the old and young, the government and military. Without unity we waste a lot of time and energy criticizing and complaining, quarreling and bickering, accusing and condemning.

But if we have unity then it is amazing what we can accomplish. When we work together our time and energy are multiplied. Towns like Geneseo can be rebuilt, a parish CCD program can be expanded, and the sick and elderly people in our society can be taken care of properly. When we join with one another to support a project, there is no expense we cannot meet. Our mission work can be increased, our hospital facilities can be extended, and our prison system reformed. When we unite for a common cause, there is no difficulty we cannot overcome. We can avert war between nations, check crime on our streets, and put an end to the fuel crisis and energy shortage.

There is plenty of room among us for difference and diversity. But there is no room for division and dissension. The former enrich us, the latter destroy us. There are so many opportunities for us to cooperate with one another. Why waste them arguing and quarreling, when we can experience the satisfaction that comes from working together?

There are so many places where we can be apostles of unity like Paul—our home, parish, school, place of work. Why sow seeds of discord and hostility when we can be the Lord's instruments of peace and unity?

Whether we live in Corinth, Geneseo or Houston, Paul pleads with us in the name of Jesus to set aside whatever divides us into factions and to be united in love as Christians.

Fourth Sunday of the Year
1 Cor 1:26-31

Jane Addams

Jane Addams is one of America's most famous women. Allen Davis has written a biography of her under the title *American Heroine: The Life and Legend of Jane Addams*. During her lifetime from 1860 to 1935 she was active in writing, social work and legislative reform. Her writings made her a sort of a forerunner of the Ann Landers type of column. Her establishment of Hull House for poor boys pioneered later projects like Boys Town. Her involvements in politics put her at the forefront of today's Women's Lib Movement.

This is a remarkable list of achievements for a woman who was a sickly child afflicted with curvature of the spine, had no American women to precede her as a model, and was attacked venomously because of her pacifist stand in World War I.

Jane Addams is an outstanding example of what St. Paul is talking about in his epistle to the Corinthians: "God singles out the weak of this world to shame the strong; he chooses those whom the world considers foolish to shame the wise."

For the most part the Corinthians to whom Paul is writing were the slaves of society. In the eyes of the educated, the powerful and the rich these early Christians were looked upon as ignorant, weak and worthless. But now their faith in Christ gave them divine wisdom, self-respect and the power of the Holy Spirit. These Christians were despised by the world because of their disadvantages, yet they were chosen by the Lord to announce the gospel and spread its message.

The Lord has done this throughout the history of salvation. In every age the Lord selects the weak and the simple to be his powerful instruments in social work, politics and religion. In our own day he wants to use us, too, in some way. In spite of our weakness he wants to work through us not only to fulfill our own destiny, but also to bring others into glory. He singles us out to secure justice for the oppressed, food for the hungry and freedom for captives. Despite our disadvantages the Lord sends us out to raise up those who are bowed down by poverty, stricken by illness or depressed by emotional problems.

If we have a negative outlook and see only our inadequacies, it is easy for us to say, "Certainly the Lord doesn't expect me to do those things. I don't have the talent or the resources." But if we take a positive approach like Paul does, then we can claim as he does: "Yes, I am foolish in many ways, Lord, but I have your wisdom to guide me." Enlightened by the Holy Spirit, then, we will do our best to bring peace where there is strife, reconciliation where there is division, and love where there is hostility.

If we have faith in God's power, then we can say with Paul: "Yes, I am weak in many things, Lord, but I have your strength to support me." Fortified with the Holy Spirit, then, we will try our best to comfort those who are in misery, offer companionship to those who are lonely, and give hope to those who are in despair.

Fifth Sunday of the Year
1 Cor 2:1-5

Power of Persuasion

In an article for *The Critic* magazine psychologist Eugene Kennedy wrote an analysis describing Cesar Chavez as "a powerful innocent." Kennedy showed how Chavez is *innocent* because his heart is free of any bitterness or hatred; *powerful* because he has the charisma to organize the migrant workers into a union; *unarmed* because his Chicanos apply nonviolent methods like demonstrations and grape boycotts; *armed* because his people have pride and dignity, patience and determination.

Born in a migrant worker's family, Cesar Chavez knows what it means to sleep in miserable shacks, to be half-starved most of the time, and to go to thirty-seven different schools before completing his eighth grade education. Yet, out of this humble background he has emerged as one of the greatest social activists of our era.

Perhaps Cesar Chavez has spoken to his brother Chicanos with the words St. Paul spoke to his fellow Christians at Corinth: "When I came among you I did not come proclaiming Christ's testimony with any particular eloquence or wisdom. No, I determined that while I was with you I would speak of nothing but Jesus Christ and him crucified. My message had none of the persuasive force of wise argumentation, but the convincing power of the Spirit."

If the power of the Spirit can operate in a simple man like Cesar Chavez, should it operate any the less in us? When we reflect upon the dedication of an ordinary man like Chavez, do we feel sort of uncomfortable about our own commitments to social justice?

In his social encyclical *Call to Action* Pope Paul VI wrote: "It belongs to the laity, without waiting passively for directives, to take the initiative freely and to infuse a Christian spirit into the mentality, customs, laws and structures of the community in which they live."

It is our proper task, then, to renew the temporal order. We can either sit back and talk about it eloquently, or else step out and get involved in social issues by personal activity. We can either simply argue persuasively about busing and housing, or else assume our responsibilities by supporting the poor and the oppressed in some real way.

Like Cesar Chavez we don't have to have any special wisdom to proclaim God's word about freedom and equality. All we need is faith in Jesus and a willingness to do something. We don't have to have abundant material resources like money and oil. Our real power comes from spiritual resources like prayer and fasting. We don't have to resort to forceful methods like armed revolution. The more effective methods are those of nonviolent social reconstruction.

As we try to transform the social order, our aim should not be to establish the superiority of one group over another. As brothers and sisters in Christ we should seek a diversity that will preserve the dignity of all groups. This happens in the liturgy. We come to the Lord's table with all our differences and diversity. By sharing in the Lord's body and blood we achieve convergence and unity. Our call is to make this happen in society. We leave the Lord's table with the command: "Go in peace to love and serve one another."

Sixth Sunday of the Year
1 Cor 2:6-10

Heaven

Music composer Burt Bacharach and lyricist Hal David are working together again writing songs. Sometimes they spend their whole day searching for that perfect tune, that right set of words. Another man who has returned to the music world is trumpet player Herb Alpert. Dissatisfied with his previous successes with the Tijuana Brass, he is again searching for that ideal musical note.

Such quests for perfection are not uncommon. All of us dream about the ideal. Skiers seek the perfect slope to descend. Surfers wait for the perfect wave to come along. Writers pursue the perfect plot for their novel. Sculptors try to create the perfect form. Scientists search for the perfect cure for cancer.

When we dream about something ideal, it might be an escape from the shortcomings of what is real. Such would be the case when a wife dreams about some movie star as a mate because her own husband is mean to her. But to dream about something ideal might also be from a drive that is deep down in our nature. Such would be the case when a mother prepares the best meal she can because she instinctively wants to please everyone.

The ideal and the perfect is what St. Paul talks about when he discusses heaven: "No, what we utter is God's wisdom: a mysterious, a hidden wisdom. Of this wisdom it is written: 'Eye has not seen, ear has not heard, nor has it so much as dawned on man what God has prepared for those who love him.' "

We all have our own dreams about what the perfection of heaven will be like—enjoying continuous music by someone like Burt Bacharach or surfing on that perfect wave that finally came along. Our visions of heaven will be surpassed by the actual experience of it. St. Paul says so.

From Scripture we know at least something about heaven. In heaven our resurrected bodies will be similar to the glorified body of Christ—incorruptible, able to penetrate matter, transfigured. Heaven will be like a wedding banquet—there will be celebration and joy, light and warmth, friendship and sharing. Heaven will consist of seeing the Lord—not from a distance or indistinctly as in a mirror, but face to face. Finally, heaven will include creation transformed—the old into the new and the temporal into the eternal.

Yet, for all that we can anticipate about heaven, Paul says that the actual experience will far exceed our wildest expectations. This means that even if we read all the books we never had time for during our life, or see all the places we never visited, or hear all the symphonies we never listened to, that won't even be the dawn of that eternal day in heaven; that won't even be the beginning of what the Father has prepared for us.

The Eucharistic meal foreshadows the banquet we will celebrate together in heaven. We still have our burdens to bear, but they become lighter when we remember that we're on our way to heaven. We still have our difficulties to endure, but they can't defeat us because we know that eventually victory will be ours.

The Eucharist is Christ's pledge that what we dream about as ideal will become real, in fact, far greater than we imagine. It is his promise that what we seek as the perfect experience will be attained, in fact, surpassed. "For eye has not seen, nor ear heard what God has prepared for those who love him."

Seventh Sunday of the Year
1 Cor 3:16-23

All Things are Yours

Famous families frequently make the headlines in newspapers because of their wealth. In recent times we've had the Patricia Hearst ransom demand and the Christina Onassis inheritance as examples. Such stories have one element in common—the importance of these children to their parents. Either the safety of these children was of greater value to their parents than any ransom payment, or their future security was carefully arranged through their parents' will.

In a sense these parents were saying to their children: "Everything we have is yours. All our property and wealth belong to you. You are the most precious thing we have."

This corresponds somewhat to what St. Paul tells the Corinthians: "All things are yours, whether it is Paul, or Apollos, or Cephas, or the world, or life, or death, or the present, or the future: all these are yours, and you are Christ's and Christ is God's."

It appears that the Corinthians had been forming factions and affirming their allegiance to different teachers like Apollos or Cephas. Paul is saying that the situation should be reversed—their teachers belong to them, not they to the teachers. In fact, he says, everything belongs to them—men, things, events. Because the Corinthians belong to Christ they are precious in the eyes of the Father and all his treasures are their inheritance.

It is the same with us. We don't have to be rivals with one another because in Christ all things are ours. We don't have to compete with one another because our Father takes care of all of us according to our needs. There is some truth in that popular song which says that the moon belongs to everyone and that the best things in life are free.

In his commentary on this text, Fr. Claude Peifer writes: "Everything is at our service: the world, which can lead us to God; life, which brings us closer to God; death, which will consummate the union; the realities of the present life, which already contain the seeds of glory; and the future which will complete it."

How dumb it is then to dedicate one's life to greed. The whole world of nature is ours to enjoy, if only we would open our eyes. The clouds, the lakes, the rocks, the flowers—all these are part of our playground, if only we would pause to appreciate them.

How foolish it is to seek power. In Christ all people already belong to us. We don't have to show our insecurity by trying to dominate or possess people. All we need for a right relationship is to approach them with respect as brothers and sisters.

How silly it is to chase frantically after pleasure. We find all the pleasures we need in using wisely the things God gives us. We don't need drugs, unlimited drinking, or sex without restraint. We have instead the simple delights of food and drink to nourish us, the sexuality of marriage to sustain us, and the recreations of books, plays, movies and sports to renew us.

When we stop to reflect, we realize that we don't have to have wealthy parents to be rich. All things are ours. It is true! Not only the good things of the created order like the sun, the water and the trees, but also the good things that come through Christ like grace, Scripture and the sacraments.

We have every reason then to dismiss all insecurity because *through* Christ all things are ours; cast out all fear because *with* Christ we have everything we need; remove all worry because *in* Christ we belong to God and are precious in his sight.

Eighth Sunday of the Year
1 Cor 4:1-5

Judgment

During the Watergate trials John Ehrlichman repeatedly asserted his innocence. Nevertheless the jury judged him guilty and he was sentenced to serve a term in prison. During her trial in North Carolina Joan Little claimed that she was innocent of the murder charges brought against her. The jury judged that indeed she was innocent and Joan Little was set free.

St. Paul, too, knew what it was like to be accused or held in suspicion. But it didn't make any difference to Paul whether people thought he was innocent or guilty. As he says in his letter to the Corinthians: "The Lord is the one who will judge me. He will bring to light what is hidden in darkness and manifest the intentions of the heart. At that time, everyone will receive his praise from God."

Judgments are an inevitable part of life in a community. Accountability is one of the marks of being a responsible adult. Paul speaks about three judgments that everyone must face.

First, we must face the judgment of our fellow man. If we are an actor on stage, our audience will praise or criticize our performance. If we are an author, our readers will accept or reject the book we write. If we manage a motel, our guests will recommend or complain about our hospitality.

Occasional mistakes are made when other people judge us, but more often than not their judgment is instinctively accurate. This is true because we tend to admire excellence and quality, goodness and virtue, sacrifice and generosity. On the one hand, we should never allow public opinion to sway us from what we believe is right. On the other hand, we should never lightly dismiss what others think. They may be telling it like it really is.

Second, we have to face judgment by ourselves. Granted that our judgment can be distorted by self-delusion and defense mechanisms, still we have to come to grips with ourselves. Unless we can achieve a healthy self-understanding we cannot grow as persons. Until we can honestly assess what is good and bad in our personalities, we will not be able to relate well to others. An alcoholic has to admit his weakness before he can overcome his habit. An athlete has to judge himself capable before he can accomplish some record breaking feat.

Third, we must face the judgment of God. This is the only real judgment. In fact, it is the final judgment. Only the Father can know all the circumstances of our lives—our opportunities and disadvantages, our talents and shortcomings. Only the Father can know all the happenings of our lives—the times we tried and the times we quit, the times we reached out to help others and the times we turned away from others. Only the Father can know all the secret motives of our hearts—our intentions to love and our intentions to hurt, our desires to do something noble and our lust for money or pleasure.

Consequently, unless it is our strict duty in some limited area, as when a teacher has to evaluate a student's work or when an employer has to assess an applicant's qualifications for a job, we should refrain from judging others. We know too little about them.

At the beginning of the liturgy of the Eucharist we bring ourselves to judgment before one another, ourselves and God. We call to mind our sinfulness, confess our guilt and seek forgiveness. This should never be an empty ritual, but a meaningful preparation to meet the Lord—not only when he comes in the Eucharist, but also when he comes as judge at the time of our death.

Ninth Sunday of the Year
Rm 3:21-28

Pioneers and Settlers

In a modern parable Wes Seeliger compares "What Christianity *really* is" with "what many people *think* it is." The former he calls "pioneer theology," the latter "settler theology." In settler theology the church is a courthouse where records are kept and taxes paid. It is a symbol of security, law and order. In pioneer theology the church is a covered wagon, a house on wheels. It is scarred with arrow marks and is always on the move to where the action is.

In settler theology Jesus is a sheriff who enforces the law and puts people in jail. In pioneer theology Jesus is a scout who daringly rides out ahead of the rest and undergoes all the dangers of the trail. In settler theology faith is believing in obedience to the law and trusting in the security of the town. In pioneer theology faith is the spirit of adventure and the readiness to risk everything in the wilderness.

This modern parable by Wes Seeliger gives us an insight into the meaning of St. Paul's words to the Romans: "For we hold that a man is justified by faith apart from the observance of the law."

In other words, our justification is not the product of our own personal achievements or from our following of the laws of the church. Instead it is a gift we receive from God and respond to in faith with our whole being. This does not deny the need for obeying laws and doing good works. It simply stresses the priority of faith.

The Jerome Biblical Commentary remarks: "For Paul, faith is an attitude by which man accepts the divine revelation made known through Christ and responds to it with a complete dedication of himself. Faith is an experience which begins with a hearing of the word about Christ, and ends in a personal commitment to Christ of the whole man."

Such a faith, then, is not merely an assent of the mind to some dogma or the conformity of the will to some moral law. Faith is a vital, interpersonal relationship of the whole person with Christ. It is not the faith of the settler who finds satisfaction in his accomplishments and security in the laws he makes. Rather, it is the faith of the pioneer who lets God lead him into adventure and is willing to take risks.

If we have such a faith, then we can never be complacent and figure that we've already got it made because of the donations we've given, the fasts we've performed or the prayers we've recited. On the contrary, we are constantly on the move looking for new surprises from the Lord and responding to the fresh challenges he issues.

Each day God gives us the gift of life and the gift of himself. Faith is the acceptance of these gifts and the commitment of our whole being to the praise of his goodness. From this kind of faith good works will follow—almsgiving, fasting and praying. From this kind of faith the observance of the law becomes easy. In fact, we are willing to do more than the law requires or demands.

Because we have faith we are willing to take risks for the Lord: to help someone even though they might take advantage of us; to surrender something to the Lord even though we feel we can't get along without it. Because we have faith we can do difficult things for the Lord: forgive someone even though they have hurt our feelings very deeply; accept suffering patiently even though we can't comprehend why.

Don't be a settler! Be a pioneer!

Tenth Sunday of the Year
Rm 4:18-25

Abraham's Faith

One of the more inspiring newspaper stories of the decade has to be the story about Glen and Ann Heikes. Glen quit his $20,000-a-year job in the government to study for the ministry as a priest in the Evangelical Church. His wife Ann has been a polio victim since age seven. She has to wear long braces and use crutches to get around. It took Ann eighteen years to finish her college education but she finally got her degree from North Park College in Chicago.

To support themselves, their two daughters and their two adopted American Indian sons, Glen and Ann did janitorial work while they went to college and served as house parents in one of the campus dorms. Then they went from Chicago to Costa Rica to receive training for the mission work they are now doing in Ecuador.

Glen and Ann Heikes bear a lot of resemblance to Abraham and Sarah as St. Paul describes them in his letter to the Romans: "Abraham believed hoping against hope, and so became the father of many nations. Without growing weak in faith he thought of his own body, which was as good as dead (for he was nearly a hundred years old), and of the dead womb of Sarah. Yet he never questioned or doubted God's promise; rather, he was strengthened in faith and gave glory to God, fully persuaded that God could do whatever he had promised."

Like Abraham and Sarah, Glen and Ann Heikes left behind their security, a $20,000-a-year job, to follow a call from the Lord in ministry. Against seemingly insurmountable obstacles they set out to become missionaries in lands then unknown to them. Their faith ran counter to hope, yet it rested upon hope. Their faith seemed absurd to human reason, yet made sense because of God's promise.

What kind of faith and hope do we have? How many times does the Lord call us to do something grand or magnificent for him, such as taking the initiative to settle our differences with someone; reaching out a helping hand to a neighbor in need; or witnessing to our faith when an opportunity presents itself? But our only response is to rationalize about the call, weigh its difficulties, and finally dismiss the whole idea. After all, why should we risk the security we already have for some foolish idea?

When the Lord calls us to leave our accustomed comforts behind and do something daring or generous for him, the only thing preventing us from stepping out in faith is our lack of trust in him. If we really had the faith and hope of Abraham and Sarah we would put more emphasis on God's promise and less on the obstacles; we would rely more on his power and less on our own resources.

If we really had the faith and hope of people like Glen and Ann Heikes, we would trust more in God's wisdom and less in our own cleverness; we would search more for the Lord's will in which we find peace and less in our own will in which we often find pain.

In the Eucharistic assembly we make an act of faith in the Lord's presence sacramentally. This is also a chance for us to make an act of faith in the Lord's presence in our life when we encounter difficulties, experience our own personal shortcomings, or run into opposition from others.

In liturgy and in life we give glory to God when we believe that nothing can prevail over his purpose for us; when we believe that there is nothing, even sin, that cannot be transformed into accomplishing his plans for us. All we have to do is believe—hoping against hope—fully persuaded that God can do whatever he promises to do for us.

Eleventh Sunday of the year
Rm 5:6-11

Lawrence of Arabia

One of the greatest movies ever made is *Lawrence of Arabia*. In an unforgettable scene from that movie Colonel Lawrence and the Arabs are traveling across the desert in a sandstorm under a scorching sun. With their food and water in short supply the situation is desperate. Suddenly one of the Arabs notices an empty saddle on a camel and asks, "Where is Jasmin?" "Who is Jasmin?" another asks. "A man from Maan who killed a Turkish tax-collector and fled to the desert" is the answer. Another Arab remarks, "Jasmin was not strong either in the head or in the body. He is not worth half a crown to worry about."

So the Arabs rode on. But Lawrence turned and rode back the way they had come. Alone and at the risk of his life, Lawrence searched for two hours before he found Jasmin—blind from the sandstorm, mad from the heat of the sun, and dying of thirst from no water. Lawrence lifted Jasmin up on his own camel, gave him the last drops of his precious water, and returned to his company. When Lawrence and Jasmin arrived the amazed Arabs exclaimed, "Here is Jasmin, not worth a half crown, but saved at his own risk by Lawrence, our Lord."

This episode about Lawrence of Arabia and Jasmin gives us some insight about what Jesus has done for us. St. Paul writes: "Christ died for us godless men. It is rare that anyone should lay down his life for a just man, though it is barely possible that for a good man someone may have the courage to die. It is precisely in this that God proves his love for us: that while we were still sinners, Christ died for us."

We have been saved not because we are so deserving and attractive, but simply because Jesus loves us; not because we are so admirable and praiseworthy, but only because he loves us. If this is the incredible love that Jesus has for us, what should our response be to him?

First, a response of profound gratitude. When we realize what Jesus has done for us at the cost of his own life, we can't help but lift up our hearts in thanksgiving. When we come to appreciate how, in spite of our sinfulness, the Lord has made us his "own special possession," we can't help but sing songs of praise to him.

Second, our response should be one of trust and confidence. If Jesus shed his blood for us when we were sinners, how much more will he do for us now that we have been saved. If his death was able to deliver us from sin, how much more will his life now do for us. There is no sin, no sickness he cannot cure. There is no obstacle, no difficulty he cannot overcome. All we have to do is trust in his everlasting love for us and have confidence in his power.

Third, our response should be one of loving and sharing. The tremendous love Jesus has shown for us inspires us to love others in the same way. His magnificence towards us prompts us in turn to reach out towards others. As the gospel says, "The gift you have received, give as a gift." Jesus urges us to love not only those who are friendly, beautiful, healthy and successful, but especially those who are hostile, repulsive, handicapped and failures. It is precisely in this that we can prove our love for others: that we lay down our lives for them in service while they are still sinners; that we seek out to minister to them while they are still separated from us.

We can imagine how often Jasmin told and re-told the story of Lawrence risking his life in the desert to save him, a worthless murderer. We do the same thing ourselves whenever we celebrate the liturgy or witness. We tell over and over again the fantastic love of Jesus for us—how he laid down his life for us when we were still sinners and how he made us his special people when we were lost like sheep.

Twelfth Sunday of the Year
Rm 5:12-15

Operation SAMM

In the *Chicago Sun Times* there was an article under the title "Three ex-cons take a message to ghetto youth." The three men are members of what is called Operation SAMM, the initials standing for Self-Awareness Motivation Movement. The purpose of Operation SAMM is to keep ghetto-born-and-bred youth from crime by talking to them, directing recreation programs for them, helping them find jobs, and assisting in other ways.

The three ex-convicts are Fred Cook, forty-six, with twenty-eight years in prison; Louis Truelock, forty-four, with twenty-three years spent in jail; and Cecil Randall-El, thirty-five, with twenty years behind bars. While in prison all three men separately underwent personal crises leading to a reevaluation of their goals. They met and now live at St. Anthony's Inn, a halfway house for parolees. Besides holding regular jobs they spend most of their time in Operation SAMM.

Louis Truelock summed up their new life by saying: "We are master failures. We are trying to struggle from lives of disgust to dignity. If we can help the kids, we can help ourselves." Another way to describe the change that has taken place in their lives is to use the words of St. Paul: "The gift is not like the offense. For if by the offense of the one man all died, much more did the grace of God and the gift of the one man, Jesus Christ, abound for all."

In connection with this passage *The Jerome Biblical Commentary* states: "Although Adam prefigured Christ as the head of humanity, the resemblance is not perfect. The resemblance is not one of equality, but of superiority. Paul emphasizes the surpassing quality of Christ's influence on mankind. The superabundance of

Christ's grace is in excess of any mercy our sins could possibly evoke."

The main thrust of Paul's comparison is that grace is mightier than sin. Grace does not just offset the results of the forces of evil. That would be merely a negative view, however important. Rather, grace does much more, as we can see in the lives of those three ex-convicts. Grace abounds without measure restoring order where there was chaos, peace where there was anxiety, and light where there was darkness.

How amazing and overwhelming is God's grace. It makes no difference how far we may stray. As long as we live we can never stray beyond the bounds of God's mercy. It doesn't matter how enormous is the weight of our sins. As long as we turn to the Lord his grace can lift any burden from us.

Moreover, grace overflows carrying us into works of healing among the sick, counseling among the disturbed and charity among the needy. Grace inspires us to release people imprisoned by loneliness and self-pity; lift up people held down by depression and discouragement; and comfort people hurt by disappointment and rejection.

Whenever we begin a Eucharistic celebration we bring the burden of our sins. But when we end it, we bear with us the abundance of God's grace. We leave to witness how God's gracious gifts abound much more than our offenses.

Thirteenth Sunday of the Year
Rm 6:3-11

New Life

Acts of violence against innocent victims have become too common an occurrence on our city streets. One such incident involved a man named Bertrand Wozniak who was beaten to death in Chicago. It was an especially tragic death because Wozniak was an active member of the Alcoholics Anonymous and he was murdered while on a mission of mercy trying to aid another alcoholic.

But even though Wozniak came to a tragic end, his life and death were marked with glory. When he was captain in the army during World War II, he became an alcoholic. Then in 1962 he joined the AA and never again took another drink. From that time on Wozniak lived a new life—a life free of the influence of alcohol, and a life of saving others who were still afflicted by it.

Bertrand Wozniak's conversion through the AA is similar to what is supposed to happen to us through baptism. As St. Paul says: "Through baptism into Christ's death we were buried with him, so that, just as Christ was raised from the dead by the glory of the Father, we too might live a new life. We must consider ourselves dead to sin but alive for God in Christ Jesus."

In his commentaries on the letters of Paul, C.H. Dodd says that there is a drastic contrast between what we were before baptism with what we are supposed to be afterwards. Before baptism the divine element within us is present only in potentiality. It is obscured by our participation in sinfulness. But after baptism this divine element within us is released and becomes operative. It manifests itself by our participation in good works.

To describe these effects of baptism in us, Paul uses three

77

prepositional phrases, namely, *into* Christ, *with* Christ, and *in* Christ. First, Paul says that we are baptized *into* Christ's death. Dodd remarks that this preposition *into* expresses our movement towards Christ. By baptism we leave behind our original condition in Adam and move *into* a new relationship with Christ. We abandon our natural inclinations in the flesh and move *into* a new life in the spirit.

Paul says that we are buried *with* Christ. On the one hand, Dodd points out that we are identified *with* the most significant of Christ's historical acts of redemption. We suffer with Christ, die with Christ, are buried with Christ, rise with Christ, and are glorified with Christ. On the other hand, we are associated *with* him in his future coming in glory. It is our destiny to be *with* Christ when his glory will be fully revealed at the end of time. In other words, we are identified *with* Christ both at the beginning and at the end of the history of salvation. In the meantime, we are *in* Christ.

This brings us to the third preposition—we are alive for God *in* Christ Jesus. Dodd says that this refers to our present state. Even though the final form of our life *with* Christ is yet to come, we already possess it in principle. We already are living *in* Christ. Just as we cannot live a physical life unless we are *in* the air and the air is *in* us, so too we cannot live a spiritual life unless we are *in* Christ and Christ is *in* us. Or, to use other examples, Christ is the vine *in* whom we must adhere in order to grow and bear fruit; he is the living bread *in* which we must share in order to survive during our pilgrimage.

Praise the Lord for baptizing us *into* Christ's death and *into* a new relationship with him. Like Bertrand Wozniak we have the power to pass out of the old order of slavery and sin *into* a new order of freedom and good works. Thank God for burying us *with* Christ and raising us *with* him. No longer are we bound by our past weaknesses and failures. Already we are living a new life *in* Christ, and we look forward to our future glorification *with* him.

Fourteenth Sunday of the Year
Rm 8:9-13

Life by the Spirit

Pat Boone, his wife Shirley, and their four daughters are considered by many as an ideal Christian family. The Boones have been outstanding in combining Christian witness with success in the world of entertainment. But it was not always so with the Boone family. Pat and Shirley were married as teenagers and Pat became an instant success on radio, TV and film. Pat tells how his hunger for success began to dilute his faith in Christ and alienate him from his wife Shirley.

Their marriage was saved from destruction when they both returned to the Lord and surrendered themselves to the Holy Spirit. Since that time the Pat Boone household has become one of the most peaceful and joyful in all Hollywood. As long as the Boones were living according to the "flesh" and pursuing fame, their marriage was dying. But as soon as they began to live by the "spirit," their marriage came alive again.

Their experience is an example of St. Paul's words to the Romans: "You are not in the flesh; you are in the spirit since the Spirit of God dwells in you. If you live according to the flesh, you will die. But if by the spirit you put to death the evil deeds of the body, you will live."

In this passage Paul is contrasting two ways of life. On the one hand, there is the life of the "flesh" leading to death. Paul is not talking about the flesh of our body, the corporeal condition of our humanity. Rather, he is talking about our natural condition with all its weaknesses and without grace.

Life according to the "flesh" is a preoccupation with all our appetites and wants, of which the physical are only a part. It is a life whose dominant interests are determined by our undisciplined desires. We can recognize the characteristics of those who live by the "flesh"—they are driven by their ambitions, controlled by their passions and imprisoned by their pride.

On the other hand, there is the life of the "spirit." Paul is not talking about an immaterial existence detached from the physical dimensions of reality. Rather, he is talking about our human nature, both body and souls, transformed by grace.

Life according to the "spirit" seeks first the kingdom of God. It seeks this world's goods in proportion to that kingdom. It is an existence whose dominant interests are the higher and more lasting values of life. We know those who live by the "spirit"—they know how to balance their like for beer with their reading of the Bible; how to participate in parties with people and in prayer by themselves; how to be competent in their work and concerned about those who can't work.

Which of these two ways of life do we follow? Which of these two alternatives do we choose most of the time? Like Pat Boone we know from our own experience that whenever we live according to the "flesh," we end up destroying ourselves. Whether it is in eating or drinking too much, seeking wealth at the expense of our integrity, or insisting on our own way without considering others, the immediate gratification we feel soon disappears and we are left disappointed, disillusioned and depressed. The vicious cycle repeats itself and we gradually put to death anything in our lives that is good, beautiful and true.

But whenever we follow the "spirit," we find life. Whether we pray or play, fast or feast, give or receive, whenever we do all these things according to the "spirit," we experience a satisfaction that is deep and lasting. Our personalities grow and become richer, we become more and more Christ-like. It's much more exciting and fulfilling to choose life and live by the "spirit."

Fifteenth Sunday of the Year
Rm 8:18-23

Creation's Destiny

A World Conference on Water was held in 1977 to study the alarming rate at which we are wasting and polluting fresh water. We need fresh water for crops, cattle, irrigation, forests, hygiene and drinking. Experts claim that unless we get international cooperation on control of water supplies, we are courting a global calamity.

The problems we have with water are only part of a larger problem involving land and air as well as food and fuel. St. Paul's words from his letter to the Romans are even more true today than they were in his time: "The whole created world eagerly awaits the revelation of the sons of God, when the world itself will be freed from its slavery to corruption and share in the glorious freedom of the children of God. Yes, we know that all creation groans and is in agony even until now."

This is one of the few places where Paul expresses himself as a poet. Elsewhere he speaks as a rabbi, a philosopher and a psychologist, but here he speaks with the vision of a poet. Paul feels the plight of the natural world: the weak devoured by the strong in the animal kingdom; the destruction of plant life by storms; the upheavals caused by earthquakes. Yet he envisions a time when the whole material universe will be delivered from bondage and transformed into glory; a time when chaos will give way to order, conflict to peace, and decay to life.

This vision is not unique to Paul. The new heavens and the new earth he foresees are expressed elsewhere in Scripture; for example, in Is 65:17; 2 P 3:13; Rv 21:1. Nor is it an idea foreign to contemporary theology. For example, the Dominican Scripture scholar Pierre Benoit says: "The plenitude of the cosmos lies in Christ. He embraces in this plenitude not only men who are saved, but the whole setting of humanity, that is to say, the cosmos."

Another example is the Jesuit theologian Stanislaus Lyonnet. In an article entitled "The Redemption of the Universe" he writes: "For a Jew instructed in the Scriptures the history of the universe was a part of the history of salvation. Created for man, the universe in some way shares his destiny. Just as the execution of the first alliance with Noah had cosmic implications so the eschatological alliance will necessarily have its impact on the whole of creation."

According to some theologians then we can envision a connection between the sacrament of the Eucharist and the re-creation of the cosmos. There is a sense in which the sacramental action of Christ goes beyond the bread and wine on the altar to embrace the whole material order with its transforming power. Sacramental elements are formed by the totality of matter in the universe, and the duration of creation is the time needed for their consecration.

Men like Paul, Benoit and Lyonnet are not pessimists. They recognize the fallen state of the world and of humanity, but they also see God's redeeming grace at work both in man and in the material world. Life for them is not a despairing waiting for an inevitable end of death and decay. Life is an eager expectation of a liberation and a re-creation, not only of man but of the whole universe.

As Christians we too have to take this planet earth seriously. We have a responsibility to use its rich resources wisely, develop its potential, and respect its sacramental character. The Eucharist reminds us of that. As Christians we have an essential part to play in its preparation for glory. The whole universe waits with us, not for destruction, but for re-creation; not for decay, but for an eternal destiny in Christ.

Sixteenth Sunday of the Year
Rm 8:26-27

Praying in the Spirit

It was like another miracle at Cana when Peter Saraceno, who was declared dead two years before, got married to his fiancee Linda Fraschalla, who refused to believe that he would die. Peter had been critically injured in an auto crash. A doctor pronounced him dead on arrival at the hospital. But the doctor tried one last time to find a pulse and found a faint one.

Peter did not die but remained in a coma for the next several months. Every night Linda came to the hospital from work and sat by Peter's side talking to him as if they were on a date. Finally, after three and a half months, Peter came out of his coma. His recovery was slow but steady. At first, he could move only his eyes, then a finger, then an arm, then a leg.

He had to learn how to do simple things all over again—how to talk, walk and eat. But with Linda's constant care and encouragement over a two year period Peter did relearn all these things and was finally able to get married to her.

What Linda was able to do for Peter Saraceno is similar to what the Holy Spirit does for us. St. Paul says: "The Spirit too helps us in our weakness, for we do not know how to pray as we ought. But the Spirit himself makes intercession for us with groanings which cannot be expressed in speech."

In a sense, all of us are somewhat like Peter Saraceno at certain times of our lives—powerless, speechless, our dreams shattered, our every effort futile. But the Lord has given us a Linda to be with us at times like these, namely, the Holy Spirit whom he has poured out into our hearts.

All of us know that feeling of helplessness in moments of

weakness—those times when we stand beside a loved one in a hospital not knowing what to do; when we feel left out like a forgotten aging parent; when we feel rejected like a frustrated youth. In situations like these the Holy Spirit supports us in our weakness, loneliness and hurt. The Spirit himself prays for us through our groanings and sighs without words.

But there is a special gift of the Holy Spirit that is being recognized and experienced more these days—the gift of tongues, the gift of praying with a new language. Fr. Rene Laurentin, a theologian, says that praying with tongues liberates us from our inhibitions in regard to man and God; it frees us from human respect and from our fear of approaching God whom no words can describe. As a result, interior energies, both mystical and apostolic, are released.

Laurentin adds that speaking in tongues meets our need for an ineffable language that attempts to reach God through a kind of discourse beyond language, beyond the profane. Praying in tongues is a way of speaking the "new language" promised by Christ in Mk 16:17. This language gives expression to the "new man" of whom Paul speaks, the man in whom God has instilled a new heart and a new spirit.

Finally, Laurentin suggests that the gift of tongues is a language of the future, a language of freedom. He who speaks it exists in tomorrow's world. Tomorrow becomes today, and the jubilant speaker experiences the beauty which some day will redeem and transform the world.

Praise the Lord for not only giving us people like Linda to help us in time of weakness and helplessness, but also the person and the presence of the Holy Spirit to pray for us when we don't know what to say. Glorify the Lord for giving us the gift of tongues with which to pray, a gift whereby we can utter a prayer so deep that our own words are inadequate, a prayer which so penetrates our being that it is beyond all speech.

Seventeenth Sunday of the Year
Rm 8:28-30

Eugene O'Neill

When he died in 1953 Eugene O'Neill was universally recognized as one of the major dramatists of the modern world. His plays are read by more people today than those of any other playwright except William Shakespeare and perhaps G.B. Shaw. A remarkable accomplishment when you consider Eugene O'Neill's background. His family was less than ideal. His father was a traveling actor, his mother became a morphine addict, and his older brother an alcoholic. His education was not altogether successful. He was a mediocre student at boarding school and dropped out of Princeton University after his freshman year.

In his early manhood O'Neill drifted for six years, deserted the first of his three wives, became a bum on the New York waterfronts, and tried to commit suicide at the age of twenty-three. His health was not the best. He had tuberculosis as a youth, was an alcoholic for two decades before quitting, and was afflicted with premature aging tremors the last ten years of his life.

Yet from all this turmoil emerged almost fifty plays, four Pulitzer Prizes, and the 1936 Nobel Prize for Literature. The life and works of Eugene O'Neill illustrate St. Paul's words to the Romans: "We know that God makes all things work together for the good of those who love him, who have been called according to his purpose."

All the difficulties of Eugene O'Neill's early life became the raw material for the successful plays he wrote later. All his sufferings were translated into powerful drama about the meaning of life. Even though Eugene O'Neill had publicly renounced his Catholic faith, the theme of most of his plays is man's relationship with

God. He became the Lord's instrument for teaching theology indirectly through his literature and drama.

It is our own experience, too, that somehow all things work together for our good: a sickness we thought was an obstacle turned out to be a blessing; a loss we thought was bad luck turned out to bring a greater gain; an adversity we thought would destroy us turned out to be to our advantage. As we look back over our past we can see that a loving hand has been guiding us and that a providential plan has been unfolding. But in order to see this we have to put our trust in the Lord.

When we go to a doctor we have to receive sometimes a painful treatment. Yet we accept this pain because we trust that what the doctor is doing is for the greater good of our overall health. In the same way, if we put our trust in the Lord, then there is no difficulty that we cannot cope with. If we believe that God's power is operating, then there are no circumstances, however bad, that cannot be converted into a source of good.

During his lifetime Eugene O'Neill had to overcome a lot of adversity in becoming an accomplished playwright. Despite his open defiance of Catholicism, he became the Lord's instrument to teach us about the meaning of life and man's relationship to God.

If the Lord could make all things work together for the good of a man who so often resisted him, how much more good will he not accomplish through us who want to cooperate with him, with us who love him. The Eucharistic bread we break together is Christ's pledge to do this. By changing the bread and wine into his body and blood, Christ promises to change all things for our good: our hindrances into helps; our obstacles into opportunities; our failures into triumphs.

Eighteenth Sunday of the Year
Rm 8:35-39

Vietnam War Vet

In 1966 Wally Clarke graduated from Coventry High School in Rhode Island as the athlete of the year. He then joined the Marines and was sent to Vietnam. Two years later he returned to rural Coventry, minus two legs and two fingers which he lost when he stepped on a tank mine. It was expected to be a sad day when Wally returned home, but he surprised the town by arriving with the same infectious smile he had when he left.

Since that time Wally has married, become the father of three young boys, and found a full time job in the state attorney general's office. Despite his handicap he is still very much involved in athletics. He coaches youth baseball and basketball teams, is the player-manager of a VFW softball team, and the player-coach of a wheelchair basketball team.

In 1978 the new high school athletic complex was dedicated to him. "He's really given of himself," said the athletic director. "He was a happy-go-lucky boy. He's still a happy-go-lucky man. There's no bitterness in his heart."

Wally Clarke knows from personal experience the meaning of St. Paul's words when he wrote to the Romans: "Who shall separate us from the love of Christ? Trial, or distress, or persecution, or hunger, or nakedness, or danger, or the sword? Yet in all this we are more than conquerors because of him who has loved us."

According to the *Interpreter's Bible* there are three stages to note in Paul's words. First, we are conquerors. Second, we are more than conquerors. Third, we are more than conquerors because of him who loved us.

At the first stage we are conquerors. Regardless of what the threat or danger may be, the human spirit is capable of rising above it. We see this in the episodes of our early American pioneers on the frontiers, in the survival of the Jews at Auschwitz, and in the determination of war veteran Wally Clarke. The greatest beauty and gallantry often emerge in the most difficult circumstances. Like stately pines that grow in clefts of rock, man's nobility can prevail in the face of any obstacle in his environment.

In the second stage we are more than conquerors. The human spirit is capable not only of overcoming difficulties, but also of converting them to its advantage. Evils are not just rendered harmless; they are changed into positive goods. We know from our own experience how often it happens that some sorrow is just a prelude to joy; a mistake serves to teach us humility; a tragedy leaves us so much wiser. The greatest blessings are sometimes disguised as obstacles. Like timber that uses the wind and the rain to develop strength, we too can use adversity to develop character.

In the third stage we are more than conquerors because of him who loved us. Only love can make us triumph in the midst of trials and transform evil into good. Because Jesus loved us and gave himself up for us, we are willing to do anything for him: endure any hardship, suffer any disappointment, risk any danger. We may not understand *why* we have adversity, but at least we have a *way* of coping with it—the love of Christ urges us on. Because we love Jesus we will not let ourselves be defeated or discouraged by difficulties. Instead we will be all the more determined to demonstrate our devotion to him.

Like Wally Clarke we can cry: "Take away my legs, my health and my possessions if you will. Nothing shall separate me from the love of Christ." Like St. Paul we can exclaim: "Strip me, starve me, persecute me, hurt me if you will. Nothing shall separate me from the love of Christ. In all these things I am a conqueror. No, more than a conqueror, because of him who loved me."

Nineteenth Sunday of the Year
Rm 9:1-5

Revitalization Corps

There is an organization known as the Revitalization Corps. It consists of more than five thousand volunteers who work in some one hundred poverty-stricken communities around the U.S. These volunteers include students for tutoring, ex-convicts to work with juvenile delinquents, business executives to provide job opportunities, and many others.

The Revitalization Corps is headed by Edward Coll, who left a lucrative insurance career to form the program. Coll says, "In pro football, they say the game is won or lost in the pit, that area known as line play. For the past ten years I've been working in another kind of pit, the ghettos of Harlem and Watts. There, it is not games that are lost, only lives. We worry about the thousands of young Americans who died in the Vietnam War, yet we ignore the thousands of young men who die in the ghettos. They die, not so much from shrapnel and mortar fire, as from diseased heroin needles or violence caused by frustration."

Because of his concern for the poor in the ghettos, Ed Coll has been called a white-pig, a nigger-lover, and a communist fanatic. But such ridicule cannot destroy his deep love for the poor. Coll says, "Christ is still dying in the pits. Christ is not dying because he is with the poor. He is dying because Christians are not there with him."

Ed Coll's feelings for the poor are similar to St. Paul's feelings for his fellow Jews. "There is great grief and constant pain in my heart," Paul says. "Indeed, I could even wish to be separated from Christ for the sake of my brothers, my kinsmen the Israelites."

When Paul became a Christian he did not abandon his heritage as a Jew. Indeed, he rejected the imperfections of the Jewish religion as regards its practice of the Law, but he preserved its many positive elements such as the word of Scripture. Paul broke with Judaism as a *system*, but found himself even more closely united with them as a *race*. The Jews were still his brothers and sisters, and he longed earnestly for their conversion.

Paul's prayer is reminiscent of Moses' plea for the rebellious Israelites during the Exodus, when he was willing to be blotted out of the Book of Life so that they might be forgiven. Paul's prayer also recalls the words of Jesus when he said that there is no greater love a man can have than to lay down his life for his friend.

We have to be moved by Paul's passionate love for his fellow Jews. We have to be inspired by Ed Coll's intense devotion to the poor in the slums. As disciples of Christ we are called to this same kind of love and devotion.

We are called to love our neighbors in other parts of the world. Their skin may be a different color than ours and they may be our rivals for wheat and oil, but they are still our companions on this spaceship earth. We are called to love our institutions of church and government. They may be imperfect and have many faults, but they are still the source of our religious and civic values.

We are called to love the communities of our parish and family. They may have members who irritate or even hurt us, but they are still our fellow members in the Body of Christ. We are called to love the poor and disadvantaged in our slums, prisons and mental institutions. They may be unattractive and even repulsive, but they are still children of God and bear his image.

The Eucharistic bread we share together is a symbol of the burdens we should share with each other in love. Because of what Christ has done for us there is no sacrifice we should not be able to make for one another. We may be ridiculed for this like Ed Coll or persecuted like Paul, but this should not weaken our commitment to love. We may be misunderstood, rejected and even hurt by the very person we try to help, but that shouldn't lessen our love for that person. Nothing is too good to sacrifice for the sake of our brothers and sisters, our kinsmen in Christ.

Twentieth Sunday of the Year
Rm 11:13-15, 29-32

Irrevocable

In the book *Fear Strikes Out* Jim Piersall tells the heartwarming story of his early life. When Jim played for the Boston Red Sox in 1952 he was one of the most sensational rookies to enter the major leagues in baseball. But he suffered a nervous breakdown that year and had to be confined to a mental institution.

It was only through the loyal devotion of his wife Mary that Jim was able to fight his way back to sanity. All through the period when Jim was doing crazy things, Mary was patient, kind and understanding. All through the recovery period when Jim was trying to piece together his life, she was sympathetic, gentle and encouraging.

Mary's fidelity to Jim is a reflection of God's fidelity toward us. St. Paul's letter to the Romans refers to this fidelity when he writes: "God's gifts and his call are irrevocable." In the context of the letter, Paul is dealing with the problem of the infidelity of the Jews. They have done crazy things like ignoring the prophets, breaking the covenant and crucifying Christ. Yet, Paul asserts, God will find a way to save them, for his gifts to them and his call are irrevocable.

There are two aspects to Paul's declaration about God's fidelity. One aspect is the confidence it should instill in us. No matter what kind of crazy things we may do, we can always count on God being faithful. In our covenant relationship with God we often carry on like the Jews and Jim Piersall—we do crazy things. The Lord protects us from serious injury in an auto accident, and two weeks later we're driving just as recklessly again. The Lord restores our health after we get sick from drinking too much, and the next time we go to a party we get drunk all over again.

Yet every time we do something crazy, the Lord does not abandon us. Like Mary Piersall standing beside her husband Jim, the Lord is always ready to help us. His patience, kindness and understanding are without limit. What confidence then we should have in him. Regardless of how unfaithful we are to him, we can always count on him being faithful to us. His gifts and his call are irrevocable.

If this is true when we are unfaithful, how much more true is it when we are faithful: when we do our best work for him, even though we fail; when we pray to him, even though it seems useless; when we trust him, even though the times are trying.

The second aspect of Paul's declaration about God's fidelity is its call to us to be faithful and loyal also. In the *Dictionary of Biblical Theology* Leon-Dufour writes: "It is not enough to praise the divine fidelity or to proclaim it in order to invoke it. We must pray to the faithful God to obtain fidelity from him and to stop answering his fidelity by our faithlessness."

It isn't enough just to admire the fidelity in the face of adversity of someone like Mary Piersall. We have to go and do the same. When our husband or wife does something crazy to hurt us, we still have to be loyal to our marriage vows and love them. When our fellow workers do something dishonest like stealing, we still have to live up to our part of the contract with the employer. When our fellow students at college practice premarital sex, we still have to be faithful to our commitment to chastity.

The Eucharist is the Lord's pledge of fidelity to us, the sacramental sign that his gifts and his call are irrevocable. Praise him for always being faithful to us, even when we do crazy things. Thank him for people like Mary Piersall who remain loyal to us, even when we hurt them. Ask him to help us live up to our promises, not only to him but also to our fellow man.

Twenty-First Sunday of the Year
Rm 11:33-36

Butterflies

One of the most marvelous happenings in nature is the transformation of a caterpillar into a butterfly. The caterpillar is a hairy worm with fourteen or more legs. It eats green things and has no interest in beautiful flowers. It makes no effort to fly but is content to crawl around.

As winter approaches, the caterpillar weaves a cocoon around itself. There in this waterproof, airproof, lightproof and heatproof cocoon the caterpillar encloses itself for the entire winter season. When springtime comes there emerges from the cocoon, not the ugly wormlike caterpillar, but a beautiful butterfly with colorful wings and a remarkable tongue to draw up nectar from flowers.

How is this metamorphosis accomplished? Scientists do not know. How does the butterfly get out of that sealed cocoon? Again, we do not know. When we observe such marvelous happenings in nature, we can't help but sing St. Paul's hymn: "How deep are the riches and the wisdom and the knowledge of God. How inscrutable his judgments, how unsearchable his ways."

If this is true about the Lord's wonders in the world of insects, it is all the more so regarding his ways with man. We can discern some of his designs unfolding in the history of man, but such knowledge is always fragmentary and incomplete.

Like Job before him Paul grappled with the great issues of life, only to end up in admiration of God's boundless wisdom. Paul probed the mystery of God's dealings with the Jews and Gentiles, only to come to the conclusion that God's ways are inscrutable. Paul searched with his mind and ended up adoring with his heart.

He applied the methods of philosophy and ended up praising the Lord with poetry.

It is no different with us. We can wrestle all we want with ultimate questions like where did I come from? How did I get to this time and place? Where am I going? But in the end we come to the realization that our questioning of the Lord is irrelevant and that it is our trusting that is important. We come to appreciate that while pondering God's plan has its place, praising him over it is more important.

Consequently, even though we may not be able to explain how caterpillars become butterflies or how sinners become saints, we know that these things happen. So we can praise the Lord for his wisdom and expect wonderful things to happen to us, too. We can expect him to transform our discouragement into hope, our fear into courage and our sadness into joy.

Even though we may not be able to explain how a butterfly emerges from its cocoon or how Lazarus left his tomb, we know that these things have happened. So we can glorify God for his mysterious ways and prepare ourselves for similar surprises, like bringing good out of evil, light out of darkness and life out of death.

"How deep is the wisdom of God and how unsearchable his ways." All through human history he has done astonishing things like making the shepherd boy David a King, the Virgin Mary the Mother of Jesus and the fisherman Peter the chief apostle. All through life the Lord does astonishing things, like overlooking our lowliness and making us his children, accepting our weaknesses and making us brothers in Christ, forgetting our sins and filling us with his Holy Spirit.

"How deep are the riches and the wisdom of God. How inscrutable his ways." Caterpillars become butterflies. Bread becomes the body of Christ. Sinners like us become saints.

Twenty-Second Sunday of the Year
Rm 12:1-2

Offer Your Bodies

One of the reasons for the rise in popularity of soccer in the United States was the signing to a contract with the New York Cosmos of the great Pele. As the Cosmos played soccer in different cities the ace from Brazil dazzled spectators with his strength, quickness and agility.

Pele is a professional athlete who makes his livelihood using his body, especially his feet. Without nimble feet the great Pele would never be the world's premier soccer player. Many other people attain excellence through the perfection of a physical skill.

For example, Rudolf Nureyev has perfected the balance of his body for the art of ballet. Alexander Calder has developed skilled hands in the world of sculpture. Marcel Marceau has created new facial expressions for his mime presentations on stage.

Such people have consecrated the use of their bodies to their careers. Through the total commitment of their bodies they have achieved prominence in the world of athletics, dance, art and drama. This same kind of consecration of the body is required of us, not necessarily to attain excellence in some career, but to attain sanctity in our relationship with the Lord.

As St. Paul says: "Brothers, I beg you through the mercy of God to offer your bodies as a living sacrifice holy and acceptable to God, your spiritual worship. Do not conform yourselves to this age but be transformed by the renewal of your mind."

The word Paul uses for body means much more than just the physical organism of flesh and blood. The word includes all the human activity in which we engage by means of our bodies. As *The Jerome Biblical Commentary* puts it, "The word *body* seems to be

Paul's way of saying *self*. We are to offer ourselves to the Lord—our whole being, body and soul and all that we do."

When we work with our body like Pele, we must offer that work to the Lord. Whether we work in mines or on farms, in factories or offices, in labs or kitchens, no matter where we work, we must offer that work to the Lord. When we play with our body like Marcel Marceau, we must offer that play to the Lord. Whether we swim or golf, play cards or tennis, go fishing or biking, no matter how we play, we must offer what we do to the Lord.

All this becomes part of the living sacrifice we make to the Lord, our spiritual worship, holy and acceptable to him. Everything we do through our body takes on a cultic sense, a liturgical dimension, a sacramental significance.

What we celebrate in church during the liturgy of the Eucharist is worship of the highest form. But it doesn't end there. Our worship extends beyond the walls of the church to include the school, shop, theater, park, or wherever we happen to be doing something for the Lord.

Our sacrifice is a living sacrifice. Even in the Old Testament the essence of sacrifice was not in the death of the animal, but in the offering of the animal's life to the Lord. The truest sacrifice is to live according to God's will, to offer him ourselves with all our powers, to consecrate to him all that we do.

When we worship in church it should not be some dull routine through which we daydream, but a dynamic offering of ourselves and everything we do through our body: our working and sleeping, our learning and loving, our playing and praying.

Twenty-Third Sunday of the Year
Rm 13:8-10

The Tramp

    Science fiction writer Robert A. Heinlein once told the following true story about his hometown when he was a child sixty years ago. One Sunday afternoon he saw a young woman accidentally get her foot caught in some railroad tracks. Neither she nor her husband could pull it free. A tramp walking on the ties came by and he tried to help, but to no avail. Then, out of sight around a curve, a train could be heard approaching.
    Perhaps there would have been time to run and flag the train down, perhaps not. In any case both men went right ahead trying to pull the woman free until the train hit and killed all three people. Neither man made the slightest effort to save himself.
    The husband's behavior was heroic, but what we would expect of a husband toward his wife—his proud privilege to die for the woman he loved. But what of the nameless stranger, the tramp? All we'll ever know about him is that he gave up his life trying to save a woman he had never seen before.
    The tramp's love for a person who was a total stranger is a unique example of the love St. Paul talks about in his writings to the Romans: "Owe no debt to anyone except the debt that binds us to love one another. He who loves his neighbor has fulfilled the law. All the commandments may be summed up in this, 'You shall love your neighbor as yourself.' "
    Earlier in the letter Paul had been urging the Christians at Rome to be good citizens: to obey authority, respect the law, pay their taxes, and so on. But besides discharging their civic duties, Christians also have a duty which they never adequately fulfill, according to Paul. This is their duty to love their neighbor. Origen once

said: "The debt of charity is permanent, and we are never free of it; for we must pay it daily and yet always owe it."

It is Paul's claim that if we honestly strive to discharge this debt to love, we will automatically keep *all* the commandments. His claim echoes the sayings of Jesus in the gospels. In other words, if we really try to love our neighbors as ourselves we would not do physical harm to them. Love does not seek to hurt but to help. If we loved our neighbors we would not take unfair advantage of them. Love is more concerned with giving than with receiving.

If we loved our neighbor we would not damage his reputation. Love does not seek to destroy but to build up. If we loved our neighbor we would not exploit him or her sexually. Love does not seek to abuse but to respect and cherish.

It is in this sense then that love fulfills the law. Love is more inclusive, spontaneous and dynamic than the static, minimal requirements of the law. There is no law that says we have to tithe. But some Christians do because they are prompted by the generosity of Christ's love for them. There is no law that says men and women should surrender sexual love. But some become priests, brothers and sisters out of love for Christ and for the sake of the kingdom.

There is no law that says we have to spend time with someone who is depressed, lonely or ill. But some share themselves with others in this way out of love. There is no law that says we have to give up our life for a total stranger. But some people like that tramp do—out of love for their neighbor.

The Eucharist in which we share is the sign of Christ's love when he laid down his life for us. It is also the promise of his daily, ongoing love for us. May the kiss of peace and the greetings we exchange in church be our pledge to love one another as we love ourselves.

Twenty-Fourth Sunday of the Year
Rm 14:7-9

We are the Lord's

In some of the most famous lines ever composed, the English poet John Donne said: "No man is an island entire of itself; every man is part of the main. If a clod be washed away by the sea, Europe is the less, as well as if a promontory were. Any man's death diminishes me because I am involved in mankind; and therefore never send to know for whom the bell tolls; it tolls for thee."

When he wrote these lines poet John Donne may not have had in mind St. Paul's words in Romans, nevertheless they seem to apply as an apt commentary on this passage of Paul's: "None of us lives as his own master and none of us dies as his own master. While we live we are responsible to the Lord, and when we die we die as his servants. Both in life and in death we are the Lord's."

Whether you prefer Donne's lines of "no man is an island," or Paul's phrase of "none of us live as his own master," the idea is still the same: we can't make it by ourselves; we are mutually dependent on one another. Moreover, we can't make it without the Lord Jesus. We are absolutely dependent upon him. Whether we admit it or not, all of us are in the same situation as Charlie Brown in the Peanuts comic strip: we need all the friends we can get; we especially need the Lord Jesus.

Consider how dependent we are on other people. To be born we needed our parents; to be educated we needed our teachers; to be accepted we needed our friends; to be challenged we needed our co-workers. We need other people to grow, mature and discover our true selves.

Then there is our dependence on our environment. To hear and see we need sounds and light; to breathe and eat we need air and food; to work and play we need tools and games. There is hardly anything around us that does not demonstrate our dependence in some way.

Our dependence is not cause for discouragement, but for delight. Praise the Lord for providing such a playground as the world to excite our senses; for giving us access to the culture of the past to stimulate our mind; for placing us with other people to perfect our personality.

Our most critical dependence is on the Lord himself. To come into contact with ultimate realities we have to commit ourselves to Christ. Only he is the way, the truth, and the life. Only he can give us a peace and joy that no one can take from us.

We can be proud of what we have accomplished in science and technology, but only the Lord Jesus can expel demons, calm storms and raise the dead to life. We can hunger and thirst for many things such as pleasure, popularity, power and possessions, but only the Lord Jesus himself can satisfy our desires fully.

Whether we live or whether we die, we belong to the Lord. Praise him for calling us into being to participate in his very existence; for becoming one of us to give us a share in his own divinity; for redeeming us so that we might live with him in glory.

Whenever we gather together for a liturgical assembly we signify sacramentally that none of us lives unto himself nor dies unto himself; none of us "is an island" unto himself. We need each other and we need the Lord Jesus. Both in life and in death we belong to each other; we are "involved in mankind." Both in life and in death we belong to the Lord Jesus; "no one shall snatch them out of my hand."

Twenty-Fifth Sunday of the Year
Ph 1:20-27

Bicentennial Saint

When the United States celebrated its bicentennial in 1976, one of the events that marked the occasion was the canonization of its first native-born American as a saint—Elizabeth Ann Seton. She was born into the Bayley family in 1774, two years before the American Revolution. The Bayleys were a socially prominent family in New York and they belonged to the Episcopalian Church.

From her spirit-filled mother, Elizabeth Ann Seton learned the value of prayer and Scripture, and from her humanitarian father, Dr. Richard Bayley, she learned to love and serve others. At age nineteen the beautiful Elizabeth Ann married the wealthy merchant William Seton. Together they had five children before William died when she was twenty-nine.

Two years later Elizabeth Ann became a Catholic convert, and, as a consequence, was denied financial assistance by her Episcopalian family and friends. So there she was at the age of thirty-one—widowed, five children to raise, rejected by her family and penniless. Yet by the time she died fifteen years later at the age of forty-six, Elizabeth Ann had founded the first American parish school in Baltimore, the first American orphanage in Emmitsburg, Maryland, and the first native American religious community for women, the Daughters of Charity.

St. Paul summarizes one of the fundamental attitudes of Elizabeth Ann Seton's life when he says: "Christ will be exalted through me, whether I live or die. For, to me, life means Christ."

Like Paul, Elizabeth Ann Seton accepted the Lord's will in all circumstances. Her letters reveal no bitterness or hopelessness when she buried her young husband and later her daughters Anna and Rebecca at ages seventeen and fourteen, respectively. Instead her letters speak only of trust and thanks. For example, in one of her early letters as a widow she writes: "God has given me a great deal to do, and I have always, and hope always to prefer his will to every wish of my own."

Since Elizabeth had been married and kept her children with her, Archbishop Carrol of Baltimore would not make her the permanent superior of the religious community she founded. She accepted this restriction as the Lord's will, but was elected by her sisters as Mother Superior three times anyway.

As a superior and educator she counseled her congregation with these words: "The first end I propose in our daily work is to *do* the will of God. Secondly, to do it in the *manner* he wills it. Thirdly, to do it *because* it is his will."

Elizabeth Ann Seton is a saint with whom we can easily identify. She was a mother, a wife, an educator, and a religious. She lived in plenty, and she lived in poverty. She knew the physical sufferings of sickness, the loneliness of widowhood, rejection by relatives, and the heartaches of a wayward son.

Elizabeth Ann Seton had no extraordinary gifts. She was not a mystic or stigmatic. She did not speak in tongues or work miracles of healing during her life. Instead she experienced God in very ordinary things like the beauty of spring flowers, the joy of a child's first step in learning how to walk, the patching of old clothes, and the paying of bills.

This is part of her popular appeal—she was an ordinary person like us. But what made her a saint was her extraordinary desire to do God's will, however difficult. She had the same hopes and fears, the same pleasures and pains as we have. What made her a saint was her extraordinary generosity to love and serve the people around her. For, to her, life meant Christ as she discovered him in every circumstance.

Twenty-Sixth Sunday of the Year
Ph 2:1-11

Unity in Space

The Apollo-Soyuz linkup in space between the United States and Russia was hailed as a significant step towards unity. It was the result of a joint effort in science by two nations who otherwise are rivals in international politics. This unique connection between the two spaceships required the utmost preparation by both nations and their absolute cooperation during its execution. To make their twin voyage a success the astronauts and the cosmonauts had to set aside their own preferences and work together as one team.

Several editorials pointed out how the unity achieved by the United States and Russia in the Apollo-Soyuz flight gives promise of an even closer unity between the two nations in the future, not only in space exploration, but also in politics, economics and culture.

This ideal of unity we dream about was also one of St. Paul's main concerns. He pleaded with the people at Philippi: "In the name of Christ, I beg you: make my joy complete by your unanimity, possessing the one love, united in spirit and ideals. Never act out of rivalry or conceit. Let each of you look to others' interests rather than his own."

It seems that the situation in which the letter is written is the series of reports Paul had received about the petty rivalries and partisan jealousies splitting the church at Philippi. His plea for their unity is reminiscent of our Lord's prayer for unity at the Last Supper: "Father, I pray that they may be one, as we are one—I living in them, you living in me—that their unity may be complete."

What are some of the elements of unity from Paul's point of

view? First, he says that we should have unanimity, or, as other translations express it, we should be united in our thoughts and in full agreement. This demands doing not just what I want, but what you want too. It involves reaching a consensus, a consensus which transcends both you and I, yet at the same time embraces both you and I.

Secondly, Paul says that we should be united in spirit. In other words, joined together in soul and having a common purpose. There can be no real community without some particular undertaking in which all the members are vitally interested. For us, this common undertaking has to be the proclamation of the Good News of Jesus Christ.

Thirdly, Paul urges us to be united in our ideals, to have our minds set on the same values. This includes reflecting on the word of God in Scripture and practicing the same moral code.

Also, Paul pleads for unity in love. Love is the essence of Christian unity—it contains the other three elements and extends beyond them. Unity in love means refraining from actions which upset my neighbor, taking up my brother's burden of sadness or depression, celebrating my sister's success or good fortune.

Unity in love means respecting my fellow worker's different culture and tradition, being sensitive to my colleague's feelings and moods, looking to the other's interests rather than our own.

The cooperation which characterized the Apollo-Soyuz space flight is certainly included in Paul's appeal for Christian unity. But Christian unity goes much deeper than the *esprit de corps* of such a joint project. It is rooted essentially in love, a love free of rivalry and selfishness, a love marked by a genuine concern for the other's needs, a love Jesus showed when he laid down his life for us on the cross and shared his risen life with us in the Eucharist.

Twenty-Seventh Sunday of the Year
Ph 4:6-9

Transcendental Meditation

Richard Kiley was the original star of *Man of La Mancha*. In an interview he revealed that he is a devotee of transcendental meditation. "It is eight times more restful than sleep," he said. "It is alert restfulness. We all have submerged layers of anxiety that we are hardly aware of. Transcendental meditation teaches you to live with them."

Actor Richard Kiley is one of thousands of people who have taken up the practice of transcendental meditation. Although TM is a 1970's phenomena as regards its form and following, it is really a return to that old Christian custom of praying. Today's gurus may have different motives and methods, but their claim is essentially the same as St. Paul's regarding some of its effects and results.

Paul outlines some of these when he says: "Dismiss all anxiety from your minds. Present your needs to God in every form of prayer and in petitions full of gratitude. Then God's own peace, which is beyond all understanding, will stand guard over your hearts and minds, in Christ Jesus."

Essentially prayer is some form of communion with God. Paul uses the expression "every form of prayer," indicating the wide variety of forms available—vocal and mental, praise and thanksgiving, petition and contrition, discursive and contemplative, and so on.

In 1964, long before TM became popular, Ed Maupin did some research and experimentation with meditation. He observed that with the collapse of Christianity in the western world and the subsequent loss of prayer, we lost some of the important benefits of meditation that had little to do with religious belief. He said,

"Meditation is a means for achieving psychological quiet and for developing contact with inner experience and with deeper resources."

In other words, one can practice TM without being a Christian or actually praying. But what of the benefits of TM which are the same as some of the benefits of Christian prayer? Ed Maupin summarizes these benefits this way: "Calm, greater ability to cope with tense situations, and improved sleep are frequently reported. Improved body functioning has been mentioned. Meditation often leads to a more positive feeling towards oneself, a more direct awareness of what one is experiencing, and a greater feeling of vitality. One psychiatrist claims that meditation results in having more energy for dealing with problems and doing constructive work."

These, then, are some of the benefits of practicing TM, Zen or Yoga. They should also be the results of Christian prayer, our personal communion with the Father through his Son Jesus. Paul knew this from his own experience. That is why he tells us to use every form of prayer to dismiss anxiety and to discover peace.

Certainly prayer does much to draw us closer to the Lord in our spiritual life of grace. But it should also have many of the psychosomatic benefits that Maupin listed. If we pray with faith we can expect the Lord to heal us sometimes physically and psychologically: we will fight off the flu, or arthritis will ease up, our worries will disappear, our self-image will improve.

But even if our sufferings or emotional problems stay with us, prayer will give us the strength we need to struggle with them and not give up, the wisdom we need to accept our Father's will in these trying circumstances, and the generosity we need to forget self and serve others.

Twenty-Eighth Sunday of the Year
Ph 4:12-20

Coping

During the 1974 NFL season Mack Herron of the New England Patriots set a new record for total yards in a season. He gained almost 2,500 yards in rushing, pass receiving, and punt and kickoff returns. New football records are made every year. But what made Herron's record so remarkable is the fact that he was only a 5'5", 170-pound runner playing against 250-pound tacklers.

Even more remarkable is the adversity Mack Herron had to overcome: he was born in a ghetto in Chicago, was convicted once in Canada for possession of illegal drugs, and had numerous injuries. Yet, in spite of these difficulties, Herron became an outstanding athlete. "It's not how tall you are," he said. "It's what's inside you. If you have that inner drive, you can do whatever you want to do."

St. Paul knew adversity too, and he too had an inner drive. Except that his inner drive was Jesus Christ. He writes: "I have learned how to cope with every circumstance—how to eat well or go hungry, to be well provided for or do without. In him who is the source of my strength I have strength for everything."

If men like Mack Herron can overcome difficulties and succeed because they have confidence in themselves, shouldn't we be able to surmount obstacles because we have Jesus as the source of our strength? Whether we are born with advantages or disadvantages, whether we are affluent or poor, whether we are healthy or sick, we should be able to cope with every circumstance because Jesus is the source of our strength.

Whether we live in a free country or in a communist country, whether we have friendly neighbors or grumpy neighbors, whether we have obedient children or rebellious ones, we should be able to cope with every circumstance because we have Jesus as the source of our strength.

When we have that inner drive like Paul or Mack Herron had, there is no trial too severe for us. We may lose money because of a blunder, or lose some part of our body because of an accident, but we won't let that overwhelm us—with Jesus we have strength for everything.

When we have confidence in Christ like Paul had, there is no challenge too big for us. We may have to undertake a new job or take care of a sick relative, but we won't let that frighten us—with Jesus we have strength for everything.

If only we could live with this kind of conviction, think how much needless worry and emotional anxiety we would avoid. If only we could put more trust in the Lord Jesus, think how much more peace of mind and inner security we would enjoy. If only we would rely more on the power and strength of God's grace working within us, think how much we would grow personally and how much more we would accomplish for society.

When we worship together we come into the presence of Jesus, the source of our strength. We come with all our weaknesses, failures and troubles. Nourished by his word and sacrament we leave renewed, determined and hopeful. Like Mack Herron said: "It's not how tall you are. It's what's inside you." St. Paul would add: "With Jesus dwelling in us we can do everything."

Twenty-Ninth Sunday of the Year
1 Th 1:1-5

Something Beautiful

One of the finest and most inspiring books ever written has to be *Something Beautiful for God* by Malcolm Muggeridge. It is about Mother Teresa of Calcutta and her celebrated work with the poor in India. The book is the result of an interview Muggeridge had with her for his TV series in England. It's especially interesting because Muggeridge is not a church-going Christian.

Mother Teresa has made such a strong impact on him as well as thousands of others that we can best describe her work with these words from St. Paul: "Our preaching of the gospel proved not a mere matter of words for you but one of power. It was carried on in the Holy Spirit and out of complete conviction."

When we apply these words to Mother Teresa's work three features emerge. First, the feature of the gospel message she preaches. It is essentially none other than the love of God and neighbor preached by Jesus himself. Muggeridge writes: "Mother Teresa regarded every derelict left to die in the streets as Christ. She heard in the cry of every abandoned child the cry of the Bethlehem child. She recognized in every leper's stump the hands of Christ which healed the lame and cured the sick."

Her gospel message is summed up in Christ's words, "Whatever you do to the least of my brothers you do unto me." Consequently, whenever she soothes the aching heads of the dying, comforts the discarded child in her arms, and bathes the stumps of the leper, she does this to Christ.

The second feature is how her preaching is not a mere matter of words but one of power. Mother Teresa tells her Sisters to preach the gospel message of love the way Jesus did—he went about doing good. The Sisters must help as he helped, give as he gave, rescue as he rescued, and comfort as he comforted. "To be beautiful their vocation must be filled with thoughtfulness for others."

The power of Mother Teresa's witness was evident in the overwhelming response she got to the TV special about her work. Mail and money poured in from everywhere because people felt they must help her cause. This prompted Muggeridge to comment: "When you get someone on the screen over-flowing with Christian love like Mother Teresa, someone for whom the world is nothing and the service of Christ is everything, then it doesn't matter what kind of TV techniques are used or what is said. The message comes through with all the power and magic as when it was first uttered by Christ."

The third feature of how Mother Teresa preaches the gospel is the way it is carried on in the Holy Spirit. Muggeridge asks the question: "How can such an obscure nun like Mother Teresa, not particularly gifted or clever in the art of persuasion, get such an incredible reaction from people?" St. Paul would answer: "It is indeed the power of the Holy Spirit manifested through her."

Muggeridge also asks: "How can her Sisters leave their comfortable upper class homes and dedicate themselves to work in the poorest sections of India? How can they be so happy ministering to the most wretched of society's outcasts?" Again, the answer is, "Only through the power of the Holy Spirit."

The love of Mother Teresa and her Sisters for Jesus and his poor is renewed each day in prayer and at the Eucharist. Inspired by their example and strengthened by the Eucharist, we too can go out to proclaim the gospel message of love and do "something beautiful for God"—not with words only, but with the power of the Holy Spirit working through us.

Thirtieth Sunday of the Year
1 Th 1:5-10

Beverly Sills

When Beverly Sills made her debut at the Metropolitan Opera House, she received a standing ovation that lasted twenty minutes. *Newsweek* magazine termed the event as "an historic debut." Beverly describes her voice as a God-given talent. She loves to sing and feels immense joy in the work she does.

But for Beverly Sills her widely acclaimed debut is not at the top of her list of memorable events. For her the most triumphant moment was the day her deaf daughter spoke her first word. In addition to her deaf daughter she has a retarded son. Her children have made her a much more compassionate and patient person.

Beverly Sills says, "When you have children with problems such as ours, either you can become bitter, or you can feel that these are very special, chosen children of God."

Paul's words to the Thessalonians seem written especially for Beverly Sills: "You, in turn became imitators of us and of the Lord, receiving the word despite great trials, with the joy that comes from the Holy Spirit."

Paul, of course, is speaking about the word of the gospel message, whereas Beverly Sills is speaking about the first word her deaf daughter uttered. But are these two uses of *word* that much different? Both uses bring out the element of good news—one about the victory of Christ over death, the other about the victory of a girl over deafness.

Both words were received despite great trials; on the one hand, for the Thessalonians because their acceptance of Christ meant their rejection by society; on the other hand, for Beverly Sills

111

because her daughter's deafness meant a lot of extra patience, therapy and tutoring.

Both words were received with the joy that comes from the Holy Spirit; joy for the Thessalonians because they had abandoned their idols and were now serving the living and true God; joy for Beverly Sills because her daughter had escaped the prison of silence and entered the world of sound.

What kind of word do we receive from the Lord? How do we receive it? The Lord's word is always primarily the good news of the gospel about Jesus Christ. But it also assumes many other forms. It can be a word of thanks, support or recognition; a report of health from a doctor; an acceptance of an application for a job; an award for excellence or service.

But many times, as it did for the Thessalonians and for Beverly Sills, the Lord's word comes in the midst of adversity. We often experience the Lord's peace in the midst of trials, his strength in our weakness, his joy in our sufferings, and his victory in our failures.

These paradoxes of the Christian life should not surprise us. A Swiss theologian, Fr. Balthasar, says: "As long as the Church is between the ages, there will always be in it a tension between the cross and joy. That is because the Church can never localize the cross as a fixed event in past history, and consider her sinfulness as a finished fact, any more than it can occupy a permanent position in the perfect joy of the Easter event."

It seems then that as long as we are still a pilgrim people we will have to walk with Christ to the cross by enduring the difficulties that enter our lives, and wait in joyful hope for him to come in glory and complete our joy.

Thirty-First Sunday of the Year
1 Th 2:7-13

Stevie Wonder

One of the most talented rock singers today is Stevie Wonder. This black, blind soul singer is also a composer and instrumentalist. In one year alone he received four Grammy Awards from the National Academy of Recording Arts and Sciences. But when he was only twenty-three years old Stevie Wonder gave up his career in the United States to move to Ghana in Africa where he could work with blind, underprivileged children.

At a press conference once, Stevie Wonder said: "I believe that you have to give unselfishly. You can sing about things and talk about things, but if your actions don't speak louder than your words, you're nothing."

Stevie Wonder's love for the blind and underprivileged blacks in Africa is similar to St. Paul's love for the Christians in Thessalonica. He says: "While we were among you we wanted to share with you, not only God's tidings but our very lives, you had become so dear to us."

Paul's preaching of the gospel to the Thessalonians is not motivated by *his* own financial gain, popularity or ambition, but rather by *their* growth in faith and in fraternal charity. Paul is not satisfied just to talk to them about love: he comes to share his very life with them, to bear their burdens, and to get involved in their struggles.

This is the essence of our own commitment as Christians—to share with others not only the good news about Jesus, but also our very lives. It's easy to declare our dedication by writing out a check for the Catholic Charities, or by stuffing our used clothing into the

St. Vincent de Paul boxes. It's easy because we can give from our surplus and avoid any personal involvement.

But we are called to be better Christians than that. Like Paul and Stevie Wonder we are called to give ourselves to others; to give our services to the family chores around the home, to the bedridden neighbor down the street, or to one of the parish committees. We are called to give our attention to the things that interest our teenagers or our senior citizens; to give our time to someone by writing a letter, calling on the telephone or making a visit. All these are ways we can share our very lives with others and demonstrate by our deeds how dear they are to us.

The imperative to be a bearer of God's tidings by our service to others is brought out in a poem written by the Hindu mystic Tagore: "Leave this chanting and singing and telling of beads! Whom dost thou worship in this lonely dark corner of a temple with doors all shut? Open thine eyes and see thy God is not before thee. He is there where the tiller is tilling the hard ground and where the pathmaker is breaking stone. He is with them in the sun and in shower, and his garment is covered with dust. Put off thy holy mantle and even like him come down on the dusty soil. Come out of thy meditation and leave aside thy flowers and incense. Meet him and stand by him in toil and in sweat of thy brow."

Tagore is not denying the need for prayer and liturgy. Like Paul and Stevie Wonder he is underlining the need to share our lives with others; like our Lord who shares himself with us under the forms of bread and wine, Tagore is challenging us to break the bread and pour out the wine of our own lives for distribution to others.

Thirty-Second Sunday of the Year
1 Th 4:13-18

Death and Beyond

A few months before he died in 1955, Albert Einstein wrote a letter to a friend in which he said: "To one bent by age death will come as a release. Now that I have grown old I regard death like an old debt, at long last to be discharged. Still, instinctively one does everything possible to delay this last fulfillment. This is the game which nature plays with us."

Einstein prepared for death by absorbing himself in his work until his last breath. Beside his hospital bed the night he died lay the pages of an unfinished calculation on the unified-field theory. He had planned to continue working on it the next morning.

Although we can admire the peace and calm with which Einstein died, we can't help but ask, "Was that really enough?" St. Paul would answer, "No," for in his letter to the Thessalonians he says: "We would have you be clear about those who sleep in death, brothers; otherwise you might yield to grief like those who have no hope. For if we believe that Jesus died and rose, God will bring forth with him from the dead those who have fallen asleep believing in him."

On the one hand, it seems that Einstein met death without yielding to grief. But, on the other hand, it also seems that he had little hope in the resurrection. How different the attitude of another famous scientist, namely Louis Pasteur.

It is reported that at the bedside of his dying daughter he said: "I know only scientifically determined truth, but I am going to believe what I wish to believe, what I cannot help but believe—I expect to meet this dear child in another world."

Here we can detect some grief, but not a yielding to it. We can

115

sense a kind of peace and calm, but only because there is hope in the resurrection. How hopeful is our own attitude toward death?

Aren't we lacking in hope of the resurrection when we regard death as the end of everything, are embittered by the death of a loved one, or become hostile over our own approaching death? Aren't we depending on a false kind of hope when we pretend not to see the finality and absurdity of death, or avoid coming to grips with its ugliness and destructiveness?

True Christian hope is neither one of these two attitudes. Instead it looks at death realistically. It recognizes the dread, disintegration and unknowability associated with death. But it looks at death supernaturally, also. It expects a time when the Father will raise from the dead all who have fallen asleep believing in his Son, Jesus.

In *The Jerome Biblical Commentary* Fr. Terence Forestell remarks: "The death and resurrection of Christ bear a causal relationship to the resurrection of Christians. A bond persists between the Christian and Christ—in death as in life. The goal of God's activity is the reunion of the believer with the risen Christ."

Because we are mortal and do not yet possess eternal life, death still calls into question the meaning of our whole human existence. It is our faith in Jesus that alone gives us hope. We believe that even though Jesus died a senseless death on the cross, death could not contain him. By rising from the tomb he proved that life is stronger than death, mortality is clothed with immortality, and corruptibility gives way to incorruptibility.

When we come together to commemorate the passion and death of Christ, we also proclaim his victory over death through his resurrection. Moreover, we anticipate our share in that victory, when, "freed from the corruption of sin and death, we shall sing his glory with every creature."

Thirty-Third Sunday of the Year
1 Th 5:1-6

Sudden Death

In 1975 the freighter Edmund Fitzgerald sank during a violent storm on Lake Superior. All twenty-nine men on board went to a watery grave without a trace. Disasters like this awaken our memories to other major disasters: the San Francisco earthquake of 1906; the sinking of the British luxury liner Titanic in 1912; the explosion of the German zeppelin Hindenburg in 1937; the fire at the Boston Coconut Grove Night Club in 1942; the Hurricane Camille in the Gulf Coast area in 1969; and so on.

Disasters like these always seem to be unexpected and swift. Their occurrence reminds us of St. Paul's warning in his letter to the Thessalonians: "You know very well that the day of the Lord is coming like a thief in the night. Just when people are saying, 'Peace and security,' ruin will fall with suddenness. You are not in the dark, brothers, that the day might catch you off guard, like a thief. No, all of you are children of light and of the day. Be not asleep like the rest, but awake and sober."

Although Paul is talking about the second coming of Christ at the end of the world, his admonitions apply equally well to Christ's coming to us individually at the end of our life.

In his commentary on this text, Bruce Vawter writes: "As the Church has grown old in history, the second coming of Christ has always remained in the future. It has ceased to be the vital motive for spiritual preparedness that it obviously once was. We tend to think of our own certain individual death, and the particular judgment that will follow it, for such motivation. Yet we know that the second coming of Christ is no less inevitable for having been delayed. Its time is quite as uncertain for us as it was for the first

Christians. It remains, therefore, in principle at least, as much a real motivation for us as it was for them.''

We must then keep both perspectives in view, namely, our own individual judgment and the final judgment of the world. Jesus Christ is the savior not only of the individual, but also of the community. Our salvation is not just a private affair with Christ when we die, but a social destiny we share in company with the saints when Christ comes in glory.

With this in mind, we can put Paul's admonition to be ready in proper focus. For many of us death will come like some of the catastrophes mentioned above—unexpectedly, when we least think it will occur; quickly, before we have time to react. When death comes like a thief in the night, as it did for the crew on the freighter Fitzgerald, it is too late to prepare. It's similar to trying to slow down a car when a skid has already started, or like trying to get out of the water when a shark has its jaws on you.

But even if we can anticipate the time of our death, say the way Private Eddie Slovik could because of his sentence to be executed, we still have to prepare ourselves. We do this for any important event in our lives. To insure the best results from an operation or trial, a doctor or lawyer has to get himself into a state of alert readiness. To produce maximum satisfaction in his audience, a performer has to spend hours rehearsing.

For all the more reason then we should prepare for that final act of our lives. To approach a death we can foresee with peace, trust and strength, we have to ready ourselves beforehand by a good life.

Whether death comes suddenly or slowly, to be able to welcome Jesus as friend and savior we have to prepare ahead of time by prayer and service. The more we welcome Jesus when he comes by word and sacrament in the liturgy, and the more we welcome him when he comes in the person of our neighbor or in the happenings of our life, then the more he will welcome us when he comes at the time of our death and then again later in his glory.

Thirty-Fourth Sunday of the Year
1 Cor 15:20-28

King Faisal

King Faisal of Saudi Arabia is hailed as one of the great leaders of modern history. Before he began his reign in 1964, Saudi Arabia was wasting its oil wealth through wild government spending. When Faisal assumed the kingship, he balanced the nation's budget and paid off their foreign debts. King Faisal also abolished slavery, opened the schools for girls and introduced the latest technology. Saudi Arabians now pay no taxes, have free medical care, and can get a free education up through the university level.

King Faisal was also the Arab's spiritual leader. He was a devout Moslem who neither smoked nor drank, and who practiced asceticism regarding the food he ate. But even with all his achievements King Faisal could not overcome every obstacle. He could not change the Arab's strict code of ethics—thieves still have their hands cut off; nor could he conquer death—he was the victim of an assassin's bullet in 1975.

All great rulers in history accomplish many remarkable things during their lifetime, but are not able to overcome every obstacle. Nevertheless, there is one exception, there is one perfect king who did overcome every obstacle—Jesus Christ. St. Paul expresses it this way: "Christ must reign until God has put all enemies under his feet, and the last enemy to be destroyed is death. When, finally, all has been subjected to the Son, he will then subject himself to the One who has made all things subject to him, so that God may be all in all."

Through his life, death and resurrection, Christ has already conquered the forces of evil—the devil, sin and death. But even though his victory is already here, it is yet to come. It is yet to come because it has to be worked out in our own lives.

In his own person Jesus has defeated the devil, but we ourselves are still often tempted by him. In his own spirit Jesus has vanquished sin, but we ourselves are still somewhat subject to it. In his own body Jesus has destroyed death, but we ourselves still have to undergo it.

But even though we still have to struggle to make Christ's victory our own, we don't have to be upset about this. As someone once cleverly remarked: "I have no need to worry. I've read the Bible, and in the end we win."

We can move forward with confidence then as we try to extend Christ's reign over his enemies and ours. We are engaged in cosmic conflicts with war, disease, famine, and so on. They are too much for any one of us to cope with. Nonetheless, we do what we can in a limited way because we realize that the ultimate victory is already in Christ's hands.

We are engaged in our own personal conflicts with fear and insecurity, habits of drinking and smoking, feelings of fatigue and boredom, and so on. Sometimes they are too strong for us to surmount or control. Nonetheless, we do what we can because we trust in the power of God's grace to triumph in the end.

When the people of God gather together to celebrate the Eucharist, they make a solemn proclamation of Christ's kingship. It is an opportunity for us to glorify the Lord for the victory he has already won in his own person; thank him for the victory he is bringing to completion both in the world and in us; praise him for the final triumph that is yet to come—that time when "all things will be subject to him and God will be all in all."

SECTION TWO

Cycle B

First Sunday of Advent
1 Cor 1:3-9

Richly Endowed

When Galina Ulanova, the leading dancer of the Bolshoi Ballet, made her first visit to the United States, she was welcomed by promoter Sol Hurok. In a special New York hotel suite ballerina Ulanova found everything she needed to make her comfortable. There was champagne and caviar in her refrigerator, flowers everywhere she looked, and even a specially constructed exercise bar backed by floor-length mirrors.

Promoter Sol Hurok spared no expense to provide the ballerina with everything she needed to make her feel important and special. This is a faint image of what our Father has done to make us feel important and special. St. Paul reminds us of this when he writes: "In Christ you have been richly endowed. You lack no spiritual gift as you wait for the revelation of our Lord Jesus Christ."

Paul is addressing the early Christians at Corinth both to remind them of the special gifts they have received and to correct them for their factions, greed and sexual license. He is positive in his approach, praises the Corinthians for their abundance of charismatic gifts, and promises fidelity on the part of God.

When we stop to think about it, we too have been richly endowed. Perhaps not personally with the charismatic gifts like tongues and prophecy, but with whatever we need to become good Christians. We have our own unique and individual talents. It might be the gift of mechanics or gardening; the gift of music or painting; the gift of entertaining or just listening. Whatever special talents we have are gifts from our Father. They are one of the ways he says to us: "You're something special to me; you're somebody important to me. Do something special with your life."

We have been richly endowed as a nation. Granted that we are imperfect in many ways, we can still claim greatness among the nations of the world. Our wheat crop and industrial output, our emergency relief, our defense of freedom, our foreign aid policy and negotiations for peace are all blessings from the Father. It is as if he were saying, "You are my chosen people; be a holy nation."

We have received special graces as Christians. Where else except in our Christian heritage would we receive the word of God in Scripture, the body and blood of Christ in the sacrament of the Eucharist, and the faith of the Christian community? Every time we read the Bible or participate in a sacrament we should hear the Father saying: "See how much I love you, how much I want to speak to you, how much I want to share with you."

Indeed, Sol Hurok did everything possible to make the Russian ballerina Ulanova feel important and special. How much more has our Father done for us to make us feel important and special to him.

As we wait during life for the coming of Christ at the end of time, we lack no spiritual gift. Failure may sometimes frustrate us, but we have the assurance that Christ's triumph will finally prevail. Sufferings may sometimes become very severe, but we have the cross of Christ to sustain us.

As we wait during Advent for the revelation of Christ at Christmas, we lack no spiritual gift. The night may get very dark at times, but we have the light of Christ to lead us. The sea may get very stormy at times, but we have the strength of Christ to see us through safely.

As we wait during the liturgy of the Eucharist for the coming of Christ sacramentally, we lack no spiritual gift. The sins we bring with us will be forgiven and we can expect the peace of Christ to fill us. The wounds we have suffered or caused will be healed and we can expect the presence of Christ to renew us.

Second Sunday of Advent
2 P 3:8-14

New Heavens

In 1962 a fire destroyed the old St. Mary's Cathedral in San Francisco. This venerable landmark was replaced by a new cathedral shortly afterwards. The new St. Mary's Cathedral is both modern and magnificent. Although its $8 million cost is still controversial, its architectural beauty is undisputed. It is a splendid symbol of the space age which has already arrived.

This new structure would never have been erected had not the old one been destroyed. This pattern of the destruction of the old followed by the creation of the new, while not a universal one, is nevertheless a common one. The grapes of the vine have to be crushed before bottles of wine can be produced. Tyrannies have to be overthrown by revolutions before a free nation like ours can be born.

St. Peter had this pattern in mind when he wrote: "The heavens will be destroyed in flames and the elements will melt away in a blaze. Since everything is to be destroyed in this way, what we await are new heavens and a new earth where according to his promise the justice of God will reign."

We must be careful not to intepret Peter's words too literally. Authors of the Bible like Peter were inspired by God to teach a revealed truth. But to express themselves they used the popular language and imagery of their time. According to Fr. Eugene Maly in the *New Testament Reading Guide*, when Peter describes the cosmic cataclysm on the day of the Lord's second coming, he does not mean total annihilation. He is using highly figurative language to depict the idea that all of nature will share with man in the final glory.

The imagery of fire then is intended to mean, not actual destruction, but some kind of transformation; not the total dissolution of the old order, but its continuation into a new order.

What a consoling and optimistic outlook this is. Sometimes a real fire will destroy what is old before what is new can be built. Such was the case with the St. Mary's Cathedral in San Francisco. But change can happen in other ways, too. The elements that make up glass are melted, not destroyed, in order to be molded into a crystal figure. The grains of wheat are broken, not annihilated, by the soil and rain in order to grow into a fruitful harvest.

It is much the same with us. As we wait during Advent for the coming of Christmas, we have to go through a conversion, a transformation. If it's something that is ruining our personal life, like too much drinking or smoking, then we might have to destroy the old habit and develop a new one. If it's something that is hurting our relationships with others, like too much time with our business and not enough with our family, then we might have to rearrange our timetable and adopt a new lifestyle. If it's something interfering with our daily encounter with the Lord, like laziness in prayer, then we might have to change our attitude and give prayer top priority.

Christmas doesn't simply commemorate Christ's new birth as man. It also proclaims the birth of a new order for us, a new heaven and a new earth. However, to make this a reality for ourselves, we have to go through a conversion. Advent is a period for just such a conversion. It is a period to purify our motives and to review our values; a time to transform our attitudes and to renew our commitments. If we succeed, then indeed Christmas will mark the beginning of a new era, an era filled with the Christmas spirit of praise and glory to God, of peace and good will among men, and of justice and generosity towards one another.

Third Sunday of Advent
1 Th 5:16-24

Rejoice Always

One of the most popular people in Northwest Indiana is a crippled man by the name of William Passmore. Even though Bill is only half a man in physical size because of an accident, he is a giant in spiritual stature. Being confined to a wheelchair doesn't keep Bill from active involvement in youth programs, civic projects and visitations to the sick in hospitals.

To overcome his physical handicaps, Bill has cultivated an enthusiasm that is contagious and a cheerfulness that is courageous. If St. Paul were here today he would point with pride at Bill Passmore and say: "Be like Bill. Rejoice always, never cease praying, render constant thanks; such is God's will for you in Christ Jesus."

In one sweeping statement Paul summarizes the Christian spirit. Fr. Terence Forestell remarks in *The Jerome Biblical Commentary*: "Paul depicts Christianity not merely as a series of obligations toward God and neighbor, but as a way of life oriented to God in joy, prayer and thanksgiving."

What is this joy that should characterize our Christian life? How can people like William Passmore "rejoice always" when there is so much pain and frustration in their own life, and so much suffering and injustice in the world? Their secret is to rejoice always *in the Lord*; to rejoice because we belong to him inasmuch as his Spirit lives within us; to rejoice because we will return to him as the fulfillment of our life.

Author Lucille Oliver uses these three points as the basis for her book *Celebrate Your Existence*. She says that when we live in the Lord we can always celebrate our existence, whether in health or sickness, success or failure, security or poverty. We can always rejoice in the Lord because in him light triumphs over darkness and life prevails over death.

Why should a Christian never cease praying? If we're cynical we might say that it's easy for a cripple like William Passmore to pray, since prayer enables him to escape from the harshness of reality into a dream world. But if we're sincere we would have to admit it's even more difficult for a crippled person to pray. For prayer puts us in the mysterious presence of the living God, a God who loves us, yet allows suffering to inflict us; a God who adopts us as sons, yet permits pain to discipline us.

William Passmore prays because it enables him to come to grips with the deepest dimensions of his existence: his relationship with the Lord; the meaning of his handicap; and the purpose of his life. He prays because when he tends to get bitter, prayer reminds him how precious he is to the Lord. When he wants to give up the struggle, prayer renews his strength to go on. When he tends to get stuck in self-pity, prayer enables him to respond to the needs of others.

What does it mean to give constant thanks to the Lord? In his book *Stress of Life* Dr. Hans Selye of Montreal states that gratitude is a remarkable antidote for stress. If we focus our attention on what we don't have and complain about it, we get uptight and anxious. But if we concentrate on the countless blessings we do have and thank God for them, we experience contentment and peace.

William Passmore knows this. That is why he doesn't let himself get depressed by what he doesn't have. He's too busy thanking God for the many gifts he does have: his life and faith, family and friends, work and activities. He's too busy praising God for the sounds he hears and the sights he sees; the air he breathes and the food he eats. As Christmas approaches, William Passmore joins St. Paul and the prophets like Isaias and St. John the Baptist to tell us how to get ready for the Lord's coming: "Rejoice always, never cease praying, and render constant thanks to the Lord."

Fourth Sunday of Advent
Rm 16:25-27

Believing and Obeying

Danny Thomas tells the story of how more than anything else he wanted to be in show business, but he was told over and over again that a hooknosed Lebanese had no chance to be a successful entertainer. So there he was in 1940, working in a beer garden in Detroit and despairing of God's goodness, when a friend told him how his wife had been miraculously cured of cancer. It happened through the intercession of St. Jude, the patron of the hopeless.

So Danny Thomas made a vow to St. Jude. He swore that if St. Jude would help him find his way in show business, he would build a shrine for him. Shortly afterwards, Danny Thomas finally got his first job on radio. Success followed upon success, and six years later he remembered his vow to St. Jude.

It was then in 1946 that he bagan to raise funds for a St. Jude's Hospital for Children. For sixteen long years he worked on this project until the hospital was finally completed in 1962.

This story about Danny Thomas illustrates what St. Paul writes about in his epistle to the Romans: "The gospel I proclaim when I preach Christ Jesus has been made known to all the Gentiles, that they may believe and obey."

Before he made his promise to St. Jude, Danny Thomas believed in the gospel message about Jesus Christ, but he didn't *believe* enough to really *obey*. In other words, he accepted Christianity, but it wasn't a real active influence in his life. But once he turned his life over to the Lord and quit worrying about success, he not only became a success as an entertainer, but also the Lord's instrument for healing sick children.

How many of us would be better off if we not only *believed* in

Jesus, but also *obeyed* his Spirit? Each day would find us spending some time in prayer with him, doing our job honestly and cheerfully, and responding generously to the needs of others.

How much more peace and satisfaction we would find if we would let the Lord influence our lives? Each Christmas would find us less self-opinionated and more understanding; hurting people less and helping them more; decreasing in self-indulgence and increasing in sensitivity to others.

How much more good we would accomplish if we would not only profess our faith, but put it into practice? Christmas would mean so much more loneliness dispelled by love; hostility removed by friendship; despair overcome by encouragement.

Once we both believe in Jesus Christ and obey his inspirations, we can do whatever he asks of us. If the Lord asks us to quit smoking or drinking for our own good, we can do that. If he asks us to quit hating someone and become reconciled with him, we can do that. If he asks us to buy less for ourselves and give away more to the poor, we can do that.

Who knows, this Christmas the Lord may even ask us to do something foolish and reckless, like building a children's hospital for him. If the Lord could build a hospital through a bartender in Detroit to serve thousands of sick children, how much can he do through us in our family, parish and place of work?

If the Lord asks us to do something extraordinary for him, we won't worry. Once we accept the Lord and make a commitment to him, we can do whatever he asks. Perhaps the best Christmas gift we can give the Lord is not only our faith that he is both God and man, but also our readiness to obey him; our willingness to do whatever he asks of us; our eagerness to let him be the main influence in our life.

Christmas
Tt 3:4-7

Christmas with Mame

In the Broadway Musical *Mame* there is a song which captures some of the meaning of Christmas. The scene is the middle of summer. Things have been going bad for Auntie Mame. She's grown a little leaner, sadder and older. To pick up her sagging spirits Auntie Mame bursts into song with "We Need a Little Christmas, right this very moment. Haul out the holly, put up the tree, candle in the window, carols at the spinet. For we need a little music, need a little laughter, need a little singing ringing through our rafter. We need a little Christmas, now."

In this way Auntie Mame teaches her nephew how to live, how to transform a hopeless situation into one of joyous expectations, how to infuse new vitality into a spiritless existence. This gives us an inkling of what Jesus did for us when he became man.

St. Paul summarizes it this way: "When the kindness and love of God our Savior appeared, he saved us; not because of any righteous deeds we had done, but because of his mercy. He saved us through the baptism of new birth and renewal by the Holy Spirit."

Yes, he saved us when things were going very bad for us. The human race had grown a little sadder and older. Its situation of sin seemed hopeless, its existence had become dreary. But then the divine Word took on human flesh and changed all that. His coming at the first Christmas transformed our darkness into light, our weeping into laughter and our dissonance into music.

And Jesus continues to come every Christmas, or, whenever like Mame, we need a little Christmas anytime of the year. His kindness and love continue to appear, if only we're willing to haul out the holly and put up the tree. A new birth and renewal by the Holy Spirit are always available to us, if only we're willing to put the candle in the window and sing carols at the spinet.

Age and illness may slow us down a bit, but we can still show a lot of vitality by keeping involved and interested. Inflation and job layoffs put us behind in our payments, but we can also rediscover that a simpler lifestyle can be a lot of fun, too. Some loss, failure or disappointment may dampen our spirits, but we can still recover our enthusiasm and write a new agenda for ourselves.

Whenever we need a little Christmas like Mame, God's love and kindness are always ready to appear to save us. Not to save us in the sense that we won't have any more physical, financial or emotional problems, but in the sense that the celebration of his new birth in the flesh will bring about a new birth for us. It will be a new birth in divine life through prayer, praise and the sacraments; a new birth in human life through a new outlook, a new approach and a new purpose.

First Sunday of Lent
1 P 3:18-22

Water

During the winter teams of bulldozers are put to work on the wind-swept steppes of Kazakhstan in Russia to pile up great mounds of snow. Their purpose is to save as much precious moisture as possible for the year's crops. This winter-long snow-saving is one of several ways in which Kazakh farmers work doubly hard to make an inhospitable region productive as one of the crucial grain-producing regions of the U.S.S.R.

When the spring thaw comes, the water from the melting snow is channeled into special reservoirs and used for irrigation during the hot and dry summers in the region. The size of the Kazakhstan crop makes the difference between bumper or bust in the Soviet Union and affects the amount of American grain the Soviets buy each year. In Kazakhstan water is like money in the bank.

Water is vital for life. Without adequate sources of water people in drought areas around the world get sick from unsanitary conditions and suffer from hunger. But once sufficient water is brought in by irrigation or by other means, the people are saved from sickness and starvation.

Water as a source of salvation is a frequent image in the Bible. St. Peter alludes to the flood when he writes: "In Noah's time, eight persons escaped in the ark through the water. Now you are saved by a baptismal bath."

Water was not only an element of destruction in the flood, but also the means of deliverance for Noah and his family. Now this happens to us, according to Peter, when we are baptized with water. Through this sacrament we come into contact with the saving power of Jesus Christ.

If we allow him, Jesus can save us from ruthless ambition that causes us to lie and cheat to get ahead, and from any deep-seated insecurity that causes us to accumulate and hoard things. Jesus can deliver us from prolonged moods of depression that dampen our outlook, and from extended periods of loneliness that cause us so much sorrow.

This is why Jesus became man—to heal us, to make us whole again. He comes into our midst to heal us of our divisions and factions, our wounds and hurts, and of our discouragement when we fail or make mistakes. He comes to liberate us from our addictions regarding gambling or drugs, and to free us from self-indulgence regarding food, drink and sex.

If water can change the steppes of Kazakhstan from a province of poverty into a place of plenty, how much more change can Jesus bring about in us. He can take our wounded pride when people reject us and change it into a free-loving spirit that continues reaching out to people in trust. Jesus can change us from people who give off negative vibrations because of our pessimistic attitude into people who bring about positive reinforcement because of our optimistic approach to life.

Water in a drought can make all the difference between life and death, nourishment and hunger. In the same way, Jesus can make all the difference between always being hungry and thirsty for fulfillment, and actually finding it here and now. He can make all the difference between a life of endless desperation and a life of deep satisfaction.

If water can save hungry people in drought regions from starvation, why don't we let Jesus save us from whatever is troubling us? If water can change a dry climate into a fertile farm area, why don't we let Jesus transform the barrenness and emptiness of our living into something fruitful?

Second Sunday of Lent
Rm 8:31-34

Top Priorities

In the movie *Turning Point* Ann Bancroft and Shirley MacLain play the roles of two women who made different choices. In her role, Ann Bancroft chooses to make a ballet career the most important value in her life. We see her as an aging ballerina past her prime of greatness. She has no husband, no children and no close friends who really care for her.

In contrast, the woman played by Shirley MacLain chooses to give up her promising future in ballet to get married and raise a family. This is her most important value. Each woman envies what the other has, yet they must live with the basic choice they've made for themselves.

Turning Point illustrates how people will sacrifice some things that are very valuable or meaningful to them in order to obtain something else they consider to be of supreme importance. Richard Burton used to spare no expense to buy precious diamonds for Elizabeth Taylor when they were married; Olympic athletes will give up their social life and even delay their education in order to train for the winning of a gold medal.

This phenomenon of people sparing no career, expense or lifestyle in order to attain something they value most highly gives us a little insight into the mystery of God's love for us. St. Paul writes: "If God is for us, who can be against us? Is it possible that he who did not spare his own Son but handed him over for the sake of us all will not grant us all things besides?"

God is for us! He created us when he didn't have to. He gave us life when he had no need of us. He called us into being out of sheer, generous, extravagant love. The very fact that we are is proof that God is for us!

But we weren't all for God, and so we sinned. We didn't believe that with him we would have all things, and so we looked elsewhere. But all we found was illusion, pain and death.

Still God was for us! He considered us so precious and so important that he did not spare his own Son for our sake; he handed him over to death to give us all the things we wanted—freedom, dignity, grandeur—and even things we never dreamed of—divine adoption, his Son in the Eucharist, eternal glory.

Can we even begin to comprehend the tremendous care God has for us? Supposing it were even possible to ask the question, "What is most precious to God?" We would have to answer, "His Son Jesus, the perfect reflection of his glory, the very image of his being."

No wonder we are startled when we ponder the following paradox. As we saw in *Turning Point*, people are willing to surrender something of value to them, though in a secondary way, to gain what they consider a supreme value. But here we have the Father surrendering his supreme value, his own Son Jesus, to gain us, who by comparison have to be of lesser importance. How crazy can God get?

Yet, it is precisely here that we are at the heart of the mystery of God's immense, foolish, reckless love for us. What more can he do to convince us that he is for us! That we are precious to him! That he wants to give us all things besides!

Who then can be against us? Certainly no hurt or anxiety, disappointment or failure. We know that God is for us. Certainly no sickness or suffering, sin or loss. We believe that in God we have all things besides.

Third Sunday of Lent
1 Cor 1:22-25

Christ Crucified

A new book released recently is entitled *Dostoevsky: Reminiscences*. Its author is Anna Dostoevsky, the wife and stenographer of the famous 19th century Russian novelist, Fyodor Dostoevsky. On the one hand, it gives us a folksy picture of their family life—morning coffee, chats with their children, practical jokes. On the other hand, it portrays much of the pain of their experiences together—the depressions which followed Fyodor's epileptic seizures; his compulsive gambling when they traveled abroad; their financial woes that more than once made them pawn their winter coats to feed their children.

Yet from out of this pain came the great novels we know so well today such as *Brothers Karamazov*. The life and influence of Dostoevsky is somewhat like the life and influence of Jesus Christ as described in the gospels. On the one hand, the gospels give us a folksy picture of Jesus in public life—picnics on a hillside, fishing on the lakes, chats with his disciples. On the other hand, the gospels portray much of the pain he experienced—insecurity and poverty when he traveled; suspicion and hostility from the Pharisees; rejection and crucifixion at the end.

From the life and death of Jesus emerged the whole New Testament about his teachings as well as the power and the glory of his resurrection. Perhaps this is why St. Paul could exclaim when he writes to the Corinthians: "We preach Christ crucified—a stumbling block to Jews, and an absurdity to Gentiles. But to those who are called, Jews and Greeks alike, Christ the power of God and the wisdom of God. For God's folly is wiser than men, and his weakness more powerful than men."

During Lent there is much we can learn from Dostoevsky and Paul as to how the life of the crucified Christ becomes part of our own life. Like the Jews and the Greeks we come to Christ with our own expectations. And, in a sense, these are realized, but not necessarily in the way we anticipated.

Dostoevsky would like to have written more polished prose, but he never had the leisure to do this. We too might want to improve our home or take a trip, but we may never have the time or money to do these things. Dostoevsky would like to have written more novels, but he never enjoyed robust health. We too might want to advance in our career or finish our schooling, but we may never have the opportunity because of illness. Dostoevsky would like to have been delivered from his compulsion to gamble, but he never quite made it. We too might want to be released from some compulsion toward food, drink or smoking, but we find ourselves still struggling after years of effort.

All these are ways in which we share in the passion of Christ, ways in which the life of the crucified Christ is reproduced in us. All these are ways whereby the Father transforms our foolishness into his wisdom and our weakness into his power; converts our stumbling blocks into stepping stones leading to glory; changes the absurdities in our lives into something meaningful and purposeful.

One wonders if Dostoevsky's own personal sufferings were what he needed to acquire that profound understanding he had when he wrote about the pain felt by the characters of his stories. Sometimes we too may have to suffer with the crucified Christ as the price we have to pay to acquire something precious—that goal we seek, that intimacy we desire, that ideal we dream about. For us who are called to be like Christ the foolishness of the cross proves to be the wisdom of God and our weakness becomes the very power of God.

Fourth Sunday of Lent
Ep 2:4-10

God's Handiwork

Author Arthur Berger claims that comic strips are popular because they tell us something about ourselves. In his book *The Comic-Stripped American* Berger shows how comic creations are characters with whom we can easily identify. For example, Dagwood Bumstead's episodes are symbols of what a typical American male has to go through—battles with his boss, paying shopping bills for his wife, getting provoked by his next-door neighbor.

In cartoon characters like Nancy or Ziggy we can see reflected our own little triumphs and defeats. In the drawings about Miss Peach or Peanuts we can relive our own dreams and disappointments. Consequently, even though comic characters are fictional, they serve a real purpose in our culture. Even though they are only the creation of artists, they enable us to laugh at ourselves, release our hostilities and identify with heroes.

Comic characters in the hands of their creators, the artists, give us some idea of what we are in the hands of God. St. Paul says in his letter to the Ephesians: "It is owing to God's favor that salvation is yours through faith. This is not your own doing, it is God's gift. We are truly his handiwork, created in Christ Jesus to lead the life of good deeds which God prepared for us in advance."

In a sense, we are like comic characters. We owe our very existence to the creative power of God. And even when we were dead in sin he brought us back to life by raising us up with Christ. As Paul points out this is not anything we have accomplished, so why pride ourselves on it? Humble gratitude on our part would be more appropriate.

There is another sense in which we are like comic characters. They are drawn to carry out the designs of the cartoonist. We, too, are created to carry out some purpose in God's plan. Does this mean that we are not free? That we can exercise no initiative of our own?

The answer is that we are free and this is one of our main differences from comic characters. We must use our own initiative, make our own decisions and assume responsibility for what we do. This is our glory: we are human, not fictional; we are co-creators, as well as created; we are artists, too, not just a work of art.

Even though our life of good deeds has been prepared for us by God in advance, we still have to use our intelligence and exercise our free will. We can choose the kind of good deeds we will do during Lent: cheer up someone who is sad; encourage someone who is disappointed; listen to someone who is troubled; assist someone who is overburdened.

Pray that what we do during Lent will reflect our dignity as God's handiwork. Pray that what we do all our life will be a worthy example of Shakespeare's words: "What a piece of work is man! How noble in reason! How infinite in faculty, in form, and moving, how express and admirable! In action, how like an angel! In apprehension, how like a god! The beauty of the world! The paragon of animals!" (*Hamlet*).

Fifth Sunday of Lent
Heb 5:7-9

Obedience

The Empire Strikes Back is the second of the space sagas written and produced by George Lucas. In one of the episodes we find Luke Skywalker on the planet Dagobah to be trained as a Jedi Knight by the great master himself, Yoda. Part elf and part wizard, Yoda has been training Jedi Knights for 800 years.

At first Yoda hesitates to teach Luke. He says that the boy has no patience, too much anger, never has his mind on what he is doing, and craves adventure and excitement. Eventually Yoda relents and trains Luke to be a true Jedi Knight.

To learn how Jedi Knights use the ways of the Force, that energy which surrounds and binds us, Luke Skywalker has to obey his master Yoda. To discover how to feel the flowing of the Force and apply its power to move objects, Luke has to suffer through a rigorous training program under the direction of Yoda.

Obedience characterized the life of Christ, also. As it is written in Hebrews: "Son though he was, he learned obedience from what he suffered, and when perfected, he became the source of eternal salvation for all who obey him."

We see in Christ's life a twofold paradox. First, obedience is connected with suffering, but only for the sake of achieving some kind of perfection, excellence or value. Second, obedience involves some kind of restriction or limitation on oneself, but as a means of enriching the lives of others.

In his book *Open to the Spirit* Fr. Ladislaus Orsy points out how Christ obeyed the Father through the institutions, persons and events of the created world. These same created realities are for us too the normal way to discover and obey the Father's will.

Institutions like the Church, government, family, and business touch many areas of our lives and sometimes create tensions between our personal freedom and obedience to authority; people enter our lives to make demands on us for such things as material assistance, psychological support or spiritual assurance; and events arise to test us—sickness, accidents, job layoffs, car breakdowns, rising costs, fires, floods, and so on.

In all these areas we are bound to experience some suffering—whether in the form of conflict with our own convenience or in the setting aside of our personal preference. But it is here that the first paradox of obedience operates. These sufferings serve to stimulate new growth within us, challenge us to become more than what we are, and bring about some kind of perfection in us.

Our obedience to the Father's will in these three areas enable us to become a source of new life for others. This is the second paradox of obedience. When we respond intelligently and creatively to the demands institutions make on us, we contribute to the development of the community in question. When we respond generously and cheerfully to people's needs when they make reasonable requests from us, we make them feel more important and cared for. When we have the faith to see the Father's will in the things that happen to us, we release within us the power of the Spirit to bring good out of evil.

To accomplish anything worthwhile—like becoming a Jedi Knight—some sort of submission and some degree of suffering is required of us. But when we obey as a positive response to the Father's purpose as it is revealed to us through institutions, people and events, we not only attain the excellence we seek, but also become a source of life for others.

First Sunday of Easter
Col 3:1-4

Raised Up With Christ

America's Number One female singer—disco star **Donna Summer**—has now joined Bob Dylan, Arlo Guthrie and other popular musical entertainers in making God the most important part of their lives. Donna said that her renewed relationship with God is something she had to get back to, particularly as world stability deteriorates.

Donna's return to the Lord is a kind of mini-resurrection story. It is not as spectacular as Christ's resurrection story, but nonetheless one that gives us some insight into the meaning of resurrection.

St. Paul announces the good news of Easter when he writes to the Colossians: "Since you have been raised up in company with Christ, set your heart on what pertains to higher realms where Christ is seated at God's right hand. Be intent on things above, rather than on things of earth."

From Paul's point of view, not only has Christ been raised from the dead, but we too have been raised up with him. This event of our resurrection has already begun with baptism, it continues through life each time we turn away from sin to live for Christ, and it will be completed after we pass through death.

That we have been raised up is part of the good news, the joyous news of Easter. All around us there are signs to remind us of this and to show us what it should mean in our life.

People are being raised up to new life: people like Donna Summer being born again after leaving the Lord; people like engaged couples preparing themselves for a new life in marriage; people like athletes in spring training pushing themselves to new levels of achievement.

143

Nature is being raised up to new life: the sun is getting warmer; daylight is getting stronger; buds on the trees are bursting; the grass is growing greener.

Business is being raised to a new life: garages are busy tuning up cars for summer travel; builders are constructing new homes for dwellers; clothing stores are advertising new fashions for us to wear.

Surrounded by so many signs of new life being raised up, we too instinctively want to get caught up in this kind of momentum. We too want to feel the rhythm of new life on different levels of our being—physical, emotional, mental and spiritual.

If this impulse is real and deep, and not just a whim or something superficial, then we will do something like Donna Summer did to experience being raised up. We won't allow ourselves to become unduly depressed, imprisoned by fear or paralyzed by worry.

Instead we will show that we have left behind these things that lead only to sickness and death, and have been raised up with Christ to a new way of life—a life of joy that surmounts every sorrow; a life of freedom that overrides every fear; a life of peace that withstands every pressure.

When philosopher Karl Jaspers was asked to describe his vision of a great and noble life he answered: "To endure ambiguity in the movement of truth and to make light shine through it; to stand fast in uncertainty; and to prove capable of unlimited love and hope."

Any Christian who has been raised up with Christ will share Jasper's vision of life—he will move with faith in the midst of doubt and difficulty; be steadfast in times of struggle and suffering; and risk reaching out to others with trust and love.

Second Sunday of Easter
1 Jn 5:1-6

Faith Conquers

Today Marian Anderson is among the world's best loved and most respected singers. But it was not always so. According to music-drama critic Jean Isaacs, "Doors opened slowly for this celebrated black woman with a golden voice. Things happened repeatedly which could have defeated or embittered her. She rose above all the obstacles as they appeared."

With only one parent, her mother, Marian Anderson grew up in poverty. But her mother was a woman of faith and she instilled that strength in Marian. After high school Marian tried to enter an outstanding conservatory near her Philadelphia home, but she was refused admittance because of her color.

So she spent more than ten years in the musical minor league. She moved from one third rate auditorium to another. She even had to pay $500 for her first European concert. But from then on success came swiftly. Royalty bowed to her, New York welcomed her recital, and the White House invited her for a solo performance.

Marian Anderson has already lived what St. John writes about in his first letter: "Everyone begotten of God conquers the world, and the power that has conquered the world is this faith of ours. Who, then, is conqueror of the world? The one who believes that Jesus is the Son of God."

The faith her mother instilled in her enabled Marian to conquer the early obstacles in her life—poverty, prejudice, obscurity. Her belief in Jesus enabled her to rise above hatred and hostility to become today one of America's greatest singers.

Should it be any different for us? Our faith in the risen Lord empowers us to conquer whatever difficulties confront us. All we have to do is claim Christ's victory as our own. By faith we can convert sorrow into joy and discover light amid darkness. By faith we can transform despair into hope and see new life rise out of death.

When we believe in Jesus we can forget injuries and forgive people; we can scatter our fears and acquire confidence. Regardless of what it is that enslaves us, threatens us or stymies us, with faith in the risen Lord, we can conquer it. If we are enslaved by self-deception, faith can free us to face the truth about ourselves. If we are threatened by unemployment, faith can support us until the crisis passes. If we are stymied by our own mistakes, faith can strengthen us to search for new ways to create our own future.

One of the most inspiring declarations of faith ever written was scribbled on a wall in a concentration camp during World War II: "I believe in the sun, even when it is not shining. I believe in love, even when I feel it not. I believe in God, even when he is silent."

This is the kind of faith we pray for—a faith that can conquer even the conditions of a concentration camp; a faith that can empower people like Marian Anderson to rise above adversity and become a celebrity; a faith that will enable us to endure our own disappointments without being discouraged, and to hope for our own victory even when the worst happens to us.

Who, then, is the conqueror of the world? The one who believes that Jesus is the Son of God.

Third Sunday of Easter
1 Jn 2:1-5

Forgiveness

Suppose you became an alcoholic even before you became a teenager and lived that way for more than forty years. Suppose, further, that your oldest daughter began tripping out on drugs at age ten, had spaced out on every drug at fourteen, and was on the brink of death at twenty-one. Imagine how difficult it would be to quit drinking and to change your way of life.

Yet, this is what Curtis Parker of Houston was able to do. Not only has Curtis Parker straightened out his own life by joining Alcoholics Anonymous, but he is now instrumental in straightening out the lives of others through a Drug Abuse Alert Committee he founded in 1971.

After four decades of running away from life, Parker now dedicates his time to talking to parents and students about drug abuse, and to rehabilitating drug addicts through group therapy and individual counseling. Parker's program encompasses twelve steps from twilight to sunset. One of the twelve steps is: "We become willing to allow a Higher Power, through the love of the group, to help change our way of life."

Parker's conversion from drink to sobriety can be described with these words from St. John: "If anyone should sin, we have, in the presence of the Father, Jesus Christ as intercessor. He is an offering for our sins."

It is through Christ, then, that we find forgiveness for our sins. We may have disowned the Lord like the Jews did before Pilate, or abandoned the Lord like the apostles did during the Passion, yet he is ready to greet us with the words, "Peace be to you." We may have become an alcoholic for forty years like Curtis Parker, or a drug addict like his teenage daughter, yet the Lord is ready to heal us and renew us.

No matter how bad is the habit we may have formed, or how far we have drifted from the right path, through Christ we can become reconciled with our Father. No matter how much we may have hurt people, or how much damage we may have caused, through Christ we can become reconciled with one another and rebuild our relationships.

Such is the Lord's power to forgive sin, deliver us from futility, and restore peace to our lives. But his power doesn't just operate in us. It operates through us to reach others. As St. John says, "Christ is an offering for our sins, and not for our sins only, but for those of the whole world." Or, as Christ says in the gospel, "Peace be to you. Now go, and be witnesses to this."

Our gift of pardon and peace then is meant to be shared with others. The new life we've found through forgiveness should be communicated to others. Like Curtis Parker helping his drug-addicted daughter return to the Lord, we too are being sent by the Lord to help others experience his healing power.

The sins of the whole world are waiting for our witness. All kinds of people are still imprisoned by sin and bound by guilt. All kinds of people are still searching for peace and haven't found it. Among these people are members of our own family who look to us for hope; people in our own neighborhood who turn to us for light; fellow workers in our own job situation who seek encouragement from us.

In his book *Shalom: Peace* Fr. Bernard Haring writes: "The Sacrament of Reconciliation is primarily the liturgical proclamation of the Easter mystery applied here and now to the faithful. When the disciples first encountered the risen Christ, he proclaimed his peace to them. This encounter freed the disciples from their crippling fear and filled them with joy."

This is what our whole life should be: a proclamation of the Easter mystery to those around us; a witnessing to the freedom and new life we've found in the Lord's forgiveness. Like Curtis Parker we should be so filled with peace and joy that we should want to tell others about this; we should want them too, to experience this in Christ Jesus.

Fourth Sunday of Easter
1 Jn 3:1-2

Becoming

Graduation exercises are usually marked by the conferring of honors in recognition of what students have already become: outstanding scholars and athletes, musicians and artists, writers and leaders. What graduates are now we can see and acknowledge. What they shall be later has not yet come to light.

When it comes to light—ten, twenty or thirty years from now—we shall see distinguished doctors and lawyers, inventors and explorers, engineers and entertainers, painters and poets, professors and politicians, and so on.

This is something like our situation with respect to life now on earth and life later in heaven. St. John says: "We are God's children now. What we shall later be has not yet come to light. We know that when it comes to light we shall be like him, for we shall see him as he is."

That we are God's children now is, indeed, a wonderful thing, almost incredible. It wouldn't be true unless God himself had told us so. Our future is no less fantastic—we shall be like the Lord; we shall see him as he is.

What we are now by our own doing is something we may be proud of or ashamed of. That's OK with the Lord—he accepts us as we are. He is more interested in what we can become, now in this life, and later in heaven.

We never know what we can become unless we test ourselves or are tested by others. For example, we never know how heroic we can be until we have to act in some emergency. We never know how generous we can be unless we have an opportunity to share

149

with someone in need. We never know how creative we can be until we try to build something like a home.

In an article on growing awareness, psychologist Sidney Jourard writes: "Suppose I decide to try some new project—to write a book, climb a mountain, change jobs. Suppose, further, that I don't believe I have the capacity to succeed. But if you encourage and try to support me when the going gets rough, I can experience within myself transcendent powers I never imagined I had. I cannot transcend my possibilities. But I can transcend my concept of what my possibilities might be. When this happens, then I am ready to grow. Then I am ready to discover deeper dimensions of my being. Then I am ready to find out who I really am."

If this is true about personal growth, how much more so is it about our growth in the life of Christ. To allow this life of Christ to operate and expand within us, we have to step out in faith. For example, we will never spread happiness among people in need, unless we risk getting involved; we will never inspire joy in people whose feelings are hurt, unless we offer our friendship.

What we are now may be good or bad. But what we can become in the time we have left, fills us with hope and enthusiasm. We can become more like the Lord so that through us people will see him. All we have to do is open ourselves up to the power of his Spirit within us. Then he can use us to bring faith to people who have lost it, hope to someone who is discouraged, and love to a person who has been rejected.

What we can still become now is exciting in its possibilities. What we shall become later after the resurrection exceeds our wildest dreams—"We shall be like the Lord, we shall see him as he is."

Fifth Sunday of Easter
1 Jn 3:18-24

Show Me

In one of the songs from *My Fair Lady* Eliza Doolittle sings: "Words, words, words—I'm so sick of words. Don't talk of stars burning above. If you're in love, show me! Tell me no dreams filled with desire. If you're on fire, show me! Here we are together in the middle of the night. Don't talk of spring, just hold me tight."

It seems then that Eliza didn't want to hear any more of Freddy's words about how much he cared for her. She wanted him to demonstrate it. She didn't want to listen any more to his promises about love. She wanted him to prove it.

This is similar to St. John's exhortation: "Little children, let us love in deed and in truth, and not merely talk about it. His commandment is this: we are to believe in the name of his Son, Jesus Christ, and are to love one another as he commanded us."

We wonder if the Sermon on the Mount by Christ, the Gettysburg Address by Lincoln, or the teachings of Gandhi would have such a deep influence on us if these men had not died for what they believed in. All of them spoke fine words. But these words would have been empty rhetoric without that finest deed a man can do—to lay down his life for his brother, his country, or for what he believes in.

But we don't have to make such a supreme sacrifice to prove our love. Everyday we have countless opportunities to express our love in lesser, but nonetheless important ways.

In his commentary on this passage of John's writings Fr. Bruce Vawter says: "Our duty to love cannot be fulfilled merely by good intentions. It must be proven by deeds. Indeed, a concrete act of charity in a relatively inferior matter such as almsgiving may be a more valid proof of this love than the willingness to lay down one's life."

It is possible then that one small act of kindness can be more valuable than a volume of grandiose pledges. For example, the simple gesture of a husband taking his wife out to dine and dance once in a while proves more than years of unfulfilled promises to take her on some expensive vacation to Bermuda; taking the initiative to actually go out and help your neighbor with his lawn means much more than bragging about how good a gardener you are and how willing you are to help him some day; volunteering to help on some parish committee now does far more good than offering to help at some indefinite future function when you might have more time.

All of us want the real thing; all of us want what is authentic. Nobel peace prizes are not given to people who preach about peace, but to people like Solzhenitzyn who do something to make it happen. Pulitzer prizes are not given to writers who promise to produce interesting stories, but to writers like Saul Bellow who turn out works like *Humboldt's Gift*.

It is no different in our Christian life. Mere talk about how much we love the Lord and our neighbor is useless. The only true test about the quality of our love is performance. If we want our love for the Lord to be the real thing, then every day we will spend some time with him in prayer, listen to his word in Scripture, and seek his help in the sacraments.

If we want our love of neighbor to be authentic, then everyday we will try to be more sensitive to his needs and hurts, reach out with both material help and psychological support, and offer friendship and understanding. In other words, we will show our love, and let others say something about it; prove our love, and let others proclaim it; do things, and let others talk about them.

Sixth Sunday of Easter
1 Jn 4:7-10

God Is Love

In his book *If God is God* campus pastor Richard Koenig makes reference to several modern dramas. One of the dramas he cites is Archibald MacLeish's play *J.B.* In this play the main character J.B. is taunted by another character named Nickles with the chant: "If God is God, He is not good. If God is good, He is not God."

Fr. Koenig comments that Nickles' couplet articulates man's shocked reaction to a God who seems to pay no attention to man's suffering. How can a good God permit children to be born deformed, people to starve because of drought, or senseless accidents to occur?

Yet, in spite of all the past atrocities of camps like Auschwitz and recent tragedies caused by tornados and hurricanes, we hear St. John insist: "Beloved, let us love one another because love is of God. The man without love has known nothing of God, for God is love. God's love was revealed in our midst in this way: he sent his only Son to the world that we might have life through him."

Who then is right? Nickles in the play *J.B.* who says, "If God is God, He is not good?" Or John in the Scriptures who says, "God is love?" As Christians we line up with John's position. This does not mean we ignore evil in the world. Rather, it means that we see evil for what it is, but do not let it obscure our vision of God's goodness. When we say that God is love, we do not pretend that there is no problem of innocent suffering. Instead, we search for an answer on a deeper level than Nickles was willing to go.

We might conclude that God is love from what we see in nature or history, but the strongest proof is the one John gives us: the

Father sent his only Son into the world so that we might have life through him.

Fr. Koenig comments on this love of God this way: "Innocent suffering seems absurd, but not when God identifies and suffers with his creatures. For then God turns out to be not one who cruelly sports with man, but one who stands beside him to share his pain. The problem of evil ends with no philosophical answer, but is taken up into a reality that is greater than itself—the suffering love of God."

If God so loved us as to suffer and die for us, no wonder John urges us to love one another. If God is love, should we, his children, be anything less? Like Christ then we won't stand at a distance, but become involved in the sufferings of others. We may not understand why the innocent suffer, but this won't stop us from trying to relieve their suffering in some way.

An unknown author once wrote: "What does love look like? It has eyes to see misery and want. It has ears to hear the sighs and sorrows of man. It has feet to hasten to the poor. It has hands to help others. That is what love looks like."

As the Father sent his Son Jesus into the world to bring his love to us, Jesus now sends us into the world to bring his love to others—to speak a word of sympathy when sorrow strikes; pick up the telephone when someone is lonely; volunteer assistance when emergencies arise; be present to someone who is in deep physical or emotional pain.

God is love. Our purpose in life is to extend his love to others—to reach out to that unlovable member in our family; show forgiveness to that hostile son or daughter; practice patience with people who upset us; recognize and praise the good work that someone does.

God is love, and now that Christ has ascended to heaven God's love is revealed through the way we love one another. Jesus now sends us into the world so that people might have his life through us and have it more abundantly.

Seventh Sunday of Easter
1 Jn 4:11-16

Seeing God

The Miracle Worker tells the story of the early struggles and the first triumphs of Helen Keller and her teacher Ann Sullivan. Its immense success as a play, film and TV drama demonstrates what an inspiring and moving story it is. Blind, deaf and mute from her nineteenth month, Helen Keller learned how to speak, read Braille and write books. Through her teacher Ann Sullivan, Helen Keller learned how to live a full human life. She could neither see nor hear people, but through the loving care of Ann Sullivan she learned to communicate in their presence and feel the warmth of their friendship.

All of us are in a similar position to Helen Keller's when it comes to experiencing God. St. John says: "No one has ever seen God. Yet if we love one another God dwells in us, and his love is brought to perfection in us. The way we know we remain in him and he in us is that he has given us of his Spirit."

What John seems to say is that through the love of people like Ann Sullivan for us we come to experience God as somebody who is really real; we learn how to sense his presence, communicate with his person and enjoy his friendship.

This is why Christ became man—so that in him we could see the Father, through him hear the Father speak, and from him receive the Father's love. This is what it means for us to be Christian—to so love one another that in us people will see Christ, through us hear his words of forgiveness and encouragement, and from us receive his light and healing.

Perhaps this is the explanation of the appeal of people like Mother Teresa of Calcutta, Jean Vanier and Cesar Chavez. The love they show to the dying, the retarded and the oppressed enables these desperate people of our society to see God in the midst of death, feel his care despite their handicaps, and experience his support in their struggle for justice.

But we don't have to be exceptional women like Mother Teresa or Ann Sullivan to help people see God. At home or at work we have all kinds of opportunities to show Christ to others. Wherever there is a burden to bear, a pain to be relieved or an emptiness to be filled, that is where we can love someone and enable them to say, "I've seen the Lord."

We don't have to be extraordinary men like Jean Vanier or Cesar Chavez to help people experience the Lord. We have all sorts of chances of our own to let people feel the surpassing kindness of the Lord. Wherever there is a need for encouragement, a sorrow to share or a second chance to be given, that is where we can love someone and make it possible for them to feel the presence of the Lord and say, "I know he's with me."

We don't have to look far to find people in the position of Helen Keller as regards their knowing the Lord—unable to see or hear him because no one cares enough to show him to them. So many people are living a marginal human existence in ghettos, prisons, hospitals, retirement homes and flop houses. They will never discover the goodness of the Lord as long as we deny it to them by our indifference.

So many people are living lives of desperation—alcoholics, the jobless, the depressed and drug addicts. They will never know that God is love unless we reveal it to them through our genuine concern, generous support and loving kindness.

No one has ever seen God. But every time we become an Ann Sullivan to care for the Helen Kellers around us, we show them an aspect of God's glory and extend the Incarnation of Christ. No one has ever seen God. But through the love we show one another, people will come to know that, indeed, God does dwell in our midst; that he does remain in us and has given us of his Spirit.

Trinity Sunday
Rm 8:14-17

Adoption

Bob Hope is famous for his humor on film and television, and for his entertaining of soldiers during World War II and the Vietnam War. But one of the lesser known facts about Bob Hope and his wife Dolores is that they have adopted and raised four children—Linda, Tony, Nora and Kelly. The Hope family was childless. But thanks to the process of adoption the Hopes found fulfillment as foster parents and their four foster children found a family.

St. Paul speaks about adoption when he writes to the Romans: "You have not received a spirit of slavery leading you back to fear, but a spirit of adoption through which we cry, 'Abba.' (that is, 'Father'). But if we are children of God, we are heirs as well—heirs of God, heirs with Christ."

Since Paul was writing to the early Christians in the city of Rome, we have to understand the term adoption according to the Roman Law of his time. In his commentary on this passage William Barclay outlines four main consequences of adoption under Roman Law.

First, the adopted son lost all rights in his old family, and gained all the rights of a natural son in the new family. Second, together with any natural sons, the adopted son became coheir to his new father's estate. Third, the old life of the adopted son was completely wiped out; all legal debts were cancelled; he was a new person beginning a new life. Fourth, the adopted son became the absolute possession of his new father, for in Roman Society a son never came of age; he was always under the complete control of his father.

These four points give us an insight into the meaning of our own adoption into the Family of God, the Holy Trinity. First, we gain the same right as Christ to be on personal, intimate terms with the Father. Literally, we can call him "Papa" or "Daddy," our equivalents to the Aramaic term of endearment, "Abba." Second, by our adoption we become coheirs with Christ. All that the Father has, he has given to Christ. All that is Christ's inheritance now becomes ours. But we must first suffer with him so as to be glorified with him. Third, by adoption our old life of sin is wiped out and the past is cancelled pertaining to our debts. We actually become new creatures beginning a whole new life of grace. Also, by our adoption we become the absolute possession of God. Once we were under the control of sin, but now we are under the complete control of the Spirit.

No wonder then that we want to praise and thank the Holy Trinity—we've been adopted into their family! We did nothing to earn or deserve this privilege. Yet our gracious Father has taken us sinners as his adopted sons and daughters. He has taken us when we were lost, helpless and debt-laden sinners, and adopted us into his own family to give us a new identity, a new freedom and a whole new way of life.

Moreover, this gift of adoption is renewed each time we celebrate the Eucharist. The gift of adoption is already ours—we are, indeed, children of God—but it is not yet perfect—we still sometimes sin. That is why we need the sacraments, Scripture and prayer—to reaffirm our divine adoption, make us more aware of our deliverance from sin, and increase our capacity to move with freedom under the Spirit.

That is why we need Charismatic Movements, Marriage Encounters and Cursillos—to make us realize more and more our new life as coheirs with Christ and the glory that awaits us. That is why we need to support causes like Right to Life, grape boycotts, Bread for the World and prison reforms—to make it possible for others to live decently within the human family here, and to share in the fullness of life in God's family hereafter.

Corpus Christi
Heb 9:11-15

Blood

At the beginning of World War II there was a medical breakthrough that later saved the lives of thousands of soldiers. Dr. Charles Richard Drew introduced the use of plasma on the battlefield as an emergency substitute for blood. Dr. Drew's research also established ways to store and preserve whole blood. He then organized the world's first blood bank in Britain and established the American Red Cross Blood Bank.

It was ironic that Dr. Drew, a Negro, would later have to resign in protest to an armed forces policy that would accept only Caucasian blood for the Red Cross. At a press conference Dr. Drew said: "I speak not as a Negro but as a scientist. The blood of individual human beings may differ by blood groupings or type, but there is absolutely no scientific basis to indicate any difference according to race."

Blood is the theme of the text used from the letter to the Hebrews for the Feast of Corpus Christi: "Christ entered the sanctuary, not with the blood of goats and calves, but with his own blood, and achieved eternal redemption. For if the blood of goats and bulls can sanctify those who are defiled so that their flesh is cleansed, how much more will the blood of Christ cleanse our conscience from dead works to worship the living God.!"

To grasp somewhat the significance of Christ's blood in the Eucharist under the form of wine, we need some understanding of the use of blood in the Old Testament sacrifices. When animals were slaughtered in sacrifice the idea was not to symbolize that the people were deserving of death, nor was the blood shed some sort of price paid to appease an angry God.

The purpose was much more positive. Blood was identified with life in the Old Testament because breath was thought to be in it. So when an animal's blood was shed in sacrifice, it was believed that its life was being offered to God, and, symbolically, the life of the worshiper, too. And when the animal's blood was sprinkled on the people, it was believed that the people were purified of their sins and that their covenant with God was renewed.

Consequently, when Christ comes along to be both the priest and the victim as his blood is shed on the cross, he fulfills, even surpasses all these Old Testament expectations. Moreover, by giving us his body and blood in the Eucharist, Jesus makes available to us all the blessings of his sacrifice on the cross. His blood in the Eucharist signifies life more than it does death—his risen life made present for us sacramentally.

But our meeting the risen Christ in the Eucharist is meaningless unless we also meet him in people. Joe Wise expresses this understanding of Eucharist in his song *Re-member Me*: "Take and eat. This is my body. Broken on crosses too lonely to mention. Take and drink. This is my blood. Spilled on your alleys and lost in your hallways. Re-member me. I ride on your buses, walk on your streets and sleep by your highways. Re-member me. I put on your ring, give you my lifetime and count on you always. Re-member me. I live in your house, play in your yard and call you my father. Re-member me. I sit in your jails, lie on your sickbeds and wait for your footsteps. Take and drink. This is my blood. Spilled on your alleys and lost in your hallways. Re-member me."

If we understood Eucharist that way, then we would never hurt people like Dr. Drew because his skin was black, or be unwilling to help refugees from Vietnam because they're Oriental. Instead we would see each other as brothers and sisters who share the same human life because of our common blood; we would remember that Christ is present in each one of us because through the Eucharist we share his blood and life.

Second Sunday of the Year
1 Cor 6:13-15, 17-20

The Body

When grandfather Gordie Howe retired from playing at the age of fifty-two, he had completed thirty-two seasons of professional hockey. His record achievements in games played and goals scored will stand a long time. Gordie Howe accomplished these feats by taking good care of his body. The secret of his athletic stamina, strength and agility was in the way he conditioned and trained his body.

Actress Katherine Hepburn is one of Hollywood's all-time great movie stars. She has already won more than one Academy Award as the Best Actress of the Year. Katherine Hepburn says that she keeps her seventy-year-old body healthy and trim by not getting fat, sleeping enough, and exercising out of doors in any weather and everyday.

Both Howe and Hepburn are examples of people who rely on their body in order to excel in their chosen profession. Both athletes and actresses have to be in good physical condition to give their maximum when they play or perform.

The body is the subject of St. Paul's teaching to the Corinthians when he uses the word "body" seven times in this passage: "The body is not for immorality; it is for the Lord, and the Lord is for the body. Do you not see that your bodies are members of Christ. Whoever is joined to the Lord becomes one spirit with him. Shun lewd conduct. Every other sin a man commits is outside his body, but the fornicator sins against his own body. You must know that your body is a temple of the Holy Spirit, who is within. You are not your own. You have been purchased, and at what a price! So glorify God in your body."

According to Paul, then, the body is an essential dimension of our human condition. We are not pure spirits who can get along without a physical body. Rather, we are embodied-spirits who have been redeemed in the flesh now and will be raised in the flesh later.

Because our bodies are members of Christ, we can glorify God with them. Whether we eat or sleep, work or play, speak or sing using our own body, we can do all these things to glorify God. Moreover, when we respect the bodies of other people, we show respect for Christ, too. Whether we feed or nurse the bodies of the sick, clothe or comfort the bodies of the poor, kiss or embrace the body of a loved one, we do all these things for Christ, too.

In other words, because our bodies are members of Christ, they are like sacraments. They are instruments through which we contact Christ. They are extensions of the very presence of Christ in the world.

The practical consequences of Paul's teachings about the body are staggering. With regard to ourselves, it means that like Howe and Hepburn we have a duty to keep our body in good health. A sensible diet, sufficient sleep and some exercise for our bodies are not optional but essential.

We also have a duty to use our body for good moral conduct. To use our body for lying, stealing or sexual abuse is immoral, whereas to use our body for artistic creativity, professional work or to render some service to the community is praiseworthy.

With regard to others, it means that we have a responsibility to provide conditions for their physical well-being such as safe surroundings for workers, humane prisons for criminals, adequate housing for the elderly, and protection for the unborn child.

Third Sunday of the Year
1 Cor 7:29-31

Time Is Short

In 1959 rock 'n' roll pioneer Buddy Holly died in an air crash at the age of twenty-two. He is the subject of a current film entitled *The Buddy Holly Story*. Holly was a clean-cut boy from Texas who became a professional when he was nineteen. He was the first white performer to adapt black rhythm to country music, from which evolved modern rock. Holly was the first rock star to write, play and sing his own music. In his brilliant three-year career he wrote forty-five hit songs, six of which were still on the charts when he died tragically.

If Buddy Holly were with us today he would probably want to say to us what St. Paul said to the Corinthians: "I tell you, brothers, the time is short. Those who make use of the world should live as though they were not using it, for the world as we know it is passing away."

When Paul wrote those words he was still under the impression that the Second Coming of Christ would happen very soon. It was only later that he realized that the return of Christ would be delayed until some undetermined time in the distant future. Nevertheless, what Paul says is true for all of us, at least in a personal sense. Time is short for each one of us, whether we live to be only twenty-two like Buddy Holly or eighty-four like Arthur Fiedler.

When we're young we have so many dreams about the future. We wonder if we will have enough time to meet all the people, see all the places and do all the things we dream about. When we're old we have a lot of unfulfilled dreams from the past. We wonder where the time went that we didn't get to know some of our family better, didn't take that planned vacation trip somewhere or didn't ever learn that hobby we'd thought about.

Time is short. Take time, then, to find Christ around you. Take time to find him when you dine with your family or laugh with your friends; when you see the beauty of nature or listen to good music; when you read a book or work in the garden.

The world as we know it is passing away. We have only a limited amount of time to live, and some of it passes away with each day bringing us closer to death. This should not make us sad, but realistic. The challenge is to use this time wisely.

As the ancient Roman poet Juvenal put it: *"Carpe diem"*—"Seize the Day." Seize today to meet Christ as he comes now in different ways. Seize today with its opportunities and possibilities, its duties and responsibilities, its surprises and wonders.

Time is short. Already this hour is half over, this day is half gone. Seize this moment, then, and say to the Lord this prayer written by an unknown author: "Lord, I shall pass through this world but once. Any good that I can do to any human being, let me do it now. Let me not defer it or neglect it, for I shall not pass this way again."

Fourth Sunday of the Year
1 Cor 7:32-35

Marriage and Celibacy

Among the developments we've seen in the Church since the time of Vatican II has been the emergence of the Charistmatic Movement, Marriage Encounter, Family Guilds and Covenant Houses. A common characteristic of all these developments is the closer contact that exists between married couples and their children with priests, brothers and sisters. They illustrate the intimate relationship there is between marriage and celibacy.

This relationship was also the subject of St. Paul's thoughts when he wrote: "The unmarried man is busy with the Lord's affairs, concerned with pleasing the Lord; but the married man is busy with this world's demands and is occupied with pleasing his wife. This means he is divided. The virgin—indeed, any unmarried woman—is concerned with things of the Lord, in pursuit of holiness in body and spirit. The married woman, on the other hand, has the cares of this world to absorb her and is concerned with pleasing her husband."

Too often this passage is interpreted to mean that Paul is saying that celibacy is superior to marriage. He isn't. He says that the celibacy he is promoting is good, but so too is marriage in its own way. Too many people read this passage as if Paul were setting up an opposition between marriage and celibacy. He isn't. He is only contrasting them to show that they really complement one another.

The marriage-celibacy relationship is not a question of a higher-lower scheme of things, but one of different callings within the same Christian community. Marriage and celibacy are not rival vocations that compete with each other, but rather vocations that complete each other by way of mutual inspiration and edification. How is this possible?

One answer is to distinguish two kinds of love. On the one hand, marriage gives evidence of the singular, individual character of Christ's redemptive love—his love for each person with a unique particularity. On the other hand, celibacy witnesses to the absolute universality of Christ's love. The celibate is pledged to love all those whom he contacts, especially the outcasts of society.

These two kinds of love are distinct but not separate. Every Christian must love in both ways. A husband and wife look to the celibate for a reminder that their married love must not become a selfish egoism for two, but must open their hearts to the poor of the world. The celibate looks to the married couple for a reminder that his universal love must not mean that he never gets close enough to anyone to get hurt, but must come to grips with the pain of loving this or that particular person the Lord sends.

Another approach is to distinguish the Incarnational and Eschatological aspects of the Christian life. Again, all Christians, married or celibate, must witness to both of these aspects. Nevertheless, by their overall visible and permanent lifestyle the married couple and the celibate become a sign of one of these aspects more so than the other.

The married couple especially expresses the Incarnational aspect; they cooperate with Christ in the sanctification of all human values. By their sexual love they proclaim that the body is sacred and holy; by their work they say that material things like property and money are good; by their participation in learning, art and culture they show that the things of the mind are noble. Marriage signifies in particular our human fulfillment.

The celibate especially expresses the Eschatological aspect of the Christian life. The final accomplishment of the Kingdom will not happen in this life, but only when Christ comes again in glory at the end of time. By freely giving up in this life the possible experience of high, positive, human values like marriage, sexual love and raising children, the celibate puts his faith and hope in values of the next life—the resurrection of the body and seeing God in the beatific vision. Celibacy signifies especially our transcendent destiny through union with the Trinity.

Fifth Sunday of the Year
1 Cor 9:16-23

All Things

One of television's favorite father figures is Dick Van Patten who plays the role of Tom Bradford in *Eight is Enough*. The secret of his popularity may be the love and care he has for both his real-life family of three sons who are now young men, and the eight lively kids who make up his television family.

Family closeness, family priorities and family faith have always been important in Van Patten's life. He shows a lot of interest and spends extensive time with his television children outside their working hours. His paternal support, affection and affirmation are quickly sensed by television viewers.

Dick Van Patten and his wife Pat know well the meaning of St. Paul's words when he writes: "Although I am not bound to anyone, I made myself the slave of all, so as to win over as many as possible. To the weak I became a weak person with a view to winning the weak. I have made myself all things to all men in order to save at least some of them."

Paul is referring to his ministry as an apostle. But what he says about preaching the gospel applies to being good parents also. Good parents like the Van Pattens have to become all things to all their children. They have to become all things from cooks and tailors to counselors and psychologists. To raise children, parents have to become part-time practitioners in almost anything from nursing and chauffering to teaching and coaching.

Child psychologist Dr. Mary McNeill of Chicago says that most of the problems children face center around self-esteem, security and success. She adds that parents play an indispensable role in guiding children and youth to find these values.

As regards self-esteem, parents can help their children to feel important and wanted. By showing genuine interest in what their children do and appreciation for their efforts to win approval, parents can enhance their children's self-image; by taking pride in their progress and praising them for it, parents can give their children good feelings of self-worth.

Parents can stimulate in their children a sense of security. By their gentleness parents can do much to assist their children to overcome any fears that threaten them. Whether it's the first time to go to school, to a camp or to a dance, children need their parents' support to overcome anxieties and acquire self-confidence.

Parents should also be sensitive to their childrens' feelings of success. Young people need encouragement and positive reinforcement from their parents in order to achieve success. Whether the activity is academic, dramatic or athletic, young people have to be shown how to overcome mistakes, cope with failure and keep on trying to succeed.

Parents always have to be ready to respond to their children according to changing conditions. Now they have to show them how to brush their teeth, later how to dress for the prom; now how to walk, later how to swing a bat; now how to pray before they go to bed in their nursery, later how to pray when tempted to go to bed with someone in a college dorm; now how to drive to get a beginner's license, later how to drive without the influence of drink.

Thank the Lord for our parents who have been all things to us during our childhood and youth. Praise the Lord for parents like Dick and Pat Van Patten who are so unselfish and generous. Ask for God's blessings on parents who are trying so hard to be all things to all their children.

Sixth Sunday of the Year
1 Cor 10:31-11:1

The Glory of God

There is a story told about an old man who ran the engines on a tugboat. The engines were kept spotlessly clean. The man took immense pride in his work, his face beamed with a radiant glow. When asked about his shining engines and the beam in his expression he answered, "Well, it's this-a-way. I've got a glory."

This tugboat man had a glory because he enjoyed what he was doing. He had a glory because he took nice care of his equipment. This kind of attitude about what we do or use is reflected somewhat in St. Paul's letter to the Corinthians when he urges: "Whether you eat or drink—whatever you do—you should do all for the glory of God."

If only more of us would learn from the tugboat man and St. Paul, we would avoid many of today's problems. Too many of us are not enjoying or finding satisfaction in what we do. We hear of surveys about students being bored with school, workers finding their jobs dull and housewives suffering from depression.

The causes for these problems are many and complex. But one of the causes may be that we are not doing what we do for the glory of God. If we did, then many other things would fall easily into place. Take our work, for example. If we did our work for the glory of God, then we would take pride in our performance, take good care of our equipment, be fully informed about procedures, and show a genuine interest in our co-workers.

We might ask, "How can a person get enthused over a task that is routine and repetitious? How can a factory worker putting in the same part, or a mother ironing clothes make their work enjoyable?" Some answers are given by Prof. Csikszentmihalyi of the University of Chicago in his book *Beyond Boredom and Anxiety*.

He believes that it is necessary to change the attitude of workers *and* to change the nature of their boring job. He points out how workers can play mental games, try new strategies and establish their own standards. He proposes that employers redesign jobs, shift workers around to different tasks and allow employees to make some minor decisions.

Take our play, for example. If we did our leisure activities for the glory of God, then we wouldn't watch TV all the time. Instead we would find something to stimulate our mind, like playing chess or reading a book; try something to exercise our body, like swimming or jogging; get involved in something to calm our nerves, like gardening or ceramics.

If we had God's glory in view when we took our recreations, then we might enjoy a few beers without getting sloshed, see a movie without it being pornographic, or play a game of cards without losing our temper.

Take our meals, for example. If we ate and drank for the glory of God, then we would eat nourishing food instead of junk food, consume a sensible amount instead of stuffing ourselves, and make conversations pleasant instead of upsetting.

Like the tugboat man, we too can have a glory about whatever we do, if we do it for the glory of God. Praise God for his gifts, thank him for his blessings, and glorify him for his favors.

Seventh Sunday of the Year
2 Cor 1:18-22

Yes

When Guatemala was struck by earthquakes in 1976 more than twenty-three thousand people were killed and one million people left homeless. Juan Chay and his family were among the survivors of this disaster. Despite the many deaths among his friends and the severe damage to his neighborhood, Juan accepted this as God's will. Instead of becoming bitter and cursing God, Juan prayed to God and began the back-breaking task of clearing away the rubble in order to rebuild what was destroyed.

It is easy to say "Yes" to God's will when everything is going well—we feel well, our job is secure and we're getting along well with everyone. But it is very difficult to say "Yes" to God's will when everything seems to be going poorly—those times when we feel sick, lose our job or people anger us. Yet, if we're going to be Christ-like, we have to accept God's will in all circumstances, good or bad.

St. Paul points out this characteristic when he writes about Jesus to the Corinthians: "Jesus Christ, whom Silvanus, Timothy, and I preached to you as Son of God, was not alternately 'yes' and 'no'; he was never anything but 'yes.' Whatever promises God has made have been fulfilled in him; therefore it is through him that we address our Amen to God when we worship together."

If we peruse the gospels we find that Paul is right—Jesus always did the will of his Father, whether it was to experience the pleasure of being human, or the pain of being human. Jesus often said "Yes" to the good things of life, like a home cooked meal prepared by Martha or a wedding party at Cana. But he also said

"Yes" to the difficult things of life, like the criticism of the Pharisees or death on the cross.

In his book *Invitation to Greatness* Fr. Frank McNulty discusses how God enters into our lives and calls us to greatness. Whether we say "Yes" or "No" to God's invitation may be life's most basic and most important decision. This is called our fundamental option. Our "Yes" or "No" to God's invitation is a commitment so radical that it may affect our value system, our attitudes, our habits. In a word, it affects our whole lifestyle and destiny.

But our basic "Yes" or "No" to God is not a once and for all response. It grows and deepens with the "Yes" or "No" we make to the Father's will at each moment of our life. If, like Christ, we want to be always "Yes" to the Father, then we will praise him for all the good things: the security of a happy home, the refreshing taste of a cold beer on a hot day, the entertainment of a good movie, the sleep that restores us after a day of activity.

To be always "Yes" to the Father means using the opportunities we have to do good: to exercise patience when we feel like exploding, to visit someone who is isolated when we feel like staying away, to give generously to a good cause, such as aiding the victims in Guatemala when we feel like turning away.

To be always "Yes" to the father includes accepting the difficult things of life: the headache that comes at an awkward time, that unexpected caller who intrudes upon our privacy, that accident we never thought would happen to us, that disappointment when we were sure of succeeding.

Indeed, Juan Chay must be a very Christ-like man to be able to say "Yes" the way he did; to say "Yes" when he saw his home destroyed, his parents' bodies broken, and his children hungry and cold. Thank God for people like Juan Chay who know how to always say "Yes" to the Father's will, not only when times are good and life is peaceful, but also when times are bad and life is painful. Praise the Lord for the opportunities we have to always say "Yes" to the Father's will. He invites us to greatness. Should we hesitate to answer "Yes?"

Eighth Sunday of the Year
2 Cor 3:1-6

Recommendations

Every four years the American political scene is covered by the primary campaigns, the party conventions and the national elections to select one man for the office of the presidency. During this political ballyhoo the news media bombard us with endorsements. As we read the editorials of the *New York Times* or the *Chicago Tribune*, we see how they support either the Republican candidate or his Democratic opponent. As we watch and listen to television commentators like Walter Cronkite or David Brinkley, we detect them backing either the incumbent or his challenger.

While such endorsements persuade us to some extent, by far the biggest influence on our choice of a candidate is the man's public record. The strongest recommendation a political office-seeker can have is his past reputation for dedicated and disinterested public service.

When we switch our attention from the political sphere to the religious sphere, we see that St. Paul is saying essentially the same thing about Christian witness: "Do I need letters of recommendation to you? You are my letter—a letter not written with ink, but by the Spirit of the living God, not on tablets of stone, but on tablets of flesh in the heart."

Paul claims that he shouldn't need any formal letters of recommendation to be accepted officially as an apostle. The Corinthian community itself should be his letter of recommendation. If Paul is worth anything as an apostle of the Good News about Jesus, then it should be obvious in the lives of his disciples. Their lives should be so penetrated by the Spirit of Christ that anyone can see this: that the Christians at Corinth are a people who have been led out of darkness into light, out of despair into hope and out of death into life.

Today Paul's challenge is addressed to us. If Christ's resurrection is fact and not fiction, then its effects will be seen in the way our lives are transformed: alcoholics getting healed, misers becoming benefactors, bigots learning to be brothers, and the violent turning into peacemakers. If there is any truth to the claims we make about Jesus, then it should be seen in the way we live: we will be known as honest and trustworthy neighbors, as cheerful and generous friends, and as industrious and reliable workers.

People, and particularly our children, are going to be either attracted to or turned away from Christ by what they read in the letter of our life, either a living translation of the gospel message or else a living lie. They will love or leave us accordingly.

People are looking for the real thing, whether in politics or in religion. Thinking people will not tolerate promotional gimmickery or campaign cliches in choosing their candidate for a political office. In the same way, they will not be persuaded about the importance of Christ in our lives, unless they see that he makes a real difference for us; that his priorities and values *do* shape our own; that he truly inspires us to be more forgiving and loving, more helping and self-giving.

Regardless of our age, our life is still an unfinished letter. Each day we write a few more words, each week a few more sentences, each year another paragraph. For some of us this may be the last paragraph we will have a chance to write. But whether it is the last paragraph or the first of many good ones yet to be written, we can give our lives over more to the Spirit and let him write them in our hearts; let him write something splendid and magnificent for us.

Ninth Sunday of the Year
2 Cor 4:6-11

Struck Down, But Not Destroyed

The movie *Midnight Express* tells the story of an American, Billy Hayes, who was held prisoner in a Turkish prison for five years. It documents the unspeakable conditions of torture that he endured. Another American, Ron Emmons, was a cellmate of Hayes. After he saw the film, Emmons told his own story of how he survived.

"When they finally approved my sentence after a year's delay, my whole attitude changed. I realized that they wouldn't kill me and that I would be getting out in four years. Even with all the inhuman beatings I would try to concentrate on one beautiful thing each day, such as a beautiful sunset or a thought of home. Each day I exercised, did yoga and prayed. I read for three hours and then wrote for three hours. I was determined to survive."

The hardships Ron Emmons endured and his plucky attitude toward them are similar to those of the early disciples. St. Paul details them when he writes: "We are afflicted in every way possible, but we are not crushed; full of doubts, we never despair, we are persecuted but never abandoned; we are struck down but never destroyed. Continually we carry about in our bodies the dying of Jesus, so that in our bodies the life of Jesus may be revealed."

We may never be imprisoned in a Turkish jail or persecuted like the early Christians, but all of us experience afflictions of some sort: physical afflictions because of an injury or illness; emotional afflictions because of depression or tension; interpersonal afflictions because of misunderstanding or rejection.

Hardships are unavoidable. How we meet them is crucial. We

can sulk and lick our wounds, or we can pick up the challenge and fight back. We can complain and curse God, or we can confront the test and carry on courageously.

The difference in our attitude lies in our faith. If we really believe that being delivered to death for Jesus' sake will lead us to new life in him, then we can defy adversity and determine our own response to it. If we truly believe that by sharing in the sufferings of Christ we will one day share in his glory, then we can be stouthearted when misfortune strikes and dauntless in the face of difficulties.

With faith in Christ we won't let ourselves become bitter when something precious to us is destroyed. Instead we will search for a way to rebuild for the future. With faith in Christ we won't give up when we're dispossessed of some of our dreams. Instead we will create new dreams with a view to a destiny that is yet to be decided upon.

If we courageously meet afflictions the way the early Christians and Ron Emmons did—with faith—then it might be said of us what Earl Rovit said of one of Hemingway's heroes, the wounded major from the short story *In Another Country*: "He is badly broken, but not destroyed. He refuses to resign himself to the chaos of unmeaning, but he refuses also to deny the actuality of his fearsome defeat. He holds tight to the superficial conventions, of his soldierly training, and sits within them to begin the laborious process of making the broken places within himself strong again. His response can be characterized as neither acceptance nor denial; he is neither victim nor rebel. The least and the best that can be said of him is that he survives with dignity."

Tenth Sunday of the Year
2 Cor 4:13-5, 1

Courage

Every now and then we are inspired by some example of courage in the face of terminal cancer. We idolize men like Humphrey Bogart and John Wayne who remained stouthearted while their bodies were slowly being destroyed. We admire how women like Marvella Bayh and Ella Grasso could preserve a cheerful outlook while cancer continued to consume their lives.

The serenity of strength of such people stems from some kind of deep faith and firm sense of purpose. They believed in something or someone so strongly that they looked on each day of life that was left as a precious gift to use wisely. As far as we know St. Paul didn't die from cancer, but he had a similar outlook regarding his own burdens and sufferings.

In his letter to the Corinthians he writes: "We believe that he who raised up the Lord Jesus will raise us up along with Jesus. We do not lose heart, because our inner being is renewed each day even though our body is being destroyed at the same time. The present burden of our trial is light enough, and earns for us an eternal weight of glory beyond all comparison."

What a source of encouragement for us when we tend to get downcast because of our trials. Our trials may not be as drastic as terminal cancer, but at times they still tend to get us depressed. It's so easy to exaggerate our burdens and slip into self-pity; to lose perspective regarding our problems and to feel sorry for ourselves. At certain times we need people like John Wayne and Marvella Bayh to lift us out of the mire of self-pity. We need to hear St. Paul's words to elevate our sights to a vision of our final glory.

When troubles come we can then take a positive approach. We can take our problems as a time for turning to God in prayer to seek the strength we need to cope with them. When we suffer some kind of loss we can then look at it optimistically. We can look at it as an opportunity to gain something more excellent, to discover other resources within us. When we've been victimized by someone we can then make a new beginning. We can start a new and better relationship with other people, or enter into a closer and deeper relationship with Christ.

This latter point was especially true with Marvella Bayh. Even though she knew that she had less than a year to live because of cancer, Marvella Bayh often said: "I've never been happier because I have experienced a rebirth in Jesus Christ. I have the most wonderful peace and quiet in my soul."

If we can live with a faith like that, our own burdens will not seem so heavy. They will actually become lighter because we believe in that eternal weight of glory that awaits us in Christ Jesus. If we can struggle with our own sufferings with a hope like that, then we in turn can become a source of inspiration to others, a help in times of trial and a light to brighten their darkness.

What a marvelous way to live, what a magnificent way to die. Perhaps someone will be able to say of us what Sen. Birch Bayh said about his wife Marvella at her funeral: "Do not mourn for her, but rejoice in the lighting of a new star in the heavens."

Eleventh Sunday of the Year
2 Cor 5:6-10

We Walk by Faith

The U.S. and Russia have engaged in several Strategic Arms Limitations Talks (SALT). At a recent meeting one of the items on their agenda was the new improved cruise missile we have developed. The small size of the cruise missile makes it easy to hide and launch. It can fly two thousand miles and strike within one hundred feet of a target.

With a sophisticated guidance system the cruise missile can literally "read" the terrain of its computer-programmed flight path. This guidance system enables it to stay two hundred feet above the ground, adjust its altitude to go over mountains and fly in a zigzag pattern.

What the electronic guidance system does for the cruise missile gives us an idea of what faith does for the Christian. St. Paul talks about faith in his letter to the Corinthians: "Therefore we continue to be confident. We know that while we dwell in the body we are away from the Lord. We walk by faith, not by sight."

If we compare the faith of a Christian with the guidance system of a cruise missile, we get some insight as to how faith helps us. Obviously the comparison is not perfect because of drastic differences. Faith is not an electronic, computer-type device. Nor is the Christian a nuclear warhead-carrying missile. Nevertheless, there are some points of similarity.

First, there is a journey involved. A cruise missile is sent on its flight one and only one time. A Christian, too, is sent into the world to make one and only one journey through life. He needs faith to point him in the right direction and to guide him along the way.

Second, it is not by sight that the journey is made. There is no pilot in the cruise missile who can sight the target. The Christian, too, has no immediate view of the goal of his journey, the Lord's home. He needs faith to believe that it even exists.

Third, there is a guidance system involved. The cruise missile has a flight plan programmed into its computer and sensors to monitor the terrain. The Christian, too, has a flight plan—its contents can be found in the Bible. The Christian also has faith to monitor his surroundings and warn him when he is too close to the danger of sin.

Also, there is a note of confidence. The military is almost absolutely certain that the cruise missile can strike within one hundred feet of its target. The Christian too enjoys a kind of confidence, the kind St. Paul had. Even though our earthly dwelling in the body will be destroyed by death, we are confident that God has already prepared for us an eternal dwelling in the heavens.

As Christians, then, we walk by faith. We don't know why we feel sometimes the way we do—moody, touchy—or why we act sometimes the way we do—selfishly, cruelly. But that's not important, as long as we move ahead and walk by faith.

We can't see why we have to experience so much pain and hurt at times—illness, a broken marriage, loss of our job. But that's of no consequence, because we walk by faith. We don't understand the absurdities of our existence—wars, tragedies, poverty. But that doesn't matter, because we walk by faith.

Praise the Lord for his gift of faith. Ask him to increase our faith, so that more and more we can walk under its guidance and be confident about reaching our goal.

Twelfth Sunday of the Year
2 Cor 5:14-17

Love Impels Us

One of the quality TV programs shown recently was *A Woman Called Moses* with Cicely Tyson in the lead role. It was a four-hour drama on the life of Harriet Tubman, the black heroine of the Underground Railroad just before the Civil War. While she was a young slave Harriet Tubman was stoned for helping a fellow slave escape. Later she managed to buy her own freedom and flee to Philadelphia.

Nevertheless, she returned to the South to rescue her parents and to set up her own underground railroad. More than three hundred fugitive slaves used her route to find freedom. After the Civil War, Harriet Tubman spent the rest of her life in the East working for the disadvantaged and the Women's Suffrage Movement.

Why would a woman like Harriet Tubman struggle so much to become free, and then jeopardize her freedom by helping other slaves escape? Why would such a woman leave her security in the North and risk her life for an underground railroad in the South?

Perhaps an answer can be found in St. Pauls' words to the Corinthians: "The love of Christ impels us who have reached the conviction that since one died for all, all died. He died for all so that those who live might live no longer for themselves, but for him who for their sakes died and was raised up."

The love of Christ and of our brothers and sisters is the reason why people like Harriet Tubman do the things they do. The love of Christ impels them to risk losing what they have so that others may be enriched; to sacrifice their own comfort so that others may be comforted in some way. People like Harriet Tubman live no longer for themselves, but for others. They are not preoccupied with the satisfaction of their own needs, but with meeting the needs of others—whether these needs are great—like freedom and justice—or small—like someone to talk to or be with.

When there is love in our hearts we can't help but reach out to others or become involved with them—whether it is to take care of someone's home while they are in the hospital, or to offer them our own home because theirs was destroyed by fire. When we have the love of Christ within us we can't help but spend ourselves generously for others. That is why a mother will spend hours washing clothes for her family, or why a father will work extra hours to pay for his children's education.

People with love in their hearts don't do these things because they have to, but because they want to. They don't give of themselves grudgingly, but joyously. They don't count the cost to themselves, but the ways others are made happy.

Malcolm Muggeridge of the BBC once asked Mother Teresa of Calcutta why some of her followers—who were educated girls from wealthy homes—suddenly wished to minister to the needs of the most wretched people in the slums. Mother Teresa replied: "These girls want to give their best, to make a total commitment to God. They give up their home and their future in order to give wholehearted service to the poorest of the poor—to serve Christ in his distressing disguise."

In other words, it was the love of Christ that impelled them to take up this ministry. This same love of Christ impels us, too, to find our happiness and fulfillment by living for and serving others. This same love of Christ urges us to seek the greatest pleasure and satisfaction in life by giving and sharing ourselves with others.

Thirteenth Sunday of the Year
2 Cor 8:7-15

Enriching Others

Prisons are probably the last places in which one would look for honors to be passed out. Nevertheless, this happened at Cook County Jail in Illinois when the inmates and officials paid tribute to Rev. Theodore Harper for his forty-seven years of service as the jail chaplain. For the past thirty years this black Baptist minister had never failed to make a six-hour daily visit to the prison.

What makes this so extraordinary is that Rev. Harper never received any pay for his services. He supported himself and his wife from his other work at the Veterans Administration and as a pastor of a small church. Rev. Harper said, "I don't accept money for my Christian work. I work from my heart to serve God by serving my fellow man."

What St. Paul says to the Corinthians about Jesus could just as well be said to the prisoners at Cook County Jail about Rev. Harper: "You are well acquainted with the favor shown you by our Lord Jesus Christ. How for your sake he made himself poor though he was rich, so that you might become rich by his poverty."

Rev. Harper could have made a lot of money had he worked for pay all those forty-seven years as the jail chaplain. Instead he chose to make himself poor so that he might enrich the prisoners in other ways. He chose to make himself "rich in faith and total concern" so that he could abound in "works of charity" among the inmates.

To what extent are Paul's words realized in our own lives? Just how rich are we in faith, total concern and works of charity? Just how far we are willing to make ourselves poor to enrich others?

In his book *Toward Stewardship* Fr. William Byron writes

about concern for the poor and sharing: "The fundamental idea of stewardship is that we own nothing absolutely; we possess things in trust for others. The possession of wealth, therefore, involves serious social responsibility. Conditions of poverty will be reduced only to the extent that those in possession of property, power and prestige are willing to let go and share."

Byron's conclusions are based on the teachings of Scripture and also the Second Vatican Council. In its document *The Church in the Modern World* the Council stated: "The right to have a share of earthly goods sufficient for oneself and one's family belongs to everyone. The Church has always taught that men are obliged to come to the relief of the poor, and to do so not merely out of their superfluous goods."

We can say then that some private property and provisions for the future are necessary. But are we justified in hoarding things that are luxuries when others lack basic necessities? Our own immediate needs and those of our family do have prior claim. But does that mean we can ignore the poor and pretend that they didn't exist?

There are all kinds of ways we can share the world's goods with the poor. For example, we can support organizations like Catholic Charities; provide jobs for the unemployed; donate food and clothing to the St. Vincent de Paul Society.

There are all kinds of ways we can share nonmaterial values with the poor. For example, we can share our knowledge by teaching them skills, our time by visiting their sick, our hopes by encouraging their efforts.

As a prison chaplain Rev. Harper had his own style of serving his fellow man. We have to discover ours; we have to find our own way of making ourselves poor so that we might enrich the lives of others.

Fourteenth Sunday of the Year
2 Cor 12:7-10

Thorns in the Flesh

Rabbi Allen Blustein tells this story about one of his experiences as an army chaplain. One day in 1974 he was called to attend to a twenty-one year old soldier by the name of Allen Jackson from Chicago. Private Jackson was involved in an accident during training maneuvers and had lost the entire portion of his body below the navel. For weeks he remained on the hospital critical list suffering unimaginable pain despite considerable medication. There were days when he plunged into deep depression, broke down in tears and wanted to die.

Nevertheless, under the constant care of the hospital staff and his family, Allen began to heal and change his attitude. He was eventually transferred to Hines VA Hospital where he is a member of an exclusive fraternity—amputees who are enduring hardship but who will not give up; amputees who are determined to learn how to walk again, drive cars and do so many other things we take for granted.

These words from St. Paul must have special significance for Allen Jackson: "I was given a thorn in the flesh. Three times I begged the Lord that this might leave me. He said to me, 'My grace is enough for you, for in weakness my power reaches perfection.' "

Allen Jackson suffered from more than a thorn in his flesh—the lower half of his body was amputated. He too begged the Lord to end his misery—even by death if this were necessary. Nevertheless, the Lord's grace proved to be enough for him; enough for him to accept his severe handicap; enough for him to change his attitude from despair to hope; enough for him to resolve to live a useful life.

When Paul uses the word "flesh" he is not just referring to our material body, but to our whole human condition of weakness without the transforming grace of God's spirit. In this sense the thorn in our flesh can take on many forms. It might be an actual physical handicap like Allen Jackson's amputation, a nervous disorder or a bad ulcer.

This thorn might be a psychological handicap like an inferiority complex, an emotional weakness like uncontrolled anger, or an ego problem like the need to dominate.

This thorn might also take on forms of temptation in the moral order, like the temptation to read pornography or commit adultery, the temptation to steal or lie, or the temptation toward envy or hatred.

Finally, there are thorns of the flesh that are just part of our human condition, like fatigue and lethargy, monotony and boredom, disillusionment and loneliness.

Many are the thorns that afflict our flesh. Many are the times when we beg the Lord to remove them. Yet the Lord answers us with the same words he spoke to Paul: "My grace is enough for you, for in weakness my power reaches perfection."

Then it is our turn to make a response. Do we continue to complain and cry because we have an affliction we can't get rid of, or do we accept our condition the way Paul did when he said: "I am content with weakness for the sake of Christ. For when I am powerless, it is then that I am strong."

Do we feel sorry for ourselves and sulk because we have to suffer some trial, or do we see things optimistically the way Allen Jackson did: not looking at what we lack, but at what we have; not looking over the things we can't do, but over the many things we can do; not looking back with regret to bad experiences, but looking forward to the good things yet to happen.

Praise and thank the Lord for whatever weakness we have to experience. For when we are powerless by ourselves, it is then that we can be strong with the grace of God.

Fifteenth Sunday of the Year
Ep 1:3-10

Our Deepest Needs

When Barbara Walters left the *Today Show* she was given a one million dollar-a-year contract by the ABC network to become co-anchor with Harry Reasoner on their evening news program. When pitcher Nolan Ryan became a free agent he was given a multimillion dollar contract by the Houston Astros to play for them for the next several seasons.

These are two examples of organizations turning to a particular individual with the hopes that this individual will bring success to their organization. ABC hopes that Barbara Walters will give it the Number One rating among news programs. The Houston Astros hope that Nolan Ryan will bring them a World Series victory.

Seeking success or some special benefits from a particular person is very common among us: business corporations are always on the lookout for some super-salesman to make their profits soar; playwrights are always screening talent for some new star who will make their play a hit on Broadway. It seems that we're always looking for the right marriage partner, the right doctor, the right politician, the right contractor, and so on, who will bring us some special benefit or meet a definite need we have.

Perhaps St. Paul had something like this in mind when he wrote: "Praised be the Father of our Lord Jesus Christ, who has bestowed on us in Christ every spiritual blessing. It is in Christ and through his blood that we have been redeemed, so immeasurably generous is God's favor to us."

What Paul seems to be saying is that Christ is the only one who can satisfy all our deepest human needs. Certain individuals can

187

take care of some of our needs, at least in a limited way, but only Christ can fulfill our deepest human needs in a complete way.

For example, our marriage partner can take care of our need for sexual love and close companionship, but only Christ can bless our marriage with profound peace and lasting joy; our business associates can provide us with opportunities for promotion and higher salaries, but only Christ can bless our work with a deep sense of personal satisfaction and self-realization.

The *Interpreter's Bible* underlines the two adjectives Paul uses with the word blessing, namely, the adjectives *every* and *spiritual*. The adjective *every* emphasizes the comprehensiveness of the Father's gift to us. His blessings are not partial or limited. He withholds nothing that could enrich us or perfect us.

The adjective *spiritual* emphasizes the special character of the Father's gifts to us. His blessings are given by the Holy Spirit in Christ. They are experienced in the depths of our human spirit. They belong to the realm of the imperishable and eternal.

It is not surprising, then, that we want to praise the Father for his immeasurable generosity towards us. No matter what it is that we need spiritually, we can find it in Christ. If we are isolated or lonely sometimes through no fault of our own, we can find companionship in Christ. If we are beset by worry or depressed because of some disappointment, we can find our equilibrium in Christ. If we are struggling with temptations or doubts about our faith, we can derive our strength from Christ.

Praise and thank the Father for bestowing on us in Christ every spiritual blessing. People like Barbara Walters and Nolan Ryan can bring certain advantages to us, but only Christ can bring the most important advantages to us. People like our spouse or closest friend can meet some of our needs, but only Christ can fulfill all our deepest human needs in a complete way.

Sixteenth Sunday of the Year
Ep 2:13-18

Brought Near

In his book entitled *Bill W* author Bob Thomsen tells the story of Bill Wilson, one of the co-founders of Alcoholics Anonymous. When Bill Wilson was riding high on Wall Street in the 1920's he would spend as much as $500 in an afternoon in a speak-easy. But then the crash came—first in his health when in a period of two years he was dried out four times, and then in his finances when he lost everything. It was the depression era.

The turning point in Bill Wilson's life came when he was in a drying-out hospital and experienced a mystical conversion. Later he met Dr. Robert H. Smith, and together they established the AA program in 1935.

If Bill Wilson were here today, he would listen with pride to St. Paul's words when he says: "In Christ Jesus you who were once far off have been brought near through the blood of Christ. It is he who is our peace."

Paul's words were addressed to the Gentile converts. Before their baptism they were far off. Unlike the Jews, the Gentiles never had a covenant with the Lord; they were not promised a Messiah; they were not members of God's Chosen People; they did not hear God speak through the Scriptures.

But all this was changed when Christ came. He brought them near by becoming their savior; by uniting them to the People of God; by establishing a covenant with them; and by announcing the good news to them.

During those long years of terrible drunkenness Bill Wilson was also far off—from his Lord Jesus Christ, his wife and his business associates. Then, thanks to his conversion experience, he was brought near—to the Lord, his family and the thousands of alcoholics he has helped to recover health.

Our situation is different from that of the Gentiles without Christ, and from that of Bill Wilson when he was an alcoholic around the depression time. Nevertheless, there are times when we have been far off in some sense, only to be brought near by the grace of God. For example, we've seen married couples who drifted apart become reunited with help from the family; teenagers who ran away from home in a state of rebellion return when they realized their mistake; priests and religious who deviated from their high ideals rededicate themselves after a powerful retreat experience; professional people who wandered from the path of integrity renew their commitments when called to account.

But it isn't only in extreme situations that God's grace operates. It also brings us near the Lord when we are far off in less critical circumstances. For example, consider the times when we receive the Sacrament of Reconciliation, follow an inspiration to help someone, or spend some time in prayer. At such times as these we turn away from the things that separate us from the Lord, things like our sins, selfishness and laziness, and allow ourselves to be brought nearer to the Lord by the power of his grace.

Alcoholics Anonymous has what they call a twelve-step program. The third step reads: "We made a decision to turn our will and our lives over to the care of God as we understand him." We don't have to be an alcoholic to make such a pledge. Every baptized Christian is called to make it. Our Sunday worship is a weekly renewal of this commitment—a commitment to leave behind whatever keeps us far off; a commitment to pursue those things that will draw us ever closer to the Lord.

Seventeenth Sunday of the Year
Ep 4:1-6

Bearing Lovingly

Irving Howe is the author of the book *World of Our Fathers*. In this book he tells the story of the migration of the East European Jews to America starting in the late 19th century. He described how these Jewish immigrants lived in crowded, impoverished conditions in New York's East Side. The population density there was so great that people literally slept in three shifts on the same beds.

Most of these Jews worked long hours in sweatshops, first of all to squeeze out a living for themselves, and secondly to scrape together enough money for their childrens' education. These immigrant Jews looked upon themselves as a sacrificial generation so that the things they valued and lacked, like education, status and culture, would be enjoyed by future generations.

St. Paul's words to the Ephesians could very well be spoken by these Jewish parents to their children and grandchildren: "Live a life worthy of the calling you have received, with perfect humility, meekness, and patience, bearing with one another lovingly. Make every effort to preserve the unity which has the Spirit as its origin and peace as its binding force."

In our contemporary conditions, Paul and these Jewish immigrants are speaking to us. In effect they are saying: "Make sacrifices for one another. Have a strong sense of solidarity and community."

If only we could take these words seriously, how different our world would be. For example, in our families how many non-speaking brothers and sisters would be reconciled and reunited; in our places of work how many fellow employees would quit complaining against each other and cooperate more; on the international scene how many Jews and Arabs, Irish and British would live together in peace.

When people bear with one another lovingly, together they can endure the worst of hardships, whether they are hardships like inadequate and crowded living quarters, or intolerable and unhealthy working conditions. When people bear with one another lovingly, they can overcome the greatest obstacles, whether they are obstacles like prejudice and bigotry, or physical disabilities and nervous disorders. When people bear with one another lovingly, they can accomplish extraordinary things, whether building parochial schools, or taking in Vietnamese refugees.

Bear with one another lovingly. To do this means having a strong feeling for family and community, and a willing spirit of sacrifice and commitment. To do this means being sensitive to the needs and moods of those around us, and ready to surrender our own preferences. To do this means recognizing the presence of Christ in the people we meet, and responding to his presence with respect.

By ourselves we can't do these things. We need the example of people like those immigrant Jews in New York at the turn of the century. We need the example of Christ when he died on the cross for us. We need the power of the Spirit who is sent into our hearts.

In the Eucharist we not only recall what Christ did for us, but also receive from him the grace to do the same for one another—to bear with one another lovingly, and to strengthen our bond of unity.

Eighteenth Sunday of the Year
Ep 4:17-24

A Fresh Way

In California there is an eighty year old woman by the name of Mrs. Eula Weaver. She couldn't walk more than one hundred feet without getting severe chest pains and was afflicted with heart disease, high blood pressure and arthritis.

By the time she was eighty-two, Mrs. Weaver could run a mile and ride a stationary bicycle for another fifteen miles everyday. She quit taking medication and is no longer bothered by chest pains, high blood pressure or arthritis. A miracle? No, her rejuvenation is credited to a new carefully controlled diet and a regulated exercise program.

Mrs. Weaver was one of several examples in a series of health articles in the *Chicago Tribune*. Science editor Ron Kotulak pointed out how two-thirds of the deaths in this country are caused by heart disease, cancer and strokes. Moreover, the major factors contributing to these three causes are the following: cigarette smoking, excessive alcohol, too many rich foods, overeating, lack of exercise, and stress.

If transformations like Mrs. Weaver's can happen on the physical level, can they occur on the spiritual level too? St. Paul seems to think so when he says: "You must lay aside your former way of life which deteriorates through illusion and acquire a fresh, spiritual way of thinking. You must put on that new man created in God's image."

Sometimes drastic changes in our spiritual lifestyle are required of us. Our present form of living may be hurting others and destroying ourselves. Perhaps we're polluting our minds with filthy literature and X-rated movies. Then we can switch to reading the Bible and some of the good Christian periodicals available, and see what a difference this makes in our speech and thoughts.

Perhaps we're hypercritical and prone to making rash judgments about other people. Then we can switch to complimenting and praising them for their good qualities, and see what a brighter outlook we'll have.

Perhaps we're worried and anxious. Then we can put more trust in the Lord and rely more on him, and see how much our confidence and self-assurance increase.

Sometimes changes in our daily spiritual habits are needed because we're living dull, mediocre and half-hearted lives. Perhaps we're too indulgent and selfish regarding food, drink and sex. Then we can fast occasionally and discipline these appetites, and see how much more peace and order we'll experience.

Perhaps we're too rich and materialistic. Then we can try giving more to the poor and getting along with fewer luxuries, and see how free this makes us feel.

Perhaps we're lazy and don't feel like praying. Then we can set aside a regular time for prayer and stick to it regardless of how we feel, and see how much our attitudes improve.

We don't have to wait until we're eighty-two years old like Mrs. Eula Weaver to change our daily habits; we can start now to acquire a fresh, spiritual way of thinking and living. We don't need any expert guidance or special exercise to become a new person in the image of Jesus Christ. We already have all we need in the word God speaks to us in Scripture and in the graces he gives us in the sacraments.

Nineteenth Sunday of the Year
Ep 4:30-5:2

The Way of Love

Shortly after the black riots in South Africa, an article was published in the Johannesburg Star newspaper. It was written by Alan Paton, a world famous South African novelist. He wrote: "What do we, the white people of South Africa, after that week of desolation, do first? The first thing we do is to repent of our wickedness, of our arrogance, of our complacency, and of our blindness. The blacks who looted and killed are evil, but we made them. They are the outcasts of our affluent society. Who are the real agitators of these riots? They are the discriminatory laws. Do you as Christians believe that you should spend 400 rands a year on the education of each white child and only 40 rands a year on each black child? Do you as Christians believe that white industry should be maintained at the cost of the integrity of black family life? The blame lies with us all. After repentance comes amendment of life."

Alan Paton sounds like a modern day St. Paul. What St. Paul says to the Ephesians underlines what Alan Paton is saying to the South Africans, and in a sense to all of us: "Get rid of all bitterness, anger and harsh words. Be kind to one another, compassionate and mutually forgiving. Follow the way of love, even as Christ loved you. He gave himself for us as an offering to God."

When we consider how much Christ loved us, we can't help but feel like Paul and Paton do. We want to put an end to the things that divide and destroy us: hatred and greed, prejudice and injustice, selfishness and blindness.

When we reflect on how Christ gave himself up to death for us, we can't help but want to follow his way of love: the way of forgiving and understanding, accepting and supporting, sharing and inspiring.

It's not important where we are—Ephesus, South Africa, or the United States—at home, in the parish, or at work. What is important is that wherever we are we replace hostility with fraternity, exchange bitterness for kindness, and forge agreements out of arguments.

The Jerome Biblical Commentary says that these lines from Paul outline the new motivation for a good moral life that belongs to those who have shared Christ's renewed humanity. "It is no longer a question of right and wrong; it is a matter of respect for brothers in Christ and a realization of how our actions can affect them."

It is not important what our particular problem is: an international problem like territorial disputes; a national problem like racial discrimination; a local problem like busing school children; or a family problem like quarreling or not talking to a certain member.

What is important is that we replace ill will with good will; settle disagreements with dialogue; and heal resentments with reconciliation. What is demanded of us as disciples of Jesus is to give ourselves to each other the way he gave himself for us: freely, not reluctantly; generously, not meagerly; lovingly, not heartlessly.

The Eucharist reminds us of how Christ gave himself for us as an offering to God. It calls for a response from us to follow his way of love—to get rid of all bitterness, anger and harsh words, and to be kind to one another, compassionate and mutually forgiving.

Twentieth Sunday of the Year
Ep 5:15-20

Present Opportunities

A TV program that made quite an impact on its viewers was *The Migrants*. It was a drama presented on *CBS Playhouse 90* and told the story of a migrant family as it picked its way north along the east coast. Every day was just another field of beans or tomatoes. Every day was just another struggle for existence. Hope was always at the next stop.

The drama especially revealed the character of the mother of this migrant family. Her hair was stringy, her face worn by poverty and her mouth set against adversity. Only in her eyes was there hope. She was lean, but had inner strength. She was desperate, but not defeated. She suffered, but still survived. Somehow she was always a bit larger than the tragedies that struck her down.

The mother of this migrant family could easily have made her own the words of St. Paul when he wrote to the Ephesians: "Make the most of the present opportunity, for these days are evil. Give thanks to God the Father always and for everything in the name of our Lord Jesus Christ."

Times are different for us than they were for Paul or the migrant family. We don't live under Roman domination or have to sqeeze out a living by picking someone else's crops. Yet, in a sense, our times are not different, for there are ways our days too can be called evil. If we look at the world scene we often see war, violence, crime, hunger and oppression. If we look into our own personal lives we often see disappointments, frustrations, failures, worries and illness.

We, too, have to make the most of the present opportunities. We can't sit idly and hope our situation will get better. It won't, unless we act to improve it. Regarding social problems we have to use our voting power, write our congressmen and support financially human development projects.

For some of us it might mean direct participation in government, assuming a leadership role in some social cause or contributing our time and talents in actual service. Whatever the form, we have to make the most of the present opportunity. Social issues cry out for our personal involvement, however limited it might be.

As regards our personal problems, we have to use setbacks in one area to step ahead in other areas, meet difficulties as challenges to grow in character, and turn the loss of one thing into the gain of something else. Like the migrant mother we may suffer disappointments sometimes, but never be defeated; have one dream destroyed, but begin building another; experience helplessness, but discover inner strength.

Whatever obstacles we encounter, we have to make the most of the present opportunity. Every obstacle is an occasion to either grow in maturity or regress; to strengthen our faith in Christ or weaken it.

Without Christ we cannot overcome the evils of our day. We need his power in order to prevail, his light to see our way and his inspiration to reach our goal. Without Christ we would get discouraged in our struggles and give up when the odds against us seem too great. We need him to move ahead like the migrant mother with hope in our hearts and a dream in our eyes.

Even if the days are evil, then, we can with St. Paul "give thanks to the Father always and for everything in the name of our Lord Jesus Christ."

Twenty-First Sunday of the Year
Ep 5:21-32

Married Love

Even when she was fifty-seven years old, Margot Fonteyn was still the prima ballerina of the world. Yet, dancing was not the most important part of her life. "My real life is with my husband," she said. "This is the true reality. The ballet is a different kind of reality, a transitory thing."

Margot Fonteyn's husband is a lawyer from Panama, Dr. Roberto Arias, whom she calls "Tito." Back in 1964, Tito suffered almost total paralysis after being shot during a political assassination attempt in Panama. For two years Tito was treated in a hospital forty miles outside London. Everyday Margot would go back and forth between the hospital and London to be with Tito during breakfast and dinner and to be at the theater for rehearsals.

Along with the medical care, it was Margot's loving devotion that enabled Tito to make an amazing recovery. He is still partially paralyzed, but he can speak again and is practicing law in New York.

Margot's love for Tito is a beautiful example of Paul's description of married love: "Defer to one another out of reverence for Christ. Wives, be submissive to your husbands as if to the Lord. Husbands, love your wives as Christ loved the Church."

In his book *The Christian Family* Larry Christenson interprets Paul's words this way. In a chapter about wives, he says that for a wife to be submissive is not to be degraded. Rather, it is for her glory.

Submission guarantees her protection by her husband; physically she needs his protection in a world of violence; emotionally she is freed from the burden of representing the family in the community; psychologically she is protected from any disrespect from their children.

Submission is a means of social balance and harmony in the home. It is not to be confused with servility, since the wife is obliged to express her opinion. Nor is it to be identified with the stifling of the wife's personality, since she must exercise her own initiative and creativity.

Submission is a means of spiritual power. The wife tries to get her husband closer to the Lord, not by pushing or nagging him, but by her loving service and kind words; not by force, but by her gentleness and generosity.

In a chapter on husbands, Christenson makes these points. First, the husband's authority is not one by which he lords it over his wife. Rather, it is one by which he sacrifices himself for her and their children to provide a home, food and clothing.

Second, it is the husband's duty to care for the spiritual welfare of his wife and children. By word and example he should be the leader of family worship both at home and in the parish church.

Third, husbands should go the way of the cross before their wives. A husband dies to his ego by seeking his wife's forgiveness when they have an argument, and by seeking her advice before he makes an important decision.

Fourth, husbands must exercise their authority in humility. A husband should recognize his wife's special competence and show appreciation for her efforts; show consideration for her varying moods and treat her with loving tenderness.

Is Paul's model for Christian marriage too unrealistic and chauvinistic? Is Larry Christenson's interpretation too idealistic and outdated? Margot Fonteyn would say, "No. My real life is with my husband." This can be the response of every wife and husband, provided they see in each other the image of Christ, give themselves generously in loving service, and sacrifice themselves joyously just as Christ did for us.

Twenty-Second Sunday of the Year
Jm 1:17-27

God's Word

The *Chicago Sun Times* recently interviewed psychologists and sociologists on the question: "Does watching violence on TV and movie screens make some children more violent?" Based on massive research up to that time, the majority opinion was "Yes."

For example, Dr. Leonard Eron began a study of 875 third grade children in 1960 and ended it in 1970 when they were a year out of high school. Eron's conclusion was clear: "One of the best predictors of how aggressive a boy will be at age nineteen is the violence of TV programs he prefers at age eight." The word aggression was defined as an act which injures or irritates another person.

The power of violence on TV and movies to influence us to evil is, indeed, great. But so is the power of the word of God to influence us to good. At least St. James thinks so when he writes: "Humbly welcome the word that has taken root in you, with its power to save you. Act on this word. If all you do is listen to it, you are deceiving yourselves."

History is full of examples of people whose lives were shaped by the Bible. We think of saints like Augustine and Ignatius of Loyola in the past. A single verse from Scripture was enough to change their entire lives. We think of men like Mark Hatfield and Charles Colson in our own time. Daily reading of the Bible has helped them to rebuild their lives after everything seemed lost.

The word of God in Scripture does have power to save, change us and perfect us. But we have to hear that word, welcome that word and act on that word.

There is a difference between good and bad influences. On the one hand, bad influences like violent programs on TV have a power similar to weeds; they don't require any effort on our part to take root, grow and spread.

On the other hand, good influences like Bible reading have a power similar to the seeds of plants; they require considerable care from us in the form of cultivating, watering and spraying in order to grow and produce their fruit.

In an article in *U.S. Catholic* magazine Scripture scholar Fr. Barnabas Ahern made some suggestions about "How to Read the Bible." First, be selective. Find the passages which say the most to us, instead of battling through boring chapters out of a sense of duty.

Second, recognize the reading as a story with tremendous personal meaning. It is God's *good news* we are reading and not merely a human historical record. Read Christ's life as a mystery we have to live. Make his prayers actual in our own lives.

Third, identify oneself with the characters. Scripture is a news story in which we have a role. The characters in Scripture are real, but they are also types in which we see ourselves. But to do this we must ponder the Bible prayerfully, and not merely read it like any other book.

If we follow Fr. Ahern's suggestions, then God's word in the Bible will become a power within us to open our eyes to selfishness and to move us to repentance; a power to heal us of injuries and support us in difficulties; a power to reveal our destiny and inspire us to generosity; a power to take root in our hearts and abound in our lives.

Twenty-Third Sunday of the Year
Jm 2:1-5

Discrimination

In Chicago one day during a robbery a white man, Nicholas Comito, was shot in the head by two black youths. When Nicholas Comito found out that he would never see again he said: "I am not a hater and I don't intend to let this make me a hater."

In response to this tragedy a group of black Chicago businessmen, led by George E. Johnson, raised ten thousand dollars to start a Nicholas Comito Fund. Johnson said: "We want to show Mr. Comito that there are other black people than the ones who shot him. The great majority of black people have a feeling for him and want to help him."

We need people like Nicholas Comito and George Johnson to destroy the racial discrimination that still prevails among us. Discrimination was on the mind of St. James when he wrote: "My brothers, your faith in our Lord Jesus Christ must not allow of favoritism. Suppose there should come into your assembly a man fashionably dressed, and at the same time a poor man in shabby clothes. Suppose further that you were to take notice of the well dressed man and say, 'Sit here,' whereas you were to say to the poor man, 'You can stand.' Have you not in a case like this discriminated in your hearts?"

James, of course, was talking about discrimination between the rich and the poor. But his words apply to all forms of discrimination that keep us divided and at odds with one another; cause differences in treatment or favor which are unfair; create separations which are injurious.

When we look down on people because they are from a lower

income bracket, we are discriminating in our hearts. When we are unneighborly to people because they come from a different ethnic background, we are discriminating in our hearts. When we are unfriendly to people because they practice a different religion, we are discriminating in our hearts. When we ridicule people because they are older, handicapped or uneducated, we are discriminating in our hearts.

In all these situations we are discriminating in a negative way because we fail to recognize the other person's dignity and pride, and instead demean them; we disregard their feelings and sensitivities, and end up hurting them; we deny their disadvantages and difficulties, and only add to their already deep wounds.

In his book *Faith and Violence* Thomas Merton writes: "The American racial crisis offers the American Christian a chance to recover Christian truth by recanting a basic heresy—the loss of that Christian sense which sees every other man as Christ and treats him as Christ."

This is the key to the solution of all discrimination problems whether they involve minority groups, immigrants, women or the handicapped. This key is not in legislation, although this helps, nor in making reluctant concessions, although they may be a start. The key is two-sided according to James and Merton: first, to see Christ in others; secondly, to treat them as Christ.

To see Christ in others may sometimes be formidable, but nevertheless possible. Nicholas Comito could see Christ in the blacks who blinded him. George Johnson, a black, could see the suffering Christ in Nicholas Comito, a white. Can we see the Christ in other people regardless of their color, social class or creed? Can we recognize the face of Christ on others regardless of their sex, strength or skills?

To treat others as Christ may sometimes be a real test for us, but also our greatest opportunity. Nicholas Comito forgave his assailant. George Johnson raised money to support Nicholas Comito. Can we welcome the refugee as we would Christ? Can we feed the poor as if Christ were our guest?

Twenty-Fourth Sunday of the Year
Jm 2:14-18

Faith and Works

In 1976 World Vision International celebrated its 25th Anniversary. WVI is a nondenominational Christian agency whose current project is to stimulate awareness to the world food problem, and to set up services to assist hungry people in the poor countries. Its president, the Rev. Dr. W. Stanley Mooneyham, has written a book entitled *"What Do You Say to a Hungry World?"*

He maintains that we have the resources and technology to feed ten times the world's present population, if we had the will to change some of our systems and lifestyles. He holds that deeds of service are indispensable to proclaiming the Gospel. Great violence is done to the Gospel if it is separated into social action and evangelism. The two must go together.

In effect, World Vision International and Rev. Mooneyham are asking the same questions set forth by St. James: "What good is it to profess faith without practicing it? What good does it do to see someone naked or hungry and wish him well without giving him what he needs for the body? Faith without works is dead."

It is not a matter, then, of *either* faith *or* works, but a matter of *both* faith *and* works. On the one hand, without works our faith becomes an empty profession of words, a thing of the mind but not of the heart, a seeking after security but without any risks. On the other hand, without faith our works become superficial, a show of pride, a busyness without direction.

Both faith *and* works are needed. They do not contradict each other, but rather perfect each other. What begins in faith is brought

205

to completion by works. Belief in God's existence becomes a personal loving response to his presence in others. What is done by works derives its inspiration and value from faith. Good deeds done for our neighbor become transfigured when we see Christ in others.

Gandhi once said: "If Christ comes to India, he'd better come in the form of bread." In other words, the only way Christianity can demonstrate the authenticity of its message is by ministering to the poor.

Albert Camus couldn't accept Christianity, yet he had a deep insight into its essence when he wrote: "What the world expects of Christians is that they should speak out, loud and clear. They must get away from abstractions and confront the bloodstained face that history has taken on today."

Thus, the challenge Gandhi and Camus throw out to us is to serve in the world as well as to sing in our churches; to minister to the bloodstained body of Christ as well as to worship its head; to offer help when misfortunes happen as well as to offer prayers at some shrine.

The challenge World Vision International and St. James throw out to us, is to free others from their oppressions, instead of staying bound by our own depressions; to bring relief to people in trouble, instead of worrying about our own; to reach out to enrich others, instead of surrounding ourselves with more things we don't need.

The Eucharist reminds us how Christ just didn't talk about giving up his body and shedding his blood; he went out and actually did it. Christ calls us to do the same—not merely to talk about our faith, but to go out and actually live it.

Twenty-Fifth Sunday of the Year
Jm 3:16-4:3

Sowing

When Mrs. Hattie Pierce of Valparaiso, Indiana was asked on her ninety-third birthday what kept her so young, she answered: "Involvement—not so much with business and materialistic enterprises, but with people."

Some of her personal involvements include the Save the Dunes Council, the Retired Citizens' Volunteer Program to help tutor students, the local Chapter of Common Cause to promote better government, and the Porter County Association of Retired Citizens to help the handicapped.

Hattie Pierce has lived a healthy and happy life because of her humane interests and civic concern. If St. James were here today, he'd probably point to Hattie Pierce and say: "Wisdom from above, by contrast, is first of all innocent. It is also peaceable, lenient, docile, rich in sympathy and kindly deeds that are its fruit, impartial and sincere. The harvest of justice is sown in peace for those who cultivate peace."

When you review all the good Hattie Pierce has done in her ninety-three years, you would have to agree with James. The jealousy and selfishness, the strife and bitterness that he mentions earlier have had no part in her life. Instead, her life has been full of innocence and peace, rich in sympathy and kindly deeds—the harvest of what she has sown and cultivated.

When we look at our own lives, again we would have to agree with James. We harvest what we sow and cultivate. If we sow and cultivate our own egotism by always insisting on our own way and taking unfair advantage of people, then we reap a harvest of self-hatred from ourselves and dislike by others. If we sow and cultivate greed by lying, cheating and exploiting others, then we reap a harvest of discontent and regret.

But if we sow and cultivate authentic personal growth by developing our talents to the fullest and being friendly to others, then we reap a harvest of self-respect in our own eyes and esteem in the eyes of others. If we sow and cultivate genuine interest in others by sharing in their joys and sorrows, or by supporting them in their successes and failures, then we reap a harvest of deep human satisfaction at seeing others uplifted in spirit.

In their book *TNT—The Power Within You* authors Claude Bristol and Harold Sherman make some remarks that reinforce what we have been considering. On the negative side, they mention how holding resentments or grudges or hates poisons the mind and destroys the body. Medical science confirms that illnesses like arthritis and ulcers are caused many times by our emotional problems and disturbances.

On the positive side, they claim that whatever it is we want—money, love, status—we have within us the power to get what we desire. All we have to do is release that power and let it operate.

In other words, we harvest what we sow and cultivate. If we're miserable because we're physically run-down, emotionally depressed and spiritually unfulfilled, then it may be because we've made ourselves this way by a lifetime of indulgence, selfishness and running away from the Lord. But if we're at peace because we're physically fit, emotionally secure and spiritually alive, then it is because we've opened ourselves up to God's gifts by a lifetime of disciplining ourselves, sharing our love and praying to the Lord.

Through the word of Scripture and the sacrament of the Eucharist, Christ comes to give us his peace, to leave his peace with us. Accept this peace, cultivate it, and carry it to sow in the lives of other people.

Twenty-Sixth Sunday of the Year
Jm 5:1-6

Riches

One of the more popular songs from *Fiddler on the Roof* is the one entitled *If I Were a Rich Man*. Like Tevye most of us can't see any harm in being a little bit rich. After all, a little wealth would add to our dignity and increase the security of our family. Moreover, it would afford us the opportunity to help the poor and give us the leisure to pray.

If that were the case, then wealth would be a blessing and prosperity would be worthy of pursuit. But experience shows that too frequently this is not the case. Instead of sharing our wealth with others, we selfishly store it up for ourselves. Instead of enjoying peace to seek spiritual riches or cultural pursuits, we anxiously strive to accumulate more material things. This is why St. James speaks out so strongly in his epistle: "Weep and wail, you rich. Your wardrobe has grown moth-eaten and your gold and silver have corroded."

James is not attacking all rich people. He is criticizing the ones who make wealth their supreme value; the ones who clutter up their homes with knickknacks, but who close their hearts to alcoholics and addicts; the ones who wear the latest fashions in clothing, but who will not help other people stripped naked of their human dignity.

James is not attacking the acquisition of wealth. He is criticizing some of the ways it is acquired, like withholding a living wage from our workers or even by killing a man. We might add such ways as hurting a friend to gain a promotion, neglecting our family to work extra hours, or surrendering our integrity to cheat in a deal.

James raises some serious questions for us. What is the supreme value in our life? Is it love for our Lord and fellow man, or is it love of money and material things? What are our most prized possessions? Are they our family, friends and faith, or are they clothes, cars and record collections?

What are the activities that fill our leisure hours? Is some of that precious time spent reading Scripture and praying, or is it wasted worrying about our savings and investments?

Psychologists say that a miser is a miserable person becaue he has little self-esteem and a weak sense of security. Consequently, a miser piles up wealth to boost his ego and he surrounds himself with material things to escape his loneliness. Isn't there something of the miser in all of us? When we try to compensate for what is lacking within us by accumulating things around us, we act like a miser. When we seek our security in finances alone, instead of trusting in God's loving care for us, we act like a miser.

The key question we must ask is: what measure of material wealth is compatible with fidelity to the gospel? The answer is: wealth that is shared, not hoarded. The Lord Jesus and the apostle James never recommended the destruction of wealth, but rather its distribution among the poor.

In other words, wealth is a wonderful thing, but it is not to be worshipped. Wealth is an immense blessing from God, but it must benefit others. Another James, namely, William James the philosopher, once said about life: "The greatest use of life is to spend it for something that will outlast it." We can apply his principle to wealth—the greatest use of money is to spend it for something that will outlast it.

In liturgy we come together—rich and poor alike—to share the Lord's Eucharistic bread and wine. Would that our celebrations of the Last Supper were visible signs of the sharing we do in life with our wealth.

Twenty-Seventh Sunday of the Year
Heb 2:9-11

Leadership and Suffering

One of the most publicized events and widely covered visits of our time has been the trip by Pope John Paul II to the U.S. Why the immense popularity of this church leader? Why the almost instant success of this man? The reasons are many, but one reason is certainly his background of hardship and suffering. Born in Poland in 1920, Karol Wojtyla had to work in junior high school to help support his poor family. His university studies were interrupted by World War II when he had to labor, first in a stone quarry, and then in a chemical products plant.

While a plant worker, Wojtyla studied theology secretly since Krakow's seminary was closed during the German occupation. After the war when he was ordained and later became a bishop, he was an outspoken critic of Poland's Communist government. He decried the drafting of seminarians, defended the right of parents to give their children a Christian education, and demanded building permits for the construction of new churches.

When you consider what Pope John Paul II has been through, it's no wonder that people are so willing to accept him as a leader, not only in the Catholic Church but in the world as well. There is text from the letter to the Hebrews which captures this aspect of the pope's popularity as a leader: "It was fitting that, when bringing many sons to glory, God should make their leader in the work of salvation perfect through suffering."

The text, of course, refers to Christ, our savior and high priest. In bringing us to glory it was the Father's will to perfect Christ as our leader through suffering. But in a secondary sense the text also describes the life of Pope John Paul II. Like Christ, he too is a leader who fought to bring his people to freedom and glory in Poland, and is now striving to bring freedom and glory to oppressed people all over the world. Like Christ, he too had to suffer much through poverty, war and hard labor to become what he is today.

We may not be leaders in a position like Pope John Paul II, or in the history of salvation like Christ. Nevertheless, if we seek to share in the glory of Christ's kingdom, then we can expect to have some share in his sufferings. We have already been saved by Christ, but this is only the beginning and pledge of our glory. Our victory will only be completed when we reproduce in ourselves the suffering, dying and rising of Jesus.

This is not to say that suffering is good in itself—it isn't. Suffering becomes an instrument to perfect us only because God chooses to use it that way. The Father alone could take Christ's passion and death and use it to accomplish the resurrection. The Father alone has power to transform our pain into joy and our death into life.

Jesuit philosopoher Robert Johann once wrote: "Life has the character of an ongoing drama, still unfinished and full of surprises—many of them unhappy. The pervasive presence of pain shows that the world it frustrates is not an ultimate. Yet man's capacity to accept pain, to meet it with courage instead of cowardice, immediately lifts him beyond the realm of nature into the realm of Being itself—the infinite."

It seems, then, that without suffering Wojtyla would never have come to his destiny to lead the church as Pope John Paul II; he would never have been lifted beyond the realm of his ordinary existence to become the spiritual father of the whole world.

Perhaps this is the same purpose of suffering in our own life. It shatters our complacency and compels us to become more than what we are. It denies us certain satisfactions but also enables us to become more sensitive to the needs of those around us.

Suffering stymies some of our aspirations, but it also leads us to look to the Lord as the ultimate source of happiness. For only God can satisfy fully our needs; only he can perfect us as persons; only he can bring us to final glory.

Twenty-Eighth Sunday of the Year
Heb 4:12-13

Influential Books

In a *Family Weekly* article entitled "Authors Who Have Shaped Our Lives," Prof. Richard Armour discusses some of the most popular and influential writers in the United States. His list includes such authors as Dale Carnegie who wrote *How to Win Friends and Influence People*, Dr. Norman Vincent Peale who wrote *The Power of Positive Thinking*, Emily Post and Amy Vanderbilt who wrote books on etiquette, Dr. Benjamin Spock who wrote a book on baby care, Dr. David Reuben who wrote a book about sex and George Orwell who wrote *1984*.

According to Prof. Armour, these are the principal authors who have shaped our attitudes, values and conduct. Nevertheless, he concludes his article with the following remarks: "I have saved for last, the book that has shaped more lives than all of the above-mentioned put together. I am referring, of course, to the Bible—which is still and always our Number One Best Seller."

The Bible was also the Number One Book for St. Paul who said: "God's word is living and effective, sharper than any two-edged sword. It penetrates and divides soul and spirit, joints and marrow; it judges the reflections and thoughts of the heart."

Paul's statements outline four reasons why the Bible has shaped more lives than all other books put together. God's word is living. It is not a dead word spoken only once in the distant past to people of ancient times. Rather, it is a living word that speaks to us again and again in the here and now. It is not a lifeless word like an outdated telephone directory. Rather, it is a living word like the slogan "Che lives" during the 1960's.

God's word is effective, sharper than any two-edged sword. His word is not just a sound we hear or print we read. His word is a power—when God speaks, things happen to us. All through history men have been moved to action by great speeches, like "I Have a Dream," by Martin Luther King, Jr. This is all the more true of the word of God.

God's word is penetrating. It reaches the very center of our being—our memory and imagination, our instincts and feelings, our intellect and will. It contacts those levels of our being that are the aim of modern depth-psychology and psychoanalysis. Consequently, God's word can heal our past, illuminate the present and strenghten us for the future.

God's word exposes, evaluates and judges. It examines and weighs our secret desires and our innermost thoughts. We may be able to wear masks in front of men to disguise our motives and intentions, but not in the presence of God. His word strips away all pretense and exposes what we really are. Our response to his word reveals whether we are smug or open to change, heroic or cowardly, selfish or unselfish.

It is no marvel, then, that God's word in the Bible has shaped more lives than all other writings put together. When we look over the gospels, we see how Christ's words were living, effective, penetrating and judging. And they still are! If only we let them be.

Praise the Lord, for his words continue to invite us to generous service, just as they did the apostles when they left everything to follow him; call us to repentance and conversion, just as they did the woman taken in adultery; inspire us with joy and enthusiasm, just as they did Zacchaeus; send us out to announce the good news to others, just as they did the Samaritan woman at the well. Be alive like God's word!

Twenty-Ninth Sunday of the Year
Heb 4:14-16

He's Been There

In his two volumes of *The Gulag Archipelago* Soviet author Alexander Solzhenitsyn describes some of the horrors of the Communist slave labor camps in Russia. For example, in one episode he tells how peasant farmers called kulaks were given picks and shovels to dig a canal by hand, but had no tents or warm clothing supplied. Huddled together at night for warmth in temperatures of twenty degrees below zero, they nonetheless froze to death in pitiful numbers.

Solzhenitsyn's writings stem from his own personal experiences, first as an ardent Communist in the Red Army, and later as political prisoner himself for eleven years. This explains why he writes with such passion and why his books have such a powerful appeal. He's been there himself, he knows what it's like.

The same is true of Christ, our savior and high priest. He's been through suffering and death himself; he knows what it's like because he's been there. This is why the author of the letter to the Hebrews writes: "We do not have a high priest who is unable to sympathize with our weakness, but one who was tempted in every way that we are, yet never sinned. So let us confidently approach the throne of grace to receive mercy and find help in time of need."

Suffering and pain, anxieties and tensions, obstacles and difficulties, disappointments and failures are all part of our human condition. We struggle to minimize them, but we will never be completely rid of them. We search for ways to draw good out of them, but we will never completely understand them. Nonetheless, what gives us hope is that not only did Christ experience the same weaknesses and limitations himself, but he also overcame them by his resurrection and ascension.

Consequently, even though we may still have to suffer physical pains from rheumatism or cancer, we can do so with more courage because we know that Christ suffered before us. Even though we may still have to meet with misunderstanding and rejection from others, we can do so with more patience because we know that Christ went through the same things. Even though we may still have to be frustrated by misfortune and failure, we can still go on because we know that this is what Christ did.

Inasmuch as Christ has been through suffering and pain before us, he can understand and sympathize with our weakness. This is why we can confidently approach him in prayer and expect to find help in time of need. Christ has the power to halt pain, remove obstacles and end adversity. But even if he doesn't do these things for us, he will at least give us the graces we need to cope with them and not be conquered by them.

We can count on his grace to accept the ordeal of any sickness, endure hurts, and persist in the face of insurmountable obstacles. We can trust in him to be with us when we're lonely, encourage us when we want to quit, and inspire us when we're weary.

Christ knows what we're going through because he has already been there himself. He can help us with our struggles because he has already won the victory and gives us access to it.

Thirtieth Sunday of the Year
Heb 5:1-6

Priests

A two-hour television special that drew a large viewing audience was *A Home of Our Own*. It was a dramatization of the life and work of an American-born Franciscan priest, Fr. William Wasson. Back in 1954 he took in his first teenage boy from a jail in Cuernavaca, Mexico. Later he rented an old abandoned brewery warehouse and opened its doors to the poor, orphaned and abandoned children of Mexico.

Today Fr. Wasson directs three such homes, caring for more than twelve hundred boys and girls. He considers his collection of children neither an institution nor an orphanage, but rather an extended family. It is a family based on four principles whereby each child is given: first, love and security; second, opportunities to share; third, work to do; fourth, responsibility.

Fr. Wasson's extended family is but one model of the many kinds of work priests do. Priesthood is one of the themes of the letter to the Hebrews: "Every high priest is taken from men and made their representative before God, to offer gifts and sacrifices for sins."

Priests may be engaged in a wide variety of occupations in the community, but there is one thing they must have in common—they must represent their people before God in prayer and sacrifice. Priests may be missionaries like Fr. Wasson or lawyers like Fr. Drinan, sociologists like Fr. Greeley or psychologists like Fr. Van Kaam, parish men like your pastor or teachers in school like myself. But whatever work priests do for you, they must represent you before God in prayer and sacrifice.

This is not to say that the people don't have to pray or offer sacrifices themselves. The text says that the priest is their representative, not their substitute. Everyone in the community of God's people must pray and offer sacrifices. The priest simply serves as their representative by symbolically gathering up all these prayers and sacrifices to offer them to God at the community level. The priest presides at the Eucharistic assembly as a visible sign of God's invisible presence. He mediates to the people God's word in Scripture, God's life in the Eucharist, and God's love by his service.

The text says that the priest is taken from among men, that is, he is chosen and called by the Lord and must be approved by the people before he is ordained. This calling may be very mysterious, but it is nonetheless real. It is unique to each individual, but it is from the same Lord. Because a priest is taken from among men it means that he is human. He is not an angel; he remains a man. He experiences the same joys and sorrows, desires and passions, strengths and weaknesses as any other human being.

Consequently, the priest needs from his people, on the one hand, their understanding and patience, and their assurance and encouragement when he makes a mistake; on the other hand, their interest and recognition, and their enthusiasm and support when he is doing something well.

The priest may not be the holiest one in the community, but he does have his authority from Christ and the call to stand in his place at the altar of worship before the people. The priest may not be the wisest one in the assembly, but he does have his power from the Holy Spirit and the mandate to interpret God's word for the people.

In one of his articles theologian Karl Rahner wrote "The priest speaks to you the word of God, not his own. Perhaps he has not entirely understood it himself, perhaps even adulterated it. But he believes, and despite his fear he knows that he must communicate God's word to you. Must not someone of us say something about God and eternal life, about sin and grace? So, my dear friends, pray for the priest; carry him so that he might be able to sustain others by bringing them the mystery of God's love revealed in Christ Jesus."

Thirty-First Sunday of the Year
Heb 7:23-28

Jesus Saves

In her memoirs author Jessamyn West relates how she almost committed suicide once. She was twenty-eight years old, married, and about to receive her Ph.D. when she caught tuberculosis. After two years in a sanatorium she was sent home to die. It was then that she contemplated suicide.

But her Quaker mother nursed her back to health. She did this by reconstructing their Quaker heritage in southern Indiana through stories about courtship and farming, blizzards and prayer meetings.

Slowly wooed back to life by her mother, Jessamyn West turned her mother's gift into her own response to suicide—her writing. The Hoosier tales Jessamyn West published over the next several years turned out to be a beloved best seller called *The Friendly Persuasion*.

Because her mother intervened, Jessamyn West's life was saved from suicide. This is a faint image of the way we are continually saved by Jesus Christ. In Hebrews we read: "Jesus Christ is forever able to save those who approach God through him, since he forever lives to make intercession for them."

What are some of the ways Jesus continues to save us by his intercession? In general, Jesus saves us by delivering us from the influences of the devil, freeing us from the slavery of sin, and rescuing us from the destruction of Death.

In particular, Jesus saves us whenever we stop hurting people. For example, when we stop tearing apart someone's reputation, and start defending it; stop ridiculing people, and start showing them more respect; stop being inconsiderate of peoples' feelings, and start taking them more into account.

Jesus saves us whenever we stop destroying ourselves. For example, when we stop drinking or smoking excessively, and start exercising more self-control over these habits; stop making money or pleasure the main purpose of our lives, and start seeking higher values; stop worrying and being anxious over the future, and start living in peace by using the opportunities of the day.

Jesus saves us whenever we abandon the things that hold us back from psychological growth. For example, when we abandon our ways of self-indulgence and selfishness, and begin reaching out and sharing more with others; put off our masks of self-deceit and dishonesty, and begin being more authentic and genuine; leave behind our neurotic fears and insecurities, and begin moving about with more self-confidence and greater freedom.

Jesus saves us whenever we escape from the things that prevent us from growing spiritually. For example, when we let go of our attachment to material things, and start understanding what Christ meant when he said, "Happy are the poor in spirit"; let go of our pride and egoism, and start learning from Christ what it is to be meek and humble of heart; when we let go of our pseudo-independence and self-reliance, and begin realizing that unless we abide in Christ like branches in a vine we can do nothing.

There are all kinds of ways, then, that Jesus continues to save us by interceding for us. What a source of hope and confidence for us! Regardless of how deep our despair, even to the extent of contemplating suicide like Jessamyn West did, Jesus can revive our hopes and inspire us with a reason for living. No matter how depressed we get because of some tragic loss—our job, home or loved one—we can be lifted up by Jesus and begin creating a meaningful future for ourselves.

Glorify the Lord because he is always ready to save us from anything that separates us from him or each other. Praise the Lord because through him we can approach the Father for mercy and forgiveness, healing and strength, light and life.

Thirty-Second Sunday of the Year
Heb 9:24-28

Die Once

A movement has begun to have Dr. Tom Dooley canonized as a saint. Dr. Dooley served as a U.S. Navy doctor in Indochina, and after two years resigned his naval commission to establish privately financed medical missions in Laos. He also founded MEDICO, an organization to provide medical care to people in remote areas. Dr. Dooley died of cancer in 1961 at the age of thirty-four.

Just before his death Dr. Dooley wrote the following in his last letter to Fr. Hesburgh of Notre Dame: "But when the time comes, like now, then the storm around me does not matter. The winds within me do not matter. Nothing human or earthly can touch me. A wilder storm of peace gathers in my heart. What seems unpossessable, I can possess. What seems unfathomable, I fathom. Because I can pray, I can communicate. How do people endure anything on earth if they cannot have God?"

Indeed, Dr. Dooley was ready to die and face Jesus as his savior. Death and meeting Jesus after death are spoken about in Hebrews: "Just as it is appointed that men die once, and after death be judged, so Christ was offered up once to take away our sins. He will appear a second time, not to take away sin but to bring salvation to those who eagerly await him."

Everyone of us is destined to die once. Whether we are rich and famous like Howard Hughes and Paul Getty, or poor and obscure like a derelict on skid row, all of us are destined to die once. We can distract ourselves from the thought by keeping busy with work and play, or we can pretend that death will never come by accumulating and surrounding ourselves with nice things, but in the end we will have to die and leave everything behind.

And after death we have to face the judgment. How much did people know we were Christians by our love? To what extent did we feed the hungry and clothe the naked? In what ways did we love one another just as Christ loved us and gave his life for us?

Notice how the author of the letter to the Hebrews takes an optimistic view of death and judgment. He sees death as the prelude to Christ's second appearance, bringing with him the gift of salvation for those who eagerly await him. Certainly Dr. Tom Dooley eagerly awaited the coming of Christ at the time of his death. There is no reason why we can't do the same.

But it takes a lifetime of eager looking for the Lord to do this at death: a lifetime of looking for the Lord in the people who live and work with us, however much they may irritate or upset us; a lifetime of looking for the Lord in the poor and abandoned, sick and lonely, handicapped and imprisoned, regardless of the demands they make on our resources of time and money.

To welcome the Lord at death it takes a lifetime of eager looking for him in the circumstances and happenings of our everyday existence, whether they are advantages or disadvantages, pleasures or pains, triumphs or defeats; a lifetime of searching for the Lord's word in Scripture or his presence in prayer, especially when it is difficult because he seems so far away and we have to do it on faith.

In the Eucharist, Christ makes his appearance under the sacramental forms of bread and wine. How eagerly we await his coming now in this sacrament is a preview of how eagerly we will await his coming later at death. The best way to prepare is the way Dr. Tom Dooley showed us—a lifetime of seeking the Lord by communicating with him in prayer and by loving and serving him in our fellow man.

Thirty-Third Sunday of the Year
Heb 10:11-18

Masterpiece

Several years ago, Leonardo da Vinci's *Mona Lisa* was transferred from the Louvre in France to the Tokyo National Museum in Japan. For insurance purposes the *Mona Lisa* was valued at $40 million, and so the Japanese government had to pay an insurance premium of $400,000.

Artistic works like the *Mona Lisa* by da Vinci or the *Pieta* by Michelangelo are actually priceless. They are priceless because they are the unique creations of men who were geniuses in the world of art. Such masterpieces stand alone in the annals of history, never to be repeated, never to be reproduced. All attempts to duplicate them always turn out to be only copies, mere imitations that lack the matchless quality of the originals.

Something like this can be said about Christ's sacrifice on the cross. It is unique, unrepeatable, never to be reproduced. In Hebrews we read: "Jesus offered one sacrifice for sins and took his seat forever at the right hand of the Father. Now he waits until his enemies are placed beneath his feet. By one sacrifice he has forever perfected those who are being sanctified."

Granted that Christ's sacrifice is unique and unrepeatable, what does this mean for us? How does it affect us? It means that we have to participate in Christ's sacrifice to make it real for ourselves. The perfection of the sacrifice lies in the person of Jesus Christ who is offering it, not in us who are yet to be sanctified.

We are dealing with a paradox. The essential conditions for our sanctification are already established in principle by Christ's death and resurrection. But they have to be fulfilled and brought to completion in our own life. Consequently, while Christ's sacrifice is singular and will never be repeated, it has to be constantly applied to us individually.

It is something like those priceless artistic works mentioned above. Great masterpieces like da Vinci's *Mona Lisa* or Shakespeare's plays will never be reproduced. Yet, they are enjoyed and appreciated over and over again by people who come to see them on exhibition or performed on stage.

How do we participate in Christ's perfect sacrifice? One important way is by celebrating the Eucharist and representing his death and resurrection under sacramental signs. But we also participate by reproducing the pattern of Christ's life, death and resurrection in ourselves. We do this by dying everyday to our pride and selfishness, hatreds and resentments, worries and anxieties, and rising from these to a new life in Christ—a life of humility and service, love and forgiveness, trust and peace.

It is our pride, selfishness and so on that are the enemies Christ is waiting to overcome. Our daily rising to a new life in Christ is what being sanctified means. This demands great patience and unremitting effort from us. Such perfection and sanctification are not achieved in a day nor without great effort.

Again, it is something like the great masterpieces in the world of art—they take time and effort to create, and time and effort to appreciate. Our dying to sin and rising with Christ, then, is not an all-at-once thing. It's a life process, a gradual growth, a continuous transformation; yes, a work of art.

When we come together as God's people to worship, we praise and thank the Father for giving us the unique, unrepeatable sacrifice of Jesus his Son. Jesus has already won the victory for us—he's waiting for us to do our part. Nothing can stop its triumph—all we have to do is die to sin and rise with Christ each day to share in it.

Thirty-Fourth Sunday of the Year
Rv 1:5-8

Liberator

Actor Jack Nicholson won an Academy Award for his performance in the film *One Flew Over the Cuckoo's Nest*. He played the role of a sane convict sent to a mental institution for punishment. In this "Cuckoo's nest" his charisma arouses a group of lethargic patients to rebel against the system—a system that is doing nothing to rehabilitate them but everything to repress them.

In some respects, Nicholson plays the role of a Christ-figure, a liberator leading people from slavery to freedom, from passivity to enthusiasm. Even his death suggests a Christ symbolism, for it becomes the occasion for his Indian friend to "fly from the Cuckoo's nest" to freedom, sanity and a full human life.

Christ as a liberator leading us to freedom is one of the images used in the Book of Revelation: "Jesus Christ is the first-born from the dead and ruler of the kings of the earth. To him who loves us and freed us from our sins by his own blood, who has made us a royal nation of priests, to him be glory and power."

What are these sins from which Christ frees and delivers us? Suppose we consider sin as a failure—a failure to become fully human, a failure to grow in maturity, a failure to actualize our God-given talents. If we accept this view of sin, then we get some interesting insights from a book written by a psychologist, Dr. Everett Shostrom, called *Freedom to Be*.

Dr. Shostrom defines *freedom to be* as man, in the here and now, daring to be himself, fully and freely, in terms of four basic elements: love, anger, strength and weakness. On the negative side, he details four basic manipulative responses which avoid or resist our *freedom to be*. The first manipulative response is called "placating." It is a failure to love authentically. We cope with life by trying to please others, either as a professional Mr. Nice-guy type, or as an oversolicitous mother-protector type.

The second manipulative response is "blaming." It is a failure to use our anger purposefully. We either bully people to intimidate them, or play the role of a judge telling people where they've gone wrong.

The third manipulative response is "conniving." A person schemes to control a situation. It is a failure to be genuinely strong. We become either the forceful dictator type, or the sneaky calculator type.

The fourth manipulative response is "avoiding" any trouble situation. It is a failure to handle our weakness. We become either the born-loser type of weakling, or the clinging-vine type so dependent on others.

On the positive side, Dr. Shostrom says that to grow as a person and achieve the freedom to be, we have to learn and acquire the alternatives to manipulation: first, authentic loving so that we really care for and take delight in the well-being of others; second, being genuinely angry so that we can assert ourselves with self-confidence; third, feeling our strength honestly so that we have courage to face the difficulties of life; fourth, facing our weaknesses openly so that we can have compassion and to empathize with others.

Psychologists like Dr. Shostrom can do much to liberate us from manipulation and lead us to the *freedom to be*. But no one can do this better than Jesus Christ. He alone can free us completely from these four basic manipulations, these failures in self-actualization. In other words, only he can free us completely from our sins.

Moreover, Jesus Christ alone can transform us completely into people who are loving, self-confident, courageous and compassionate. In other words, he alone can make us into a royal nation of priests to give him glory by being all that we are meant to be as human beings.

Only Christ the King has the power to liberate us completely from the "Cuckoo nest" of our self-hatred and insecurities and deliver us into the freedom to be fully human and princely people.

SECTION THREE

Cycle C

First Sunday of Advent
1 Th 3:12-4:2

Crisis

Early in 1956 Humphrey Bogart was operated on for cancer. By the end of the year everyone in Hollywood knew that he was dying. Yet, in the face of certain, slow death Bogart refused to give in to the feelings of despair or self-pity. Every afternoon he was helped from his bed to a wheelchair and then was taken down to his den. There he continued his tradition of hospitality by entertaining guests at a cocktail hour.

When Bogart finally died in 1957, his friend John Huston had this to say about him: "No one who sat in his presence during those final weeks would ever forget his display of courage. After you got over the initial shock of his wasting appearance, you quickened to his grandeur, expanded under it, and felt proud to be there as the friend of such a brave man."

The class and courage Humphrey Bogart showed in his final scene of life are the kind St. Paul hopes the Thessalonians would show in their final scene: "May the Lord strengthen your hearts, making them blameless and holy at the coming of our Lord Jesus Christ. Conduct yourselves in a way pleasing to God. Learn to make still greater progress."

When Paul wrote this he had in mind the second coming of Christ at the end of the world. But what he says applies equally well to Christ's coming at the time of our death and to Christ's coming at Christmas when we celebrate his birth.

We don't know how much faith in Christ actor Humphrey Bogart had. But if he could prepare for his death with courage, and if he could grow as a person in meeting this crisis, then, surely, believers in Christ can do no less.

Advent is a crisis situation. It is a call to grow as a person. It is a challenge to make still greater progress as a Christian. Too often our approach to Advent is either too commercial, too sentimental or too superficial. Too often gift buying, Santa Claus parades and parties suppress within us the sense of urgency we should have about Christ's coming.

If we really take Christ's coming seriously, then we will accept his call to become more human and more Christian. If we really believe that Christ comes so that we might have life more abundantly, then we will not allow ourselves to slip into complacency, but make some move to improve ourselves.

In a book entitled *Passages* author Gail Sheehy discusses some of the crises of adult life; crises like husbands coming to the realization that they have reached their peak on the salary scale; crises like wives coming to the realization that they have become bored with their housework. Gail Sheehy contends that each crisis we encounter is an opportunity for further growth, or, unfortunately, for avoidance, regression or stagnation.

The same thing can be said of the period of Advent. It is an opportunity either to grow as a Christian, or, unhappily, to ignore Christ's call, turn further away or remain static. During Advent we need that sense of urgency which Humphrey Bogart had in preparing for his death—a realization about the shortness of time and a determination to live with more awareness and appreciation.

We need Bogart's courage to let go of the things that hold us back from growth—our fears and insecurities, materialism and greed, egoism and self-deception—and to reach out for the things that will make us grow as Christians—a deeper understanding of ourselves, a more profound appreciation of Christ's presence in the world, a richer prayer life through Scripture and the sacraments, and a greater generosity in sharing with others.

Second Sunday of Advent
Ph 1:4-6, 8-11

Things That Really Matter

Out on the coast of the state of Maine, on a bay surrounded by pine forestry, is a 140-acre farm. Here ninety-two year old Scott Nearing lives with his seventy-one year old wife Helen. Scott Nearing is a former university professor of ecomonics and his wife a former concert violinist. For over forty years the Nearings have been living their own simple lifestyle. They grow their own food, keep a vegetarian diet, provide a free guesthouse for visitors, and spend part of each day with music and reading.

In an interview one time, Nearing said: "We don't need fame or fortune ourselves. We never did. Douglas Fairbanks had 454 suits. Why? It is the merchants who fill us with the illusion that we need things. The way to live is as close as you can to the cycles of life."

The Nearings live this way in order to pursue the things that are important to them, to value the things that really matter. St. Paul had something like this in mind when he wrote to the Philippians: "My prayer is that your love may more and more abound so that with blameless conduct you may learn to value the things that really matter, up to the very day of Christ."

For us during Advent the day of Christ's coming is Christmas. Paul urges us as we prepare for this celebration to value the things that really matter. He exhorts us to seek what is good in the highest degree, and not to settle for something less. He challenges us to pursue what is absolutely the best, and not be misled by what is only second-rate.

This is why the Nearings left the mainstream of society to live on their farm in Maine. They became discouraged with the violence and competitiveness, the exploitation and injustice in today's society. They wanted to give an example of sane, healthy living in an insane, destructive society. Their desire is to help build a new society based on sharing and simplicity, cooperation and mutual respect.

We may not be able to adopt the same lifestyle as the Nearings, but we should be able to value like them the things that really matter. To seek a high paying job and to have a nice comfortable home are good things in themselves. But it is far better to seek personal satisfaction in our work and to have an atmosphere of peace and contentment in our home. To have adequate insurance for protection and sufficient food in our pantries are important. But it is far more important for us to have a heart of compassion for the unprotected and a spirit of generous sharing with the hungry.

As we approach Christmas we need the Nearings and Paul to remind us to value the things that really matter—to value the presence of Christ become man more than any material present we receive; to value the peace that comes from the sacraments more than any excitement we find at drinking parties; to value the joy of sharing friendship more than watching any program on television.

Why should we be misled by advertising about the best way to celebrate Christmas? Why should we feel that we have to have the most expensive camera, the choicest liquor, or the latest gadget to enjoy a Merry Christmas?

Value the things that really matter about Christmas—the magnificent love of God for sinners; the simplicity of the stable where Christ was born; the good news announced by the angel; the peace and joy experienced by the shepherds and wise men.

Third Sunday of Advent
Ph 4:4-7

The Circus

Most of us are familiar with Barnum and Bailey's claim to be "the greatest show on earth." But how many of us know what is the world's smallest traveling circus? It is the Royal Lichenstein Quarter Ring Sidewalk Circus which consists of three performers. One of these performers is a Jesuit priest, Fr. Nick Weber. He is both the ringmaster and fire-eater of this circus troupe which has performed at thousands of shopping centers and college campuses.

When he first started out in 1971, Fr. Weber felt that the morals drawn in the ancient fairy tales performed in the circus would justify its existence. But now he sees the value of the circus as primarily an invitation to play. "Play is something very much needed in the midst of today's pressures," he says. "When dreams fade, life becomes a barren field."

In his own unique way Fr. Weber is announcing the same good news which St. Paul proclaims when he writes: "Rejoice in the Lord always! I say it again. Rejoice! The Lord himself is near. Dismiss all anxiety from your minds."

When we review the events of the past year we might object and say that St. Paul and Fr. Weber are unrealistic. How can you always rejoice when there is still fighting on the international scene in Northern Ireland, South Africa and other places? How can we always rejoice when there are still domestic problems like inflation, unemployment and political scandals? How can we always rejoice when we still have our own personal struggles with sickness, worry or boredom?

If the cause of our rejoicing were the things that happen outside of us, then our objection would be valid. But it isn't. The cause of our rejoicing is *in the Lord*, and not in such things as our government's foreign policy or our bank statement.

If the cause of our rejoicing were in ourselves, then again the objection would be valid. But it isn't. We can always rejoice because we do so *in the Lord*, and not because we ourselves have done something spectacular.

Authentic Christian joy is independent of what happens outside of us or in us. It depends on the abiding presence of Jesus—the Lord is near, as Paul reminds us. Consequently, we can rejoice in the Lord whenever we experience the good things of life—a delicious meal, a restful sleep, an entertaining movie, the companionship of a friend. We can rejoice in all these good things because they have been sanctified by Christ. Everyone of our human conditions—eating, sleeping, praying, friendship—have been transformed by grace because Christ became a man and shared in them.

We can also rejoice in the Lord even when the worst happens to us. Fires or floods, crippling accidents or disabling sicknesses, job layoffs or failure in school—none of these things can prevent us from always rejoicing in the Lord. The reason again is that Christ is near, he is with us. By his death and resurrection he has already overcome all these things—his light is stronger than darkness, and his life is stronger than death.

This is the good news announced by Fr. Weber and his circus troupe. "Today's pressures and tensions are too much for us to bear alone," he says. "So take time out to play, to laugh, to rejoice in the Lord because he is very near."

This is also the message of Advent. Our fears and worries, our hurts and disappointments may sometimes seem to overwhelm us. Nevertheless, we can still rejoice because the Lord is near—he is coming at Christmas to renew our lives by his birth, revive our fading dreams with his words, and brighten our horizon with his light.

Fourth Sunday of Advent
Heb 10:5-10

The Hunchback

In his book *The Hunchback of Liberty Hall* author Floyd Miller tells the story of Charles Steinmetz, an electrical wizard. Charles Steinmetz did research for General Electric and made important discoveries regarding electric motors and generators, street and automobile lights, and lightning arresters.

Such success did not come easy to Steinmetz. He was almost refused admission as an immigrant to the United States because he had no family, no money and no job. He was nearly a dwarf in size, his frail body was deformed by a large hump on his back, and his head was overlarge.

Nevertheless, Steinmetz was a genius in mathematics and brilliant in electrical research. So when he died in 1923, Steinmetz was ranked with Edison, Marconi and Bell as one of the outstanding scientists of the 20th century.

The words describing Jesus in the following passage from Hebrews might very well be used to describe the life of Charles Steinmetz: "On coming into the world Jesus said: 'Sacrifice and offering you did not desire, but a body you have prepared for me. I have come to do your will, O God.' By this will we have been sanctified through the offering of the body of Jesus Christ once for all."

Steinmetz was handicapped by his dwarfed, hunchbacked body. But he accepted his condition and used his body as an instrument to make scientific discoveries, to befriend children, and to help the downtrodden. By the offering of his body to the cause of science and the service of society, Steinmetz in a sense sanctified us—he enriched our lives with his scientific discoveries, inspired us with his humility and good humor, and aroused our admiration with his love for children and outcasts.

Yet what Steinmetz did through his body is only a dim reflection of what Jesus did through his body in the Incarnation. In his book *The Meaning of Man* theologian Jean Mouroux shows how Christ becomes for us a visible image of the invisible God through his body. His voice speaks to us God's word of truth, his hands heal us with God's own power, and his heart seeks us with God's own love.

On the one hand, the Incarnation is a humiliation. It is God descending into our human condition to become one of us. It is God coming to experience our hunger and thirst, work and sleep, pleasure and pain, and finally death. On the other hand, the Incarnation is a glorification. It is God taking a human body to himself, uniting it to his divine nature, and transforming it with grace.

From the way Christ used his body to save and sanctify us, and from the way Steinmetz used his body to enrich us, we get an idea of how we should use the body God has prepared for us; how we too should offer up our body to give glory to God and service to man.

This means accepting our body as God's special gift to us. This body may have many weaknesses and imperfections, but essentially it has beauty and nobility inasmuch as it comes from God; it has glory and grandeur inasmuch as it is destined for the resurrection.

We must use our body to fulfill ourselves and enrich others. Through our body we can discover and learn, work and play in order to develop ourselves to the fullest. Through our body we can communicate and share with others, love them and be loved in return.

Finally, we must use this body to give glory to God. Like Christ's, our own body too, should reveal God's presence in the world: our words witnessing to his good news, our hands serving his people, and our hearts making his love felt. Our bodies should be visible images of God's invisible being.

Christmas
Heb 1:1-6

Reflection of the Father's Glory

In the religious epic movie *Mohammed—Messenger of God*, starring Anthony Quinn, we see a lot of stunning desert scenes, intense debates and violent battles. But nowhere do we ever see the Prophet Mohammed himself. Mohammed is never shown on the screen because Muslim law forbids his depiction. Sometimes we see his walking stick, but not the prophet himself. Sometimes he is asked questions, but he doesn't say anything in reply.

How different is the Christian understanding and approach to Jesus Christ. The author of the letter to the Hebrews expresses it this way: "In times past, God spoke in fragmentary and varied ways to our father through the prophets; in this, the final age, he has spoken to us through his Son. This Son is the reflection of the Father's glory, the exact representation of the Father's being."

Jesus is God's messenger to us. He is God's Word made flesh so that we could see his human face, hear his human voice and feel his human skin. Jesus is the revelation of God's glory to us. He embodied the very being of his Father so that we could be forgiven by his spoken words, fed with his hands and healed with his touch.

This is why he was born as a man—to make his dwelling among us and make visible the enduring love of God for us. While we no longer have his physical presence as the disciples experienced it, we have something better—his presence in the word of Scripture and in the sacrament of the Eucharist; a presence that transcends the limitations of time and space; a presence that is available to every people and race.

We ourselves are now called forth to make his presence felt among men, to make visible God's enduring love. Thomas Merton once wrote: "The mystery of Christmas lays upon us all a debt and an obligation . . . not only to preach the glad tidings of his coming, but above all to reveal him in our lives. Christ is born to us today, in order that he may appear to the whole world through us."

What the author of Hebrews says about Jesus must in a sense be said about us. In times past, God spoke through the prophets. In this, the final age, he speaks through us every time we greet the lonely, welcome the strange, comfort the sick and cheer up the downcast. Jesus was, and continues to be, the perfect reflection of the Father's glory. But now we, too, are called to image the Father's glory every time we have an opportunity to forgive an enemy, help a neighbor, feed the hungry and heal the hurt.

People don't want to just hear about Jesus, the way they hear about Mohammed in the movie. They want to experience and hear him through us. People don't want to just see Christ's walking stick or be told that he is present in the tabernacle of some church. They want to see and feel him through us.

Christmas can never just be a sentimental celebration. It's a serious obligation to relive the Incarnation. Christmas can never just be an announcement of glad tidings. It's an avowed commitment to ministering and serving.

First Sunday of Lent
Rm 10:8-13

Jesus Is Lord

During the year 1974, *Ice Follies* star Janet Lynn was the world's highest paid woman athlete. At twenty-two the five-time U.S. figure skating champion and winner of an Olympic bronze medal was earning more than $750,000 a year. Janet Lynn did not accomplish this alone. She had to put in a grueling apprenticeship under her coach, Slavka Kohout. She had to spend hours being instructed in the finer techniques of skating and drilled in certain moves until they became perfect.

While she trained, Janet Lynn literally made her coach the lord of her life. She showed respect for the coach's superiority, listened to her instructions and submitted to her discipline. It is not uncommon to make someone like a skating coach the center of one's life for a while in order to become a master oneself. This helps us understand a little of what St. Paul means when he uses the phrase "Jesus is Lord." He says in his letter to the Romans: "For if you confess with your lips that Jesus is Lord, and believe in your heart that God raised him from the dead, you will be saved."

Basically what we have here is the backbone of the Christian creed, an early faith formula: Jesus is Lord and God has raised him from the dead. But what does it mean to confess with our lips that Jesus is Lord?

On the theoretical level the word *Lord* meant several things to Paul. It was a title of respect given to someone in authority, much like our "Sir" in English; it was a royal title given to kings and emperors; and it was a divine title given to the Greek gods.

All three meanings come together when applied in Scripture to Jesus. To call Jesus "Lord" is to address him with respect, acknowledge his kingship, and proclaim his divinity.

On the practical level, to say "Jesus is Lord" is to make Jesus the center of our life and to give him the supreme place. No person, not even our spouse nor our closest friend, is as vital to us as Jesus. Nothing, not even our health or our career, is as important to us as Jesus.

To say "Jesus is Lord" also means to acknowledge our dependence on him and our need for him. Without him we will always seek for some substitute to satisfy us—power, pleasure, possessions. Without him we will never find the strength to resist temptation or overcome obstacles.

To say "Jesus is Lord" also means that we submit to his authority. We listen to his words in Scripture to learn his way and to acquire his wisdom. We accept his will in difficult times to discipline our desires and to grow in character.

To say "Jesus is Lord" means that we worship him. We respect his presence in creation by using and developing his gifts. We honor his presence in others by loving and serving them. We revere his presence in ourselves by praying to him and praising him.

Lent is a good time to look into our lives to see to what extent Jesus is Lord for us. Janet Lynn submitted to her skating coach as the lord of her life for a while in order to become a champion. How far do we go in submitting to Jesus as the Lord of our life in order to be saved? Janet Lynn accepted her coach's way of life voluntarily, eagerly and joyously. How much desire, enthusiasm and delight do we show in accepting Christ's way of life?

Second Sunday of Lent
Ph 3:17-4:1

Restoration

One of the more inspiring testimonies to the human spirit is the reconstruction of the city of Warsaw. During World War II the city was completely destroyed. Since the end of the war, more than thirty years ago, the Polish people have painstakingly rebuilt their capital city.

Not only have they rebuilt it, but they have restored all its important buildings exactly as they originally were in design and art work. On the verge of completion after seven years of labor is their royal castle, a replica of the famous 17th century structure. The castle symbolizes the historical continuity and the national pride of the Polish people because over the centuries it has served as the seat of Polish kings, presidents and parliaments.

This is a remarkable example of how the human spirit can rise and reconstruct its works of architecture, art and culture. It helps us to understand the more marvelous restoration the Lord will accomplish in our resurrection from the dead. St. Paul writes: "We eagerly await the coming of our Savior, the Lord Jesus Christ. He will give a new form to this lowly body of ours and remake it according to the pattern of his glorified body."

Although we are dealing with the mystery of the resurrection here, the gospels give us a glimpse of what Christ's glorified body is like. Before he was exalted, his body was lowly like ours, that is, it was subject to all our human conditions. Like ours now, Christ's body could feel hunger and thirst, pain and pleasure, weakness and strength. But after his resurrection Christ's body was glorified, that is, it was transfigured by his divine nature. His risen body was beyond any feeling of pain, could pass through closed doors, and could appear and disappear at will.

This is the pattern of how the Lord will remake our own body and give it a new form. Our future life, then, is not merely something spiritual. It will include our material body, but not a body as we know it now. More than that we cannot say. What matters is how our faith in the resurrection affects what we do here and now.

If we really believe that life is stronger than death, then our faith will sustain us through any loss or separation we suffer. We may lose our health or be separated from our loved ones by death, but that won't make us despair because we believe that in the resurrection a restoration will take place.

If we truly believe that the grave gives way to glory, then our faith will support us through any breakup in our lives. We may have to experience a broken marriage or a broken career, but that won't make us quit because we believe that the Lord can somehow put things back together for us.

Besides doing penance during Lent to prepare for Easter, we can also deepen our faith in the resurrection and let its power renew our lives right now. Like the Polish people reconstructing Warsaw after its total devastation in World War II, we can be *Easter* people who will not allow any destruction to leave us permanently defeated.

Like the legendary phoenix arising from its own ashes after being consumed by fire, we can be *alleluia* people who will not permit any annihilation of our dreams or damage to our ego to leave us without hope. Praise the Lord in prosperity, for we are experiencing in this life some of his risen glory. Praise the Lord in adversity, for here, too, we can experience his power to reconstruct our lives and remake them in his glory.

Third Sunday of Lent
1 Cor 10:1-12

One Step Away

The movie entitled *The Seduction of Joe Tynan* tells the story of a talented young senator whose political star is on the rise. Joe Tynan is persuaded to champion a cause which will put him in the spotlight and secure for him a national constituency. As he devotes more time and energy to political issues, he spends less time with his family. The deeper Joe Tynan gets involved with his political associates, the further he gets away from his wife and children. Finally, he commits adultery. His seduction by power, fame and sex is now complete.

The Seduction of Joe Tynan might well be captioned by St. Paul's warning when he writes: "The things that happened to our fathers serve as an example. They have been written as warnings to us, upon whom the end of the ages has come. For all these reasons, let anyone who thinks he is standing upright watch out lest he fall!"

Paul is warning the Jews of his day who think that they are very special because they are descendants of Moses. This is not so, says Paul. They are only one step away from being struck down by God's destroying angel, unless they keep God's commandments.

Today the same warning is given to us. From our own experience we know that the warning is a much needed one. Any member of Alcoholics Anonymous will tell you that he is only one drink away from becoming a drunk again. Any compulsive eater will confess that he is just one eating binge away from regaining in a week all the weight it took him a year to lose.

It doesn't matter what our weakness is—smoking, gambling,

drugs, or pornography—we know from sad experience that we are only one step away from slipping back into our old routine of self-indulgence, and only one occasion away from collapsing into our former habits of sin. Old habits die slowly, if at all, and that is why we must never be complacent about them.

Besides the negative side of Paul's warning, there is also a positive side. Perhaps like Joe Tynan we are only one step away from falling into sin, but we are also just one step away from moving towards the Lord Jesus. Like Moses we are always standing on sacred ground in the presence of God, if only to look for him in the burning bush of our everyday situation.

Like Matthew we may be only one tax collection away from becoming a real follower of Christ. Like Zacchaeus we may have to climb only one more tree to get closer to Jesus. Like the Samaritan woman at the well we may be only one drink of water away from accepting Jesus as our savior.

The Scriptures are full of examples of the opportunities which we have to repent of the past and to reform our lives. Every temptation is not only an attraction turning us away from Jesus, but also a time of opportunity and challenge to follow him more closely.

On the one hand, as Paul warns, if we think we are standing upright we should watch, because one step in the wrong direction and we may be like Joe Tynan. On the other hand, we are only one step away from the burning bush of the Lord's presence, his forgiveness of our sins, his healing of our ills, and his crowning of our lives with glory.

Fourth Sunday of Lent
2 Cor 5:17-21

A New Creature

Every now and then you find in the newspapers or magazines an article about health resorts. These resorts offer programs that include dieting, exercise, saunas, yoga and group counseling. After a week or several weeks a participant is supposed to emerge a new person—healthier because he has lost some weight and is eating more nutritious food; happier because of a better self-image and he has found some inner peace.

Such health resorts can be a good thing for some people. They may be expensive and their programs may be hard to continue on one's own, but they do make one feel like a new person, at least for a little while.

What these health resorts claim to accomplish for us physically and emotionally is comparable to what the Lord does for us spiritually. St. Paul says: "If anyone is in Christ, he is a new creature. The old order has passed away; now all is new."

There is a double meaning to these words. On the one hand, Paul is speaking about the old order of humanity begun by the first Adam—an order of sin and separation from God. This order has passed away and is replaced by the new order of humanity begun by the second Adam, namely, Jesus Christ—an order of grace and reconciliation with God.

On the other hand, Paul is speaking about the old order of Judaism under the Old Covenant of the Mosaic Law. This, too, has passed away and is replaced by the new order of faith in Jesus Christ.

How does this work in our contemporary experience and daily lives? Sometimes this means a dramatic conversion, like the reborn experiences of a Charles Colson or a Betty Hutton, a drastic turning away from sin to seek the Lord. More often it is something less dramatic, but nonetheless, just as real and radical for us personally.

Becoming a new creature in Christ can take on many forms. A list of these forms might include the following. First, a new control over our appetites—sensible dieting instead of foolhardy indulgence. Second, a new outlook on life—less complaining about what we lack and more gratitude over what we have. Third, a new interest in our leisure activities—a reduction in our indiscriminate TV viewing and an increase in our selective reading of books, like the Bible perhaps. Fourth, a new set of values—emptying our closets of accumulations and giving more generously to the poor. Fifth, a new sense of social justice—purging ourselves of prejudice and supporting causes like refugee immigration. Sixth, a new relationship with people—curbing our selfishness and expanding our concern for others. Seventh, a new self-image—quitting the game of "I'm no good, nobody loves me" and asserting "God loves me and I'm OK."

These are just a few of the ways we can enter the new order and actually experience being a new creature. These are all kinds of things in our lives that should pass away into the old era to make room for the new era of life in Christ—a life of peace and joy, prayer and praise, giving and sharing.

The Church invites us to come to its health resort during Lent. It's not an expensive health spa like some of those advertised in the newspapers, but its Lenten program of prayer, fasting and almsgiving are guaranteed to make new creatures out of us. If we take up its offer and seriously participate in its threefold program, then on Easter Sunday we will be able to sing, "Alleluia! Now all is **NEW** in Christ."

Fifth Sunday of Lent
Ph 3:8-14

Reaching the Goal

Chris Bonnington is one of the world's greatest mountain climbers. In his book *Everest the Hard Way* he tells the story of how he and his team climbed the unsurmountable southeast face of Mt. Everest. At 29,000 feet, Mt. Everest is the highest mountain in the world.

Chris Bonnington himself did not make it to the top of Mt. Everest. Four of his party did, only three came down. Bonnington writes: "At 25,000 feet you're using the oxygen mask. Every single step takes will power and the most of your physical exertion. You command yourself to take twenty paces upward without a rest. Most of the time you make eighteen before falling down in the snow in exhaustion."

Mountain climbers like Bonnington can appreciate St. Paul's desire and determination when he wrote: "I do not think of myself as having reached the finish line. I give no thought to what lies behind but push on to what is ahead. My entire attention is on the finish line as I run toward the prize to which God calls me—life on high in Christ Jesus."

If mountain climbers like Bonnington will endure tremendous hardships, suffer severe exhaustion, and even risk the dangers of death in order to climb to the top of the world, why is it that we sometimes expend so little effort to attain life on high in Christ Jesus? If some men will give their all to conquer the ultimate challenge of a mountain like Everest, why is it that we sometimes give so little to reach Christ, the living God?

Perhaps one reason is that we don't have the desire of saints like Paul. On the one hand, we want to belong to Christ and to be with him. But, on the other hand, we don't want him to get too close and take control of our lives. We're willing to sacrifice some things for Christ, especially if we find this convenient or satisfying to our ego, but we're unwilling to let go of other things, especially if the cost is too great or the changes are too demanding.

A second reason could be that we become complacent and self-satisfied. After all, in the past we have been loyal to our family and dedicated to our job. Moreover, we've been quite generous in our contributions to mission appeals, clothing collections and emergency relief funds. But it seems that as soon as we start to congratulate ourselves, we begin to settle down and slowly slip into mediocrity. We find ourselves beginning to say: "So what if we cheat or steal a little? What difference does it make if I read a dirty book or look at an indecent movie?" Pride preceding a fall is not an uncommon experience.

Perhaps a third reason why we are half-hearted in our quest for Christ is that we become discouraged too easily and lack determination. We look behind and see the many times we've fallen into the same old sin. We look ahead and wonder how we're going to meet all the demands made on us to love one another. Unlike Bonnington and Paul, we don't have their intense determination. We hesitate to let go of whatever holds us back from Christ, and to reach out in faith for the things that will bring us closer to him—things like prayer, fasting and almsgiving.

Lent is an opportune time to review how well we've been climbing with Christ to the top of Mt. Calvary. It is a time to put aside the sins that lie behind us by receiving forgiveness in the Sacrament of Reconciliation. It is a time to push ahead to a new life with Christ by fixing our attention on him through the reading of Scripture and seeing his face in the poor and the needy. Lent is a time to strip away our self-complacency and to renew our determination to endure any hardship for Christ.

First Sunday of Easter
1 Cor 5:6-8

New Unleavened Bread

Actress Gail Storm is making a comeback in her career and personal life. For many years she and her husband Lee Bonnell led a storybook, Hollywood life. They had been happily married for over thirty years, their four children were doing well, Gail was enjoying the dinner theatre circuit, and Lee was a successful insurance executive.

But Gail gradually overextended herself with too many commitments to television shows and theatrical performances. She began drinking more and more to relax until she became an alcoholic. Recovery was no easy task. She went through four hospital programs before regaining control of herself.

Since then she has spoken openly about her alcoholism on the PBS series *Over Easy* and goes every weekend to a hospital to help other alcoholics. She did a volunteer television commercial about the dangers of drinking. Now, at age fifty-five, she believes that "the best of life is still ahead."

Gail Storm must feel a thrill when she hears St. Paul's Easter message to the Corinthians: "Get rid of the old yeast to make of yourselves fresh dough, unleavened loaves, as it were; Christ our Passover has been sacrificed. Let us celebrate not with the old yeast, that of corruption and wickedness, but with the unleavened bread of sincerity and truth."

Yeast or leaven is a mixed metaphor in Scripture. In the gospels our Lord uses it as a symbol of the inner dynamism of the Kingdom of God. But in Jewish literature it stands for a corrupting influence since leaven was leftover dough which had fermented. So in preparation for the Passover the Jews were commanded by the Law to get rid of any yeast found in their homes and to bake only fresh, unleavened bread.

This is the sense in which Paul uses the metaphor. Christ's death and resurrection is the new Passover. To celebrate this new Pasch, Paul urges Christians to rid themselves of the old leaven of corruption and wickedness, and to let themselves be nourished by the unleavened bread of sincerity and truth.

That is why Gail Storm can get excited by these words from Paul. She has rid herself of the old yeast of alcoholism and self-pity, and is celebrating life again with the new unleavened bread of self-control and caring for others. She has in a sense written her own Easter story in passing over like our Lord from death to life.

This can be our Easter story too in some way. If we search our lives like the Jews searched their homes, we will find some old leaven there that we should get rid of. It might be stubbornness in dealing with our spouse, impatience with our children, unfriendliness toward our next door neighbor, or dishonesty with our employer. Whatever the old leaven is we can't be authentic *Easter* people until we get rid of it and celebrate life with the fresh unleavened bread of understanding, patience, love and truth.

If our Easter "Alleluias" are going to be sincere, then we have to remove the old yeast of petty preoccupations with trifles, brooding over lost opportunities, and bitterness because of broken relationships. We have to replace it with the fresh dough of ultimate concerns, discovering new options, and establishing new relationships.

We can't do this alone. But because Christ has already made the Passover from death to life by his resurrection, it is possible for us to make our own passage from sin and darkness—to grace and light. Because the risen Christ is with us through the power of his Spirit, we can experience our own exodus from slavery and suffering—to freedom and glory.

Second Sunday of Easter
Rv 1:9-19

Aslan the Lion

The Chronicles of Narnia are a famous fantasy adventure written by the late C.S. Lewis. Its opening story *The Lion, the Witch and the Wardrobe* was recently shown in animated form on TV. The story is a Christian allegory of the death and resurrection of Christ. It deals with four children in a magical land of Narnia, which the children reach by going through the back of a wardrobe.

One of them, Edmund, is tempted by a wicked witch into betrayal, allowing the witch to cast her spell over them. A great lion, Aslan, submits to execution to atone for the betrayal. Aslan is led and bound to a stone table where he is mocked, spat upon and shorn of his beautiful mane. He dies on this table when the witch plunges a stone knife through his heart. Then, through deep magic, the great lion roars back to life. He empowers the four children and others to fight against the witch and defeat her. The children become royalty in the now lovely land of Narnia.

This fairy tale about the great lion Aslan is reminiscent of the Son of Man in John's vision in the Book of Revelation. In one scene the Son of Man speaks to John: "There is nothing to fear. I am the First and the Last and the One who lives. Once I was dead but now I live—forever and ever."

This may be a vision John had, but it is certainly no fairy tale. It is a tenet of our faith. We believe that Jesus Christ did die on the cross to atone for our sins and that he was raised from the dead to lead us into glory. The Easter story may have much that is mystery about it, but it is no myth in the ordinary sense. It is a proclamation by the apostle that something extraordinary happened on that first Easter Sunday—Jesus was dead and now he is alive.

The apostles were not eyewitnesses of the event of Jesus being raised from the dead. They couldn't give us a videotape replay of what happened. But they did experience the appearances and the presence of the Risen Lord after he left the tomb, and they did leave us a written record in the gospels of their reflections about the effect these appearances had on them.

Since then thousands of Christians like us have also experienced the Risen Lord in someway, and we too have had our lives profoundly affected because of that. There is a song written by the Gaithers entitled *Because He Lives* which describes some of the effects of Christ's resurrection in their lives: "Because he lives I can face tomorrow. All fear is gone because I know he holds the future. And life is worth the living just because he lives."

Because Jesus was dead and now lives, we can face tomorrow with its uncertainties and challenges, its pains and joys, its troubles and delights. Because Jesus lives, all fear is gone about finding money to meet our expenses, about our future in a new marriage or job, about whether we'll fail again in our battle against drugs or drink. Because Jesus lives, life is worth living in spite of our past mistakes and foolishness, the loss of our spouse or health, being hurt or rejected.

Praise our great Lion, then, because he died on the cross on Calvary to save us. Give glory to him, because he roared back to life and leads us to victory.

Third Sunday of Easter
Rv 5:11-14

You're a Good Man, Jesus Christ

You're a Good Man, Charlie Brown is a delightful comedy based on the popular Peanuts comic strip in the daily newspaper. But it's also an insightful play about us—our fears and dreams, failures and successes, loneliness and friendships.

In this play Charlie Brown's gang gathers around him to sing the title song of the play, *You're a Good Man, Charlie Brown*. This is similar to our joining the thousands of living creatures in the Book of Revelation to sing: "Worthy is the Lamb that was slain to receive power and riches, wisdom and strength, honor and glory and praise."

In other words, we're saying, "You're a good man, Jesus Christ, because you laid down your life for us. You're a good God, Lord, because you rose from the dead to give us a share in your own life."

But our words of praise will be empty unless we also perform the works of Christ. Perhaps what the Rev. Jesse Jackson said about following Dr. Martin Luther King Jr. also applies to our own following of Christ. The occasion of Jackson's words was the 9th anniversary of King's assassination.

Jackson wrote: "It's not the *death* of a man that has the potential to save society. It's the *life* of a man. The challenge to each of us is not merely to *admire* Dr. King, but to *follow* him. We should consider the unfinished business of Dr. King. Wouldn't he still be working to end hunger and find jobs? Would he ignore the challenges of drugs and decadence—of hatred and violence? Don't honor Martin Luther King Jr. merely with words; do his works. Stop hating and killing. Feed the hungry and be merciful to the oppressed. By these works, his *followers* will be separated from his *admirers*. And the world will still know that the king lives."

It is no different in our relationship to Christ. Because he sacrificed his life for us, Christ is indeed worthy of honor and glory. But unless we do Christ's works, our words of praise will be empty. If the world is going to know us as his disciples and not just as his admirers, then it has to see us carrying out his unfinished work.

People will know we are Christians by the way we challenge the evils of our own day, evils such as abortion, pornography and prejudice. People will know that Christ is at the center of our lives by the way we respect him in others, especially as we find him in the disadvantaged, the handicapped and the neglected. The world will know that Christ still lives by the way we continue his saving actions—bringing healing where there are hurts, light where there is darkness, and gentleness where there is violence.

During the Easter season we sing a lot of Alleluias to the Lamb that was slain and rose from the dead. But alleluias without love are meaningless. As Jesse Jackson pointed out, we can't just praise great men like Dr. King and Jesus Christ to honor them. We have to pursue the ideals they left us and complete the work they began. We have to be the ones today who will bring unity where there is division, justice where there is oppression, and peace where there is strife. That is why we begin our liturgies with songs of praise and thanksgiving, but end with challenges to love and serve one another.

Fourth Sunday of Easter
Rv 7:9, 14-17

Winners

In 1977 Canadian Jerome Drayton was the winner of the grueling Boston Marathon. He completed the murderous 26.2 mile course in 2 hours, 14 minutes and 46 seconds.

A writer once compared the Boston Marathon to Dante's Inferno. You see thousands of runners in various stages of extreme exhaustion—some trotting weakly, others staggering along unevenly, others just dragging themselves to walk.

When Jerome Drayton finished first in the race, he put his swollen feet into cool water and announced that he would never again run the Boston Marathon. Never again would he have to fight off the challenge of more than 3,000 runners. Never again would he have to make that excruciating ascent of Heartbreak Hill near the end of the course.

The honor and glory bestowed on Jerome Drayton for winning the Boston Marathon is something like the honor and glory bestowed on the saints in heaven. St. John describes them in his Book of Revelation: "They stood before the throne dressed in white robes with palm branches in their hands. These are the ones who have survived the great period of trial. Never again shall they know hunger or thirst, nor shall the sun beat down on them. For the Lamb on the throne will lead them to springs of life-giving water."

All of us are hero-worshipers at heart. We admire champions like Jerome Drayton because their deeds declare that we can overcome great difficulties. We identify with saints like Thomas

255

More and Joan of Arc because their martyrdom is a statement that we can survive intense trials.

All of us have to undergo difficulties in this life—difficulties with our own personal growth because of our fears, worries and anxieties; difficulties with our family because of our hurts, angers and resentments; difficulties with people with whom we work because of our disagreements, irritations and frustrations.

But thanks to the victory won by Christ's resurrection we can conquer all these difficulties. We too can join the ranks of the saints crowned with glory before the throne of God.

Some of us have to suffer intense trials in this life—enduring a prolonged sickness because of some disease; becoming crippled because of an accident; losing our home because of a fire or flood. But thanks to the power that comes from Christ's resurrection we can survive all these trials. We too can stand with the saints to celebrate our triumph with the risen Lord.

The Easter season is intended to strengthen our courage in the struggles we still have to make, and to sustain our hopes during the trials we still have to go through. As long as we live in this world there will always be some Heartbreak Hill we still have to climb; there will always be one more problem to solve, injury to heal, disappointment to bear.

But these are opportunities for us to share in the Passion of Christ. As long as we stay close to Christ we know that we're going to end up winners; we know that we're going to arrive at that day when we will never have to hunger or thirst again; we know that Jesus himself will lead us to the springs of life-giving water.

Fifth Sunday of Easter
Rv 21:1-5

Renaissance Center

The city of Detroit has a new Renaissance Center consisting of five spectacular skyscrapers located alongside the Detroit River. It was the city's response to a steady decline that had been taking place because of increasing crime, rising costs, abandoned houses and a deteriorating downtown. Although its new Renaissance Center was never designed as a total solution to the city's problems, it did mark the beginning of a rebirth in Detroit, a new Motor City.

What is happening in Detroit is only a faint preview of what will happen to the world at the end of time. John's vision in the Book of Revelation tries to picture for us this ultimate renaissance: "I, John, saw a new Jerusalem, the holy city, coming down out of heaven from God, beautiful as a bride prepared to meet her husband. The One who sat on the throne said to me, 'See, I make all things new.'"

What will happen, then, at the end of time is something truly magnificent. Instead of being destroyed, the world will be transformed into glory. Instead of disintegrating, the world will have its hidden beauty fully revealed.

Moreover, we will share in this renaissance. By our own resurrection we too will participate in this new birth of God's creation. This is the good news of Easter—the Lord makes all things new.

Furthermore, we don't have to wait until the end of time to experience this. Even now we see new things being made by the

257

Lord. Every Spring the Lord gives us fresh blossoms so that we can feel renewed. Every Summer the Lord sends new rains so that we can have new harvests in the Fall.

In every family there is sickness and death. But the Lord makes all things new by weddings and ordinations, by births and baptisms. At the end of every school year graduates receive their diplomas. Their commencement exercises symbolize the beginning of a new era and new adventures.

When we stop and look around we see that we are surrounded by all kinds of gifts from the Lord, gifts that make all things new for us. There are stores filled with new clothes and new cars to make us feel good; theatres with new plays and new movies to refresh our spirits; places of employment with new jobs and new opportunities waiting for us; new books to read and new music to hear to enrich us; new places to visit and new people to meet to awaken our interests; new needs to meet and new services to render to challenge our generosity. We are surrounded with newness to relieve our boredom and stimulate our ambitions; to break our monotony and excite our imaginations.

When we stop and look at the liturgy, again we see ourselves surrounded by newness: new signs of forgiveness in the Sacrament of Reconciliation; newly consecrated bread in the Sacrament of the Eucharist; new words of inspiration in the reading of Sacred Scripture.

It's impossible then for Christians to be pessimists because the Lord is always starting a renaissance somewhere. It's unthinkable for Christians to be depressed very long by defeat because the Lord is renewing our lives in so many ways. It's inconceivable for Christians to be sad for any length of time even in the midst of suffering because the Lord makes all things new.

Sixth Sunday of Easter
Rv 21:10-14, 22-23

City Lights

One of the famous sights of Chicago is its skyline illuminated in part at night by the bright lights shining upon the Wrigley Building. These lights make both the Wrigley Building and the city of Chicago radiant with glory.

During the energy crisis of early 1975 these lights were dimmed for the first time since the Second World War. For several months the Wrigley Building was darkened. The effects were evident. Without these lights the city of Chicago lost some of its splendor and spirit. Without the brilliance of its famous building the city lost some of its glamour and vitality.

A place like Chicago needs its lights to flourish as a city. What a contrast with the holy city of Jerusalem envisioned by St. John when he writes: "It gleamed with the splendor of God. The city had the radiance of a precious jewel that sparkled like a diamond. The city had no need of sun or moon, for the glory of God gave it light, and its lamp was the Lamb."

Without a source of light a big city like Chicago becomes paralyzed. Its risk of crime increases and its cultural activities are curtailed. It's not that much different with us.

On the one hand, without Christ as the light of our life we become vulnerable to sadness and depression, to selfishness and self-pity. We become defenseless against temptations to greed and materialism, to sensuality and dishonesty. On the other hand, with Christ as the light of our life we begin to see ourselves surrounded with radiance instead of darkness, with brightness instead of shadows.

The lyrics of Debbie Boone's hit *You Light Up My Life* express this same theme in song. Another popular song along these lines is *Those Who See Light*. One of its verses reads: "Those who see light can walk in the dark. Those who look up will discover God's face. Those who look down will uncover his path."

In other words, with Christ as our light we become more sensitive to his presence in nature and in people. We become aware of his guidance in ordinary events in the sacraments. Moreover, with Christ as our light we can see sufferings as occasions to advance in wisdom, problems as opportunities to grow in maturity, and setbacks as chances to develop character.

We have no need then to rely on drugs or drinks to make us feel good. The Lord is our light and that is enough for us. We have no need to become rich or famous to find fulfillment. The Lord is our light and his glory our glory.

Unlike the Wrigley Building which has its own source of light we depend on Christ for our light. But like the Wrigley Building we become reflectors of the light shining upon us. With the light of our faith we can help others walk in the dark, even in the dark of death; we can help others discover God's face, even in the person who hurts them; we can help others uncover God's path, even in the midst of confusion.

Seventh Sunday of Easter
Rv 22:12-20

Come

Hannah Hurnard's book *Hind's Feet on High Places* is an allegory which narrates the story of how a young girl named Much-Afraid escaped from the Valley of Humiliation and went to the High Places. Much-Afraid was an unsightly, crippled girl with a crooked mouth that marred her appearance and speech, and crooked feet that made her limp. Moreover, her life was made more miserable by her own family of Fearings who tormented her.

But one day the Shepherd invites her to come to the High Places where no Fears of any kind exist, blemishes are healed, a new name is given and only love prevails. Much-Afraid accepts his invitation and begins her arduous and rugged journey.

With each crisis Much-Afraid encounters along the way, she learns to believe, trust and obey the Shepherd as he leads her to higher places. Finally she reaches the summit where she hears the Shepherd say: "This is the time when you are to receive the fulfillment of the promise. Never again am I to call you Much-Afraid. From henceforth your new name is Grace-and-Glory."

The shepherd's invitation to come to higher places in this allegory parallels the invitation we find in the epilogue of the Book of Revelation: "The Spirit and the Bride say, 'Come!' Let him who hears answer, 'Come!' Let him who is thirsty come forward; let all who desire it accept the gift of life-giving water. The One who gives this testimony says, 'Yes, I am coming soon!' Amen! Come, Lord Jesus!"

Phrases using the word "come" are used seven times in the

epilogue as if to emphasize its significance and impress us with its urgency. The invitation to "come" is given by Christ; his bride, the Church; and his Spirit. It is timeless and contemporary; it is given in every age, and it is given to us now.

The invitation takes on many forms: maybe a summons to leave behind our fears, worries and self-hatred, and to come into possession of confidence, calm and self-esteem; perhaps a call to abandon behavior that is destroying our family life, wounding other people or causing discontent where we work, and to move toward a new agenda of building up, healing and peacemaking.

Another possibility is the invitation in the form of a challenge to become more than what we are—to let go of our present position in personal growth, social relationships or prayer life, and to move into deeper self-discovery, keener sensitivity about other's feelings and closer intimacy with the Lord.

We need to hear the Lord's word's "I am coming soon," especially when we experience some of the things Much-Afraid did in the allegory: having Sorrow and Suffering for companions; confronting Bitterness and Self-Pity on the shores of loneliness; forced to take detours through the desert; injuring ourselves making steep ascents; going around in circles in the forest of mist; being stripped of all our gains in the valley of loss.

We need to hear Jesus say, "I am coming soon," whenever we come to grips with our own poverty and emptiness, get discouraged by our own futile efforts and failures, or lose sight of our vision or dream of glory.

But we shouldn't have to wait for extreme situations to cry, "Come, Lord Jesus." It should be our call everyday, every hour, every moment; our constant invitation to let him share our successes and triumphs, too; our adventures and explorations; our joys and ecstasies.

Trinity Sunday
Rm 5:1-5

Oh, God

When John Denver was interviewed about the movie *Oh, God* he said: "The point of the picture is that God, in form of George Burns, is coming down to talk to somebody in order to let the world know he exists and that we should cherish all the things given to us." So even though *Oh, God* was made for light comedy, its essential message is a serious one. The film makes us laugh at the one-liners George Burns throws at us, but it also makes us reflect on how sincere we are in our relationship to God.

In a sense, *Oh, God* may even tell us something about the mystery of the Holy Trinity. First, God is not dead. He exists and he cares about the world. This is God the Father. Second, God wants to speak to us. So he assumed the human form of a retiree we can see and hear. This is Jesus Christ, God the Son. Third, God has given man the means to find peace on earth—his love poured into our hearts. This is God the Holy Spirit.

The movie's message about the Holy Trinity, then, may be taken as a reflection of what Scripture tells us about one God and three Persons. In St. Paul's letter to the Romans we hear: "Now that we are justified by faith we are at peace with God through our Lord Jesus Christ. Through him we boast of our hope for the glory of God. And this hope will not leave us disappointed, because the love of God has been poured into our hearts through the Holy Spirit who has been given to us."

Admittedly Paul's words are not as simple or humorous as the lines in the movie *Oh, God*. But when you compare their meaning they are essentially the same. First, the Person of God the Father cares very much for us and wants to share his glory with us. Second, God the Son took on human form in the Person of Jesus Christ to speak God's word and to justify or reconcile us with God. Third, the Person of the Holy Spirit is the love of God that has been poured into our hearts so that we might love one another.

Neither Paul nor the movie explain the mystery of the Holy Trinity. No one can do that. But at least they give us some insight about how God reveals himself as three distinct Persons, yet sharing one divine nature. They also give us some suggestions about how this mystery may affect our lives.

Like the Father we should be concerned about the world and show genuine care for one another. The material world, with its rich resources of water, food and oil, should be respected, not destroyed; used wisely, not wasted. We may be different in race, color and culture, but as God's children we should care for and cooperate with one another in sharing the resources of the world.

Like Jesus Christ we should make God present in human form. Through us, people should be able to see forgiveness in action, feel the touch of a helping hand and hear words of comfort.

Like the Holy Spirit it should be through us that the love of God is poured out into the hearts of others. Through us the poor and the lonely should be able to feel this love of God as something real. Through us the lost and the outcast should be able to experience for themselves what the love of God means.

Corpus Christi
1 Cor 11:23-26

Handing Over

At Chicago's O'Hare Airport one of the refuelers for American Airlines is a man named Robert Wood. He is a thirty-three year old bachelor, but a foster father to twenty-five children. Robert Wood supports these twenty-five children through charitable agencies all over the world at the cost of $300 a month. He writes daily to two or three of the children and has visited some in their own countries. "I wish I were rich," he says. "It's a beautiful experience to sponsor a child."

Another person who is a foster parent is Mrs. Bridget Donahue. She raised nine children of her own on a Michigan farm and twenty-six foster children, accomplishing most of this by herself after her husband died in 1933. One of her foster sons is a Maryknoll missionary, Fr. Joe Corso. "In the Donahue home," Fr. Corso says, "I came to experience love and happiness. Ma Donahue's generosity made us children more deeply aware of our own attitude toward others."

Robert Wood and Mrs. Bridget Donahue are two people who know what it means to love and to give; who understand the significance of the Eucharist as sharing and giving. This is the meaning brought out by St. Paul in his first letter to the Corinthians.

"I received from the Lord what I handed on to you, namely, that the Lord Jesus Christ on the night in which he was betrayed took bread and said, 'This is my body, which is for you.' In the same, way, he took the cup, saying, 'This cup is the new covenant in my blood. Do this, whenever you drink it, in remembrance of me.' "

In the Greek text the two words for "handed on" and "betrayed" are very close in spelling and sound. It may be word play on Paul's part to underline this one particular aspect of the Eucharist, namely the Eucharist as handing over or giving.

The whole public life of Jesus was a giving of himself to the people. His entire ministry was a service of giving in teaching, consoling, forgiving and healing. It was the same in his Passion. At the Last Supper he gave us his body and blood in the Eucharist. In the garden he gave himself over to those who came to arrest him, On the cross he gave forgiveness to the crowd, faith to the centurion, paradise to the thief and his mother to John.

So when Jesus gives us the Eucharist and says, "Do this in remembrance of me," he is not just telling us to reenact the Last Supper; he is telling us to love and to give the way he did. "Give," he says, "some of your material goods to the poor and your time to the lonely. Give some of your attention to the unloved and your work to the helpless. Discover the joy of generosity like Robert Wood did. Experience the satisfaction of sharing like Mrs. Donahue did."

The Eucharist, then, is not just a gift we receive from the Lord for ourselves. It is a gift we are commanded to hand over to others. The Christ we receive under the forms of bread and wine has to be given over to others under the forms of forgiveness and reconciliation, care and compassion, hospitality and sharing.

There is an oriental verse by Lao-Tse which summarizes this purpose of the Eucharist. "Kindness in words creates confidence. Kindness in thinking creates profoundness. Kindness in *giving* creates *love*."

Second Sunday of the Year
1 Cor 12:4-11

Variety of Gifts

One of Hollywood's movies that has made its way into television viewing is *That's Entertainment*. It is a film that features memorable scenes from nearly one hundred musical classics produced by MGM. Among the unforgettable acts are dancing routines by Fred Astaire, romantic singing by Bing Crosby and swimming pageants featuring Esther Williams.

In watching *That's Entertainment* one has to be struck by the magnificent variety of talented people MGM has had perform in their films. These talented performers deserve to be called movie stars, because like the stars in the sky they shine with their own unique brilliance and individual beauty. Moreover, like the stars in the sky they shine for our enjoyment, entertainment and delight.

Such a variety of talents for the good of others is similar to what St. Paul describes in his writings to the Corinthians: "There are different gifts but the same Spirit; there are different ministries but the same Lord; there are different works but the same God who accomplishes all of them in everyone. To each person the manifestation of the Spirit is given for the common good."

Paul then proceeds to list nine examples of the wonderful variety of God's gifts to the Corinthian community. At the end of his listing he again stresses their common source—God—and their common purpose—the good of the community.

When we look over our own family and parish community the situation is not unlike that of the Corinthian community. There is a tremendous variety in the gifts we have from God—in occupational skills some of us are craftsmen or tradesmen, others are cooks or seamstresses; in artistic talents some of us are musicians or singers, others are writers or painters; in interpersonal qualities some of us are strong leaders or organizers, others are good listeners or available helpers; in spiritual gifts some of us have immense faith or indestructible hope, others have a capacity to pray or interpret Scripture.

What a splendid diversity in the gifts we have received from God. On the one hand, then, there is no reason for us to ever be downcast or discouraged—we all have special and unique gifts that make us shine like stars in the sight of God. On the other hand, there is also no reason for us to be proud or boastful—whatever we have as talents comes from God as their source and not ourselves.

With the gifts comes an awesome responsibility—the gifts are given to us not only to enrich us personally, but also to serve the community, to help those around us.

When we understand what Paul teaches, there is no room for rivalry or jealousy because others have gifts we don't have. Nor is there room for self-satisfaction or complacency because we are richly endowed with gifts others don't have. Our diversity is a call to unity, and our talents are a call to ministry.

In his book *The Joy of Being Human* psychologist Eugene Kennedy makes some remarks that underline Paul's viewpoint: "The world abounds with God's gifts, for they all have a human face. Everything that the rest of the human family has given to us is a gift to each of us—one that makes us aware of our responsibility to be equally generous to those as yet unborn. Charisms are gifts we have to give away—gifts that shrivel in our hands when we clutch them selfishly; gifts that get larger when we share them with others. The man who discovers that what he has been given is to be given in turn to others has come close to discovering the meaning of life."

When movie stars rejoice in their talents and share them with us on the screen—*That's Entertainment*. When we celebrate the special gifts God gives us and use them for the common good—*That's Life in the Spirit.*

Third Sunday of the Year
1 Cor 12:12-30

One Body

One year in Gary, Indiana the public schools were closed for two weeks because of a labor strike by the school janitors and secretaries. This closing of the schools showed how a school system is like a human body. It is one body, but composed of many parts—tax payers, school boards, administrators, teachers, students, office helpers, building custodians, and so on.

In order to operate properly, each part of this vast system must perform its own particular function. When one part of the school system is out of order, the whole system suffers, as happened during the Gary strike when there was no teaching or learning going on for two weeks.

This is something like what St. Paul was afraid would happen to the Christian community at Corinth. So he tried to impress upon them the importance of their unity in Christ: "The body is one and has many members, but all the members, many though they are, are one body. And so it is with Christ. If one member suffers, all the members suffer with it. If one member is honored, all the members share its joy."

For Paul this was not merely a metaphor. It was a reality. He doesn't say that the Church is like a body. He says it *is* the body of Christ. In a very real sense we are grafted into Christ through baptism and share in his risen life.

Moreover, this is not a private or individual incorporation. The whole Christian community is grafted into the body of Christ so that we are joined with each other as different members.

The practical consequences of this are staggering. Our union with each other in Christ transcends all distinction of race or nationality. We are no longer divided as Jew or Greek, Irish or British, black or white. We are all connected now as members of the one body of Christ and our fellowship with each other goes beyond any differences of status, education or wealth. We are no longer segregated as slave or free, slum dweller or suburb dweller. We are all bound together now as believers in Christ.

This is not to say that all individual differences between us are blurred into a dull uniformity. We need the variety of different cultures, ethnic customs and individual talents to add beauty to the body of Christ. But it is to say that we must set aside all the irrelevant distinctions that keep us divided, and substitute instead the common elements that bind us together in Christ—our faith, the Bible, the sacraments.

If only we could realize how much we need one another for our vitality, we would set aside our suspicions and fears, and instead mutually embrace and support one another.

If only we could understand that when one of us hurts we all hurt, we would set aside our indifference and aloofness, and instead reach out with loving concern and care for our suffering members.

If only we could appreciate how important the contribution by each member is to the growth of the body of Christ, we would cease ignoring or overlooking our brother's efforts, and instead thank him and praise him for his special service.

The Eucharist in which we participate is a sign of the common life we share in the one body of Christ. But it will be an empty sign unless we validate it by a genuine interest in each other's welfare, by a mutual bearing of every member's burdens, and by a sincere celebration of one another's successes.

Fourth Sunday of the Year
1 Cor 12:31-13:13

Gandhi and Paul on Love

More than 400 biographies have been written about Mahatma Gandhi, that great spiritual and political leader of India who devoted more than 50 years of his life to the cause of peace and freedom. In one of the more recent books about him, entitled *Mahatma Gandhi and His Apostles*, author Ved Mehta cites these words of Gandhi: "It is my firm belief that it is love that sustains the earth. There only is life where there is love. Life without love is death. Love never claims, it ever gives. Love ever suffers, never resents, never revenges itself."

Gandhi's description of love corresponds closely to St. Paul's famous passage in his letter to the Corinthians: "Love is patient, love is kind. Love is never rude, it is not self-seeking. Love does not rejoice in what is wrong but rejoices with the truth. There is no limit to love's forebearance, to its trust, its hope, its power to endure."

When we compare these edifying descriptions of love with the grinding realities of everyday life, we wonder about their accuracy. Every now and then we see outstanding examples of love, such as the selfless service of a Dr. Schweitzer in Africa or a Mother Teresa in Calcutta. But great feats of love like these seem more like footnotes in the history of man. Hatred and violence seem to make up most of our reading in history.

Occasionally we witness an individual act of kindness during rush hour traffic or a demonstration of patience by some beleaguered parent. But these seem like isolated and disconnected acts.

Rudeness and impatience seem to prevail most of the time, especially when there is a shortage of something or when people are in a hurry.

When we hear people like St. Paul and Mahatma Gandhi talk about love with such glowing terms, we tend to dismiss them as visionaries out of touch with reality. Yet the fact remains that they *did* the very things they *described*. The indifference of people near them, the difficulties that surrounded them, and their own human weaknesses did not prevent them from giving themselves to others in loving service. It should be no less true of us.

Frequently we get too wrapped up in ourselves with our own feelings and needs. We might eat or drink too much to ease our tensions, or overindulge in spending money or in taking recreation to relieve our hurts. It is at times like these that we need to be reminded by men like Gandhi that love is not selfish but seeks the good of others.

Sometimes our best efforts to show care meet with ingratitude and hostility. We might make immense sacrifices for our spouse, our children or our closest friend, and yet in return get nothing but rejection and resentment. It is at times like these that we need the example of men like Paul to realize that there is no limit to love's forebearance and its power to endure.

Often the demands for love about us seem greater than what we can supply. Cries for love come from as far away as South Africa and as near as our ghettos and prisons. It is at times like these that we need to look to Christ to see that love never fails, regardless of how great the demand becomes.

We may never be able to write poetry about love like Paul or have books written about our acts of love like Gandhi, but that isn't important. What is important is that we understand what they did about love: love is essentially the giving of ourselves to others joyously and generously. What is important is that we experience what they did of love: love liberating us from selfishness and leading us into happiness and peace.

Fifth Sunday of the Year
1 Cor 15:1-11

Roots

When the drama *Roots* was shown on television for the first time in 1977, it made a powerful impact on the American people. This story of author Alex Haley's twelve-year search to trace seven generations of his family ancestors motivated thousands of people to delve into their own roots to discover more about their identity.

In an interview Alex Haley said: "One of the most powerful things in the world is to have a strong sense of one's family history and of one's worth. I'm hoping beyond everything else that *Roots* will give my people a heightened sense of identity. In my book I tell how for centuries the Africans have had their birth rituals wherein the father holds up his newborn infant and whispers the child's name three times in his ears to make sure that he, alone, is the first to know who he is."

St. Paul too talks about roots, the roots of our Christian faith: "Brothers, I handed on to you first of all what I myself received, that Christ died for our sins, that he was buried, and, in accord with the Scriptures, rose on the third day. This is what we preach, and this is what you believe."

According to Paul the roots of our Christian faith are the death, burial and resurrection of Christ. The essence of our identity as Christians is our belief in the person of Jesus Christ. This is the tradition and the good news that Paul received from others and which he now hands on to us. This is the gospel message that transformed his whole life, so much so that he described himself as one who was reborn.

As this Christian faith has been transmitted down through the centuries it has inspired martyrs like St. Agnes and monks like St. Benedict, spurred on humanitarians like St. Hedwig and missionaries like St. Francis Xavier, motivated married people like St. Elizabeth Ann Seton and ministers like St. John Neumann.

If only we had a deep understanding of our roots as Christians, we too would share in Paul's enthusiasm about Christ and be ready to leave everything in order to follow Christ. If only we could appreciate what it cost Christ to purchase us as his precious people, we too would be willing to sacrifice anything for him.

When we know who we are—people who are special in the eyes of the Lord—we can overcome any obstacle, whether it be prejudice or ingratitude from the outside, or feelings of insecurity or self-pity from the inside. When we reflect on our Christian identity, we discover, like the black people in the story *Roots*, a capacity to endure any suffering, whether it be sickness or slavery, a slight disappointment or a crushing degradation.

To be aware of one's history and tradition is a source of strength in which we can find a resilience to recover from any setback, whether it be the loss of a loved one or the destruction of something dear to us. To be conscious of our proud heritage as Christians expands our capacity to see light where others see only darkness and sustain hope when others would despair.

Such is the power of our identity with Christ. Yes, we still have to suffer with him, and even die with him, but we can do this freely—even joyously—because we already know that his victory is our victory. Yes, we can hold our heads high because as Christians we know where we came from—we've been reborn in Christ—and we know where our destiny leads us—reunion with Christ when he comes again in glory.

Sixth Sunday of the Year
1 Cor 15:12-20

First Fruits

During World War II a certain city church in London was all set for a harvest thanksgiving. In the center of the gifts there was a sheaf of corn. The service was never held, for on that Saturday night there was an air raid and the church was destroyed by bombs.

On the bomb site where the church lay in ruins there appeared shoots of green in the spring. All through the summer these shoots grew until they were harvested as corn in the autumn. Not even the bombs and ruins could kill the life of the corn and its seeds. Life was stronger than death.

This is the same conviction St. Paul had when he wrote: "If Christ was not raised, your faith is worthless. But as it is, Christ has been raised from the dead, the first fruits of those who have fallen asleep."

Seeds fall into the ground and die. Yet new life emerges. Christ was crucified and died on the cross. Yet he rose to a new glorified life. His resurrection is the final proof that life is stronger than death.

Christ's resurrection makes all the difference for us. Without it our faith is worthless, our hopes are futile, and our life is senseless. But with the resurrection our faith becomes a sun scattering the night, our hopes an anchor in the midst of storms, and our life a planting for our own thanksgiving harvest.

Without the resurrection our time spent in prayer would be wasted, our efforts at honesty and purity would be pointless, and our concern for the poor and oppressed would be foolish. But with the resurrection, our prayer turns into a chorus of praise, our struggles with honesty and purity become builders of character, and our compassion for others leads to our own liberation.

If Christ has not been raised from the dead, then why not have abortions when it is convenient, promote pornography when it is profitable or change marriage partners when we get bored? But as it is, Christ *has* been raised from the dead, and, consequently, we must respect the life of the unborn, the aged and the imprisoned; insist on decency in literature and on the screen; and uphold the sanctity of marriage as a sign of Christ's love for the Church.

Sometimes it seems as if the forces of evil are going to prevail. Today's rising rates of crime, divorce and political scandals seem to bear this out. But like seeds of corn that proved to be indestructible and the beginning of new life, so too is our faith in the resurrection of Christ. It is indestructible in the midst of difficulties or disappointments, mental sufferings or physical sickness, ridicule or persecution. It is the beginning of new life in the face of failure or loss, tragedy or death.

Writer James Carroll once made a list of reasons why we should give up trying to build a better society. Nevertheless, he insisted that though there was reason to feel this way, biblical faith thought otherwise. He wrote: "When the times call for resignation, the Word of God calls for boldness. Where the times give us excuses to despair, the Word of God insists on fidelity. Faith and prayer are never more important than when they appear to be foolish and irrelevant."

The source of Carroll's optimism is the fact that Christ has been raised from the dead, and with him a fallen world. As Paul pointed out, Christ's resurrection is the first fruits of those who have fallen asleep, the sign of the harvest that is yet to come and is already on the way. This is why we proclaim the mystery of our faith in the liturgy: "Dying you destroyed our death, rising you restored our life. Lord Jesus, come in glory."

Seventh Sunday of the Year
1 Cor 15:45-49

The Renaissance Man

Clay Falker is the new editor of *Esquire* magazine. His aim is to give *Esquire* a new image to conform to the needs of the new, ideal man of today. The Renaissance man of the modern world is no longer interested in merely making money, driving a sleek car and admiring beautiful women. Although the new man still prizes these things, he values other things much more. The Renaissance man measures success now more by self-development and richness of life; he is absorbed with getting in touch with his feelings, personal growth and self-actualization; he is more devoted to enriching his leisure life with new hobbies and his professional life with new skills.

There are many appealing features about the new man. The same would be true of the Renaissance woman if we were to develop a similar model for her out of *Vogue* magazine. We would all like to be more self-developed and experience more of the richness of life. Nevertheless, this new image is as nothing compared to another image that should shape us. This is the image of Jesus Christ, the perfect model of what a man or woman should be, the second man St. Paul talks about in his letter to the Corinthians: "The first man was of earth, formed from dust, the second is from heaven. Just as we resemble the man from earth, so shall we bear the likeness of the man from heaven."

The context in which Paul says this is his discussion of the resurrection with Corinthians, and, in particular, the difference between the natural body we have now and the spiritual body we will have after the resurrection. Without denying all the human values so dear to *Esquire's* new man or *Vogue's* ideal woman, Paul asserts that there are spiritual values which are more important.

We can become a perfect duplicate of the *Esquire* or *Vogue* magazine model, but if we don't develop the spiritual dimension of our lives according to the Bible, we are still incomplete as human beings. We can wear the latest fashions in clothing and dance with the latest disco moves, but if we don't bear the likeness of Christ within us, our lives will be hollow and empty.

It may be good to learn about transactional analysis and psycho-cybernetics to become a more mature person. Nevertheless, it is also important to learn about the Sermon on the Mount to become more Christ-like. It is good to learn how to do the things that will enrich our professional and leisure life. Nevertheless, it is also important to learn how to do the things Jesus did: showing compassion to the poor; aiding the handicapped; welcoming the outcast; getting involved with people in trouble.

Part of our human task, then, is to improve ourselves on the natural level, to become a beautiful person—intelligent, charming, jovial. But our human task is also much more than that because our destiny goes beyond the natural order into the spiritual order of the resurrection. Our human development also means becoming more like Christ and bearing his likeness, so that when people meet us they can see the justice and strength of God; feel his kindness and forgiveness; experience his peace and love.

Thank the Lord for all his natural gifts to us and for all the opportunities we have to develop these gifts. Praise the Lord for all his spiritual gifts to us whereby we can become more and more like him to reflect his goodness in this world and his glory in heaven.

Eighth Sunday of the Year
1 Cor 15:54-58

Victory

During the 1960 Olympic Games in Rome nineteen year old Wilma Rudolph won three gold medals. It was the first time in the history of the games that an American woman had won three gold medals for running. Wilma Rudolph's record accomplishment is still more remarkable when you consider her background.

She was born in poverty in Tennessee, the twentieth of twenty-two black children. At age four Wilma was afflicted with double pneumonia and scarlet fever that caused her left leg to be paralyzed. Daily therapy enabled her at age eight to begin using her left leg again with a special reinforced high-top shoe. By age eleven she had discarded the special shoe and began running. She made her first Olympic team at fifteen and Olympic track history at nineteen with three gold medals.

Wilma Rudolph's early handicap and subsequent Olympic triumph gives us a faint idea of how death will be conquered by the resurrection. St. Paul says: "When the corruptible frame takes on incorruptibility and the mortal immortality, then will the saying of Scripture be fulfilled—'Death is swallowed up in victory.' Thanks be to God who has given us the victory through our Lord Jesus Christ."

Paul's words are taken from his reflections about the resurrection. The changes he describes and the victory he proclaims refer to the resurrection of our body. Using our example above, if Wilma Rudolph's handicapped frame took on swiftness and her weakness strength, how much greater are not the changes which Paul mentions regarding incorruptibility and immortality?

This would be too good to be true except that the victory has already been claimed for us by Jesus Christ when he was raised from the dead. All we have to do is accept this victory and make it our own. Christ's resurrection is our proof that even though true goodness is often crushed in the world, yet somehow it endures; even though total goodness in the person of Jesus was utterly destroyed and killed, yet indeed it triumphed in the end.

Lutheran minister Dr. Carl Braaten of the Chicago Divinity School once wrote: "On the cross it appeared that the life-giving love of God himself was cut down and that injustice had prevailed. So, too, in much that happens in the modern world—the strong trampling the weak—the corrupt exploiting the innocent—the rich victimizing the poor—disasters, wars and disease taking their toll—it appears as if violence and death have the final say. But Christ's resurrection proclaims that they *will not* win in the end."

Christ's resurrection promises that despite the worst that the world can inflict on the best, the best will triumph when it's all over. Justice, love and life will ultimately prove to be stronger than injustice, hatred and death.

The same applies to our own personal struggles. Sometimes it appears that a serious illness, intense loneliness or excessive anxieties will prevail over us and destroy us. But if we have faith in Christ and carry on the fight, we have his pledge that in the end, victory will be ours.

Despite the worst that can happen to us—becoming addicted to drugs or alcohol, losing our job, or having our marriage broken up—we can exclaim with Paul: "Thanks be to God who has given us the victory through our Lord Jesus Christ."

Ninth Sunday of the Year
Gal 1:1-10

Values

In June of 1979 Russian author Alexander Solzhenitsyn gave the commencement address at Harvard University. He charged the U.S. with losing its courage and destroying its spiritual life through a devotion to man's appetites instead of God's design. Solzhenitsyn cited sensationalism in the press, irresponsible freedom and movies full of crime and pornography as examples of how the West has lost its idealism and moral fibre.

The very next month President Carter addressed the nation concerning the energy crisis. He began by speaking about a more fundamental issue which he called a crisis of confidence in the American spirit. He said that in a nation that was proud of hard work, strong families and faith in God, too many of us now tend to worship self-indulgence and consumption. Instead of continuing on the path leading to self-interest and fragmentation, he urged us to return to the path of common purpose and American values.

What Solzhenitsyn and President Carter felt about the U.S. deserting its traditional values is similar to what St. Paul must have felt about the Galatians abandoning the gospel values. He writes: "I am amazed that you are so soon deserting him who called you in accord with his gracious design in Christ, and are going over to another gospel. But there is no other."

Since this is the beginning of Paul's letter it gives the keynote of what he has to say, especially about how Christians are justified by faith, not by works; are called to live in freedom, but not in irresponsible freedom; and are to fulfill the law of Christ by loving one another.

Basically the problems we face are the same as those of the Galatians. We have substituted other works in place of the Jewish law, but we still tend to believe to some extent that by doing them we will be saved. We think that if we give money to construct church buildings, get married in church and attend Sunday services, then we are good Christians. We may well be, but not if we forget that faith is a gift from God instead of something we do, or if we ignore the fact that discipleship means relationships with people in love and ministry instead of following a few rules.

We tend to abandon the radical values of the gospel whenever we selfishly hoard what we have without sharing with the poor; want freedom for ourselves and allow discrimination against others; proclaim respect for life but hurt the unborn, handicapped and aged. We tend to desert the gospel values whenever we pursue a lifestyle of materialism instead of simplicity; bombard our senses with entertainment and seldom pray to nourish our spirits; are preoccupied with instant gratification and avoid self-denial.

Occasionally we delude ourselves with thinking that there might be an easier way to be a Christian, a way without commitment, responsibility or the cross. But there is no other gospel Jesus gave us. We want to have our own way. settle down and accumulate more. But Jesus says, "Deny yourself, wash one another's feet and store up heavenly treasures."

We want to be secure with our advanced technology, scientific knowledge and military might. But Jesus says, "The kingdom of God is within you, learn to be meek and humble of heart, and trust that your Father will care for you like lilies in the field."

There is no other way to self-fulfillment except the way of Jesus. There is no other gospel for world peace except the gospel of Jesus. It's time to return to it. At least Solzhenitsyn, President Carter and St. Paul think so. Do we?

Tenth Sunday of the Year
Gal 1:11-19

He Set Me Apart

In the *Chicago Sun Times* there was a news item about Eldridge Cleaver. He had given a talk to some two thousand people at Wheaton College. In the late 1960's Cleaver was one of the founders of the Black Panther Party, a revolutionary group that advocated violence to overthrow the government in the U.S. and had shootouts with the police.

Now in the late 1970's Cleaver is back in the U.S. to face a murder trial. In his speech at Wheaton College he related how he had experienced a religious conversion during his exile and that he is now a Christian with a heart full of good will. "Since becoming a born-again Christian," he said, "I haven't met one single person I haven't loved. There are people who don't like me and say nasty things about me, but I like them anyway and pray for them."

St. Paul too went through a conversion experience, and his words to the Galatians might easily have been used by Cleaver to summarize his talk: "You know the story of my former way of life in Judaism—how I tried to destroy the Church of God. But the time came when he who had set me apart before I was born chose to reveal his Son to me, that I might spread among the Gentiles the good tidings concerning him."

Cleaver's former way of life was one of anger, hatred and violence. This was much like Paul's in his early days. But now, also like Paul, he had been set apart by the Lord to spread the good tidings of forgiveness, love and peace.

Is there any place in our own lives for this kind of experience?

While our former way of life may not be characterized by the extremes of Paul and Cleaver before their conversions, perhaps it did contain certain elements we have left behind. For example, maybe our former way of life identified us as materialistic, moody or phony. But now that we've come to know Jesus, people see us as someone interested in spiritual values, cheerful and authentic.

Perhaps our present way of life needs some changing before we can point to it as former. For example, we might be presently troubled with a poor self-image, compulsive eating or resentment toward others. To make these pass into the former-way-of-life category we have to come to know ourselves better, first of all, and then come to know the Lord more intimately so that he can heal us of these ills in our personality.

If we do this, then we will be experiencing a kind of mini-conversion and others will be able to recognize the changes in us. Perhaps they will even be surprised to see us with a positive self-image, eating meals sensibly and enjoying the company of others.

We may never travel to Galatia like Paul or preach at Wheaton College like Cleaver, but we are all set apart in some way to announce the good news about Jesus. Whether we are in Chicago or Houston, at home or at work, in a supermarket or in a gas line, no matter how we find ourselves we should be spreading the gospel, sometimes by word, but most often by what we do.

People should be able to sense spontaneously the peace, joy and fulfillment we have found in Christ. Regardless of what our former way of life was or what our present way of life is, all of us are set apart in a unique way to proclaim what Jesus is doing for us.

Eleventh Sunday of the Year
Gal 2:16-21

Alexander the Great

In his book *Alexander the Great* author Robin Lane Fox narrates several episodes which made Alexander so popular with his soldiers. For example, when his soldiers hesitated to climb ladders at the wall of a besieged city, Alexander himself scrambled up. When the ladder broke he jumped down into the city and fought alone, suffering a near fatal wound before he could be rescued.

At another time, when the river Oxus was finally reached, the army was so scattered that fires had to be lit on a hill to direct them into camp. Alexander stood by their route and refused to take food or drink or refresh himself in any way until the entire army had passed him by. Time and again Alexander refused the privileges of rank and preferred instead to share the hardships of his soldiers. He always led his troops personally in battle, getting wounded on nine different occasions. No wonder he inspired his army to endure extraordinary hardships without complaint and to risk their lives heroically under his leadership.

The way Alexander the Great's men loved him is strikingly similar to the way St. Paul loved Christ. St. Paul expressed his strong allegiance to Christ when he said to the Galatians: "I have been crucified with Christ, and the life I live now is not my own. Christ is living in me. I still live my human life, but it is a life of faith in the Son of God, who loved me and gave himself for me."

Paul was so overwhelmed by the thought that Christ was crucified and laid down his life for him, that he wanted to devote his whole life to Jesus. He was so overcome by Christ's love in calling him to be one of his apostles after he had persecuted Christ's church, that he wanted to dedicate his very being to Jesus.

Does Jesus move us as deeply as he moved Paul, or as Alexander the Great moved his soldiers? Do we have the same profound realization that Jesus loved us and gave himself for us? If we did, then perhaps we would be much more enthused about our commitment to him. Like Alexander's army we wouldn't complain about any difficulties we had to endure, because we would know that Christ bore them before us. We wouldn't be bothered so much by a physical pain or the privation of some comfort, because we would see ourselves as crucified with Christ and rejoice to be counted worthy to suffer with him.

If we were truly inspired by the way Christ shared our human condition, then perhaps we would be more eager to accept challenges for him. Taking care of a senile parent, working patiently with an undisciplined child, getting reconciled with an unfaithful spouse—all such challenges would be met with faith, because we would believe in the strength of our leader, Jesus Christ. We wouldn't cry about the enormity of the task. We would show our pride at being in the service of Christ and confront the task with daring.

When we have to face some crisis and there is no way out but only a way through, remember Paul's words: "He loved me and gave himself for me." When we are weary from the monotony of our work or discouraged and want to quit, remember these words: "He loved me and gave himself for me." When we are afraid to speak out for some moral truth or hesitate to stand up for some right, remember once more: "He loved me and gave himself for me."

Twelfth Sunday of the Year
Gal 3:26-29

Unity

1979 was designated as "The Year of the Child." The United Nations International Childrens' Educational Fund, more commonly known as UNICEF, organized the activities for that year. One of its projects was to make a film featuring actor Peter Ustinov.

While part of the film was being made in Jordan, Ustinov said: "I'm not here to get involved in Middle East politics; I'm concentrating on the children. Kids are all alike everywhere. It's like filming a cross-section of head waiters—but on kids across five continents. The point is that children are much more similar than adults. When you hear children screaming—as you do often in this film—they're still holders of the secrets of the only universal language. Children screaming have no accent. You can't tell if they're from Arabia or Israel."

UNICEF exists because it believes in and promotes the unity of the world symbolized by the children it supports. St. Paul too believed strongly in unity, especially the unity symbolized by our fellowhsip in Christ. He wrote: "All of you who have been baptized into Christ have clothed yourselves with him. There does not exist among you Jew or Greek, slave or freeman, male or female. All are one in Christ."

When we compare what Ustinov and Paul say about our unity, two points stand out. First, there is a similarity in what they say from the point of view of children. Ustinov says that crying babies, playing children and dancing youth all speak the same universal

287

language. Paul says that because we have been baptized into Christ we are now sons and daughters in the one family of God—we are now God's children.

Second, there is a different emphasis in what the two men say. On the one hand, Ustinov is stressing the unity stemming from our common roots in human nature and from our sharing the same human condition. On the other hand, Paul focuses more on the unity flowing from our common participation in divine life and from our common destiny in God's glory.

Would that we saw the same vision of these two men about our unity as human beings and as Christians. We wouldn't be torn apart by wars, suspicion and greed, but united in peaceful cooperation. We wouldn't see yellow, black, white and red skin, but people colored by "God's skin."

Would that we felt the excitement Paul and Ustinov have about our fellowship. We wouldn't separate ourselves according to status symbols like academic degrees, annual income or where we live, but would come together to build, work, play and celebrate. We wouldn't waste or selfishly consume food and natural resources without any care about the consequences, but would share what we have with the poor and the disadvantaged to demonstrate our bond of solidarity with them.

Unity is absolutely essential for the vitality of families, parishes, local communities, individual nations and international organizations. Without unity, hostilities arise, barriers are built and little is accomplished. But with unity, reconciliation is possible, interests are shared and mutual support becomes a way of life.

It is a common saying that the longest journey must begin with the first step. In a similar way, the strongest chain of unity must be forged by the first link. We can be that link by promoting unity wherever we are and in whatever we do. We have the power to do that because we are united with Christ and his power is now ours.

Thirteenth Sunday of the Year
Gal 5:1, 13-18

Freedom Festival

Summertime is freedom time—a time for vacations from our daily routine of work or study; time for a little leisure and traveling. In summertime we begin to notice the vacation ads in the newspapers. For example, American Airlines had a full page ad which had this caption at the top: "Great planes to great places. What to expect besides a tan."

Summertime is Freedom Festival time—the time when we celebrate on July 4 the birthday of our nation's Declaration of Independence. Activities like fireworks displays, picnics and parades all serve to remind us of our origins as a free nation.

St. Paul has his own way of reminding us about our freedom as Christians: "It was for liberty that Christ freed us. So do not take upon yourselves the yoke of slavery a second time. You have been called to live in freedom—but not a freedom that gives free rein to the flesh. You should live in accord with the spirit. Out of love place yourselves at one another's service."

On the one hand, we might imagine freedom to be a release from our responsibilities or an escape from our burdens: "If only I didn't have to take care of the kids or paint the house, how free I would feel." On the other hand, we might imagine that freedom is the right to do what we want or the power to have our own way: "If only my parents would let me stay out as late as I want or get my own car, how free I would feel."

In his book *Building the Human* author Robert Johann of Fordham University discusses freedom. He says that the central problem of freedom is less a matter of *doing* what we *want to do*, than of really *wanting to do* what we *do*. This is why so many of today's quests for greater self-determination end in disillusionment.

In other words, we can seek to have our own way, not so much because we really have our heart set on it, but because other people expect it of us. We can insist on doing our own thing, not so much because it is inherently worthwhile, but because our desires are undisciplined and disordered. To be truly free and to really want to do something, we have to reflect on reality, not just react to it; we have to discipline our desires, and not just indulge in them; we have to respect the rights of others, and not just override them.

Johann's insights about freedom are reflected in Paul's words above. In one sense, we have been freed by Christ *from* the slavery of sin and our disordered desires. In another sense, we have been freed *for* living in accord with the spirit.

Paul says further on that if we are guided by the spirit, we are not under the law—we are free. This means that we will not yield to our undisciplined appetites, not so much because the law *says not to*, but because we *want to* do what is best for our own growth and development; we will love our neighbors as ourselves, not so much because we *have to* according to the law of charity, but because we really *want to* see other people happy as ourselves.

If we follow the guidance of the spirit, we won't run away from our responsibilities. Instead we will do far more than what duty demands of us. If we are led by the spirit, we won't always insist on having our own way. Instead we will be more sensitive to the needs of others.

Moreover, we will do these things spontaneously because we *want to* do them; we will do these things gladly because we *desire to* do them. Like Paul says, it will be out of love that we will place ourselves at one another's service.

We don't have to wait for July 4 to celebrate our liberty. Every Eucharist is a Freedom Festival celebrating the coming of the Holy Spirit to set us free *from* sin so that we can live *for* Christ.

Fourteenth Sunday of the Year
Gal 6:14-18

The Marks of Jesus

Corrie ten Boom's book *The Hiding Place* has been made into a major motion picture. It tells the story of the two years she spent in Nazi concentration camps where she witnessed her father and sister die of starvation and exhaustion. The ten Booms's only crime was that of hiding Jews from extermination at the hands of the Nazis when they invaded Holland.

She recalls one day when she and 700 others were herded into a room built for 200. Their cold and starved bodies were stripped naked and they were made to stand exposed to the cruelty of their captors. Many years later after Corrie was baptized in the Holy Spirit, she was able to sing: "Hallelujah! Because I am suffering, Jesus is glorified."

Her song strikes a familiar chord in the writings of St. Paul when he says: "I bear the brand marks of Jesus in my body. May I never boast of anything but the cross of our Lord Jesus Christ."

None of us can fully understand the mystery of the cross and sufferings, let alone explain it. Nevertheless, we can discover some insights about their purpose. The cross seems to be a necessary condition for bringing out what is best in us; it reveals our hidden possibilities. Violets have to be crushed to become perfume; grapes have to be pressed to become wine; wheat has to be ground up to become bread. In the same say, it seems that we have to experience some pain to reach perfection; we have to share in some suffering to attain excellence; like Corrie ten Boom we have to carry our cross with courage before we can make any claim to greatness.

Also the cross teaches us about the true values of life. It detaches us from what is trivial, superficial or only momentary, and attaches us to what is essential, profound and eternal. When a heavy drinker is "feeling good," alcohol is his main preoccupation. But when he is sick with a bleeding ulcer, his survival alone assumes supreme importance. When a man is enjoying success, he sometimes becomes proud of himself and insensitive to others. But when he suffers failure, he begins to realize his dependence on others and his need for friendship. Without the cross some of us would never come to know what are the real and lasting values of life.

The cross completes our prayers. What prayer by itself cannot obtain, prayer with suffering does. Christ once said that some cures are brought about only by prayer and fasting. He might also have said, "By prayer and suffering." Someone once said that we instruct others by talking, but we save them by suffering. By carrying our cross as Christ did we make our prayers more authentic and powerful.

The cross comes in many forms: sufferings of the body, like sickness or handicaps; sufferings of the mind, like doubts or worries; sufferings of the heart, like disappointments or discouragement. Certainly we must make reasonable efforts to relieve these sufferings. But if they persist, we can accept them as the cross of Christ.

Like Paul and Corrie ten Boom we can be proud to bear the brand marks of Jesus in our body. We can be proud because we know that the cross will call forth our true greatness; teach us to value what is most important in life; and make our prayers more authentic and powerful. May we never boast of anything except how we carry the cross of our Lord Jesus Christ.

Fifteenth Sunday of the Year
Col 1:15-20

Image of the Invisible

Entertainment reporter David Lewin writes: "The Muppets are more than puppets on a glove. In just three seasons on television and in one film, *The Muppet Movie*, they have become real life people with passions, sorrows, fears and fun of their own."

This "real life" quality explains in part the Muppets' popularity. The unique expressions, gestures and voice of each character reveal something about ourselves in a playful way. We identify easily with them because they reflect something of our own personality, traits and lifestyle.

For example, in Miss Piggy we might see an image of our own vulnerability, and our need to survive in a competitive world, and our dreams of marrying someone like Kermit. In Kermit the Frog we might see mirrored our own happy-go-lucky attitude toward life and our leadership capabilities.

The way the Muppets reveal our human foibles and qualities parallels somewhat, however imperfectly, the way our Lord reveals the Father to us. St. Paul writes: "Christ Jesus is the image of the invisible God; the first-born of all creatures. It pleased God to make absolute fullness reside in him and by means of him, to reconcile everything in his person, making peace through the blood of his cross."

When the Word became man the invisible God took on human flesh so that we could see, hear and touch him in someway. As the perfect image of his Father, Jesus made it possible for us to come to know and love the God we cannot see. Jesus himself told Philip, "He who sees me sees the Father."

Theologian John Shea talks about Jesus' presence. When people were with Jesus they somehow sensed the presence of God; were energized by him; felt touched by God; had their desire for the divine flare up. Moreover, when Jesus left, they lost the intensity of this experience.

The words and actions of Jesus image the invisible God. For instance, through his parable of the Good Samaritan we come to know God as one who wants to take us in his arms, dress our wounds, give us shelter and take care of us. Through his treatment of the woman caught in adultery we see a God who understands our weakness, restores our self-esteem and gently invites us to greatness.

Jesus is the image of the invisible God. But now that he has returned in glory to the Father's right hand, we in turn must be images of the invisible God. Now it is our care for the weak and oppressed that gives expression to God's compassion for his people; our kindness to the downtrodden and addicts manifests the mercy of God; our love for the lonely and the alienated shows the presence of God's love in the world.

This call to image the invisible God is put to song in a Methodist hymn: "Called from worship into service, forth in your great name we go; to the child, the youth, the aged, love in living deeds to show. Hope and health, good-will and comfort, counsel, aid and peace we give; that your children, Lord, in freedom may your mercy know, and live."

The Muppets have a "real life" appeal because they image so well our human qualities. Jesus is the really real who images perfectly the invisible God. We become more real the more we ourselves become a true image of the unseen God, and the more people are able to sense God's presence through us.

Sixteenth Sunday of the Year
Col 1:24-28

Joy in Suffering

Clement Tigar's book *Forty Martyrs of England and Wales* is a collection of forty different biographies unified by one theme: joy in suffering. Everyone of the forty saints, from Philip Howard the Earl of Arundel to John Rigby the farm hand, witnessed to Christ not only by the fact of their martyrdom, but also by the way they died—all walked to the scaffold radiant with joy.

Everyone of these forty martyrs of England and Wales could exclaim with St. Paul: "I find my joy in the sufferings I endure. In my own flesh I fill up what is lacking in the sufferings of Christ for the sake of his body, the Church."

These are rather startling assertions. Are we to take them merely as fancy rhetoric on Paul's part, sort of pious exaggeration, or are we to take them as an authentic revelation, a genuine insight on the paradox between suffering and joy?

It will help to make some remarks about what his words do *not* mean. He is not saying that suffering is a good to be desired for its own sake like listening to good music. The mystery of the cross does not mean an unhealthy preoccupation with suffering nor an exaltation of it. On the contrary, suffering is not a good in itself. It is a reaction against some sort of pain and a yearning for a good that is lacking.

Also, Paul is not saying that Christ's death on the cross was inadequate, or that his sufferings were insufficient to save us. On the contrary, he says elsewhere that the sting of death is sin and we should thank God for giving us the victory over it through Jesus Christ.

Taking a more positive approach, we can say that the completion of the sufferings of Christ is connected with the completion of

295

the preaching of the gospel. Whenever Paul proclaimed the good news in a new locality he caused a division among the people. Some received the word with joy and became Christians, while others rejected the word with hate and persecuted Paul. It seems then that just as Jesus himself suffered in announcing the gospel and establishing his Church, so too must his disciples suffer as they continue his mission. The disciple is not above the master.

We can also say that even though suffering is not a good in itself, it can serve a good purpose. Without the suffering of training and practice an athlete or an actor cannot perform well. Sometimes suffering is the price we have to pay to achieve excellence; sometimes suffering is the means we have to use to obtain a higher good, like being conformed to Christ.

This leads us into another thing we can say about suffering. It enables us to enter into a deeper fellowship with Christ. Our identity with Christ is incomplete until we experience in ourselves some of his sufferings on the cross. In this sense, suffering for Christ is not a penalty or a punishment but a privilege, because by it we become more Christ-like. When people see us carrying our crosses with courage they come to know Jesus himself; when people see us at peace in the midst of affliction they encounter the Christ living within us.

Paul could find joy because he suffered not only for Christ, but also for his body, the Church. In bearing the burdens of the people he served, Paul rejoiced that the greater part of the weight fell on his shoulders. Like a soldier who carries his wounded buddy so that he will hurt less, we too can bear one another's burdens with gladness because we know that our sufferings will lessen theirs.

Most of us won't be sent to the scaffold to die like the forty martyrs of England and Wales, nor be sent to prison like Paul for preaching the gospel. But all of us can be like them in the way we find joy in the sufferings we endure for others. In our own flesh we can fill up for what is lacking to make us conform to Christ and continue his work.

Seventeenth Sunday of the Year
Col 2:12-14

Baptism of the Holy Spirit

In a paperback compiled by Fr. George Kosicki entitled *The Lord is My Shepherd* we find a collection of thirteen personal stories by priests who have experienced the baptism of the Holy Spirit. For example, Fr. William O'Brien tells how he began his work as a priest in a Jersey City parish. After seven years he felt a general sense of frustration. His ministry seemed to have no impact on people's lives nor on the urban community.

So he left the parish ministry for campus ministry. As a chaplain at Fairleigh Dickinson University he had great expectations for the liturgies, retreats and social action programs that he would offer to the students. After six months he was again disillusioned by failure.

It was then that he experienced the baptism of the Holy Spirit. Through his contact with a Cursillo Workshop and the Charismatic Movement he realized how weak his faith was and how inept his prayer life was. So he prayed for and received the baptism of the Holy Spirit.

This meant a deepening of his faith in the Lord Jesus as the center of his life, and not his own ego; an increased awareness of the Holy Spirit as the source of his ministry's success, and not his own efforts; a stronger hunger to hear the word of God in Scripture, and not the voice of his own hurt pride.

To understand further the significance of the baptism of the Holy Spirit, we turn to St. Paul and begin with the sacrament of baptism: "In baptism you were not only buried with Christ but also raised to life with him. Even when you were dead in sin, God gave you new life in company with Christ."

In this passage Paul is talking about adult baptism by immersion. The convert descended into a pool of water as a symbol of his going down into the grave to die with Christ. He then rose from the waters as a symbol of his rising to a new life with the resurrected Christ.

Paul does not think of baptism as a magic rite. He considers it as a sacrament whose effectiveness depends on faith, for as he says, "You were buried and raised with Christ because you *believed* in the power of God who raised Christ." Through our faith we believe that baptism puts to death our old sinful selves and releases within us a new life of grace.

No longer then do we have to be enslaved by selfishness, driven by uncontrolled desires, or victimized by false promises. Instead we can live a new life of generosity and sharing with others, a life of freedom to follow our most noble impulses, and a life of joy because of our hope for final victory.

If all this is true, then why don't more baptized Christians live like this? Because our faith is weak, our hope is unstable, and our love lacks enthusiasm. That is why we need a new and deeper experience of God and a fresh outpouring of the Holy Spirit into our hearts—we need the baptism of the Holy Spirit like Fr. O'Brien received.

The baptism of the Holy Spirit is not a second sacrament of baptism, nor is it a rebaptism. It is an in-depth renewal of the life we have already received in baptism and a release of the gifts we received in confirmation. Some of its effects include a keen awareness of the presence of God, an eagerness to read the Scriptures, a strong desire to pray, a deep peace and inner joy, a greater compassion and care for people in need, and a manifestation of spiritual gifts like tongues.

When we are baptized in the Holy Spirit our dying to the old ways of sin is made more definitive and our rising to a new life of grace is heightened. We experience a more drastic turning away from sin and a more intense life of prayer and praise, peace and joy, service and ministry. All this because we believe in the power of God who raised Christ from the dead.

Eighteenth Sunday of the Year
Col 3:1-5, 9-11

Things Above

When he was sixty-five years old Dr. Walter Alvarez retired from his position in the Mayo Clinic. Twenty-five years later, on his ninetieth birthday he was still helping patients seven days a week and writing medical articles. His whole life as a physician has been devoted to serving people. He never was terribly interested in making money. "If I had wanted to be a millionaire," he said, "I would have charged patients $15 for a five minute examination or written a popular diet book."

Instead Dr. Alvarez spends a lot of time with his patients listening to their problems and making them feel important. No wonder so many of his patients in the Chicago area come in red-eyed and in tears, but go out smiling.

Dr. Alvarez is a man who has practiced St. Paul's words: "Since you have been raised up in company with Christ, set your hearts on what pertains to the higher realms where Christ is seated at God's right hand. Be intent on things above rather than on things of earth."

Does this mean that Christians must not seek after material wealth but only spiritual riches—put aside physical pleasures and experience only the delights of the spirit—withdraw from the temporal concerns of secular society and involve themselves only with things that are eternal?

No, this is not what Paul meant when he said that we must be intent on things above rather than on things of earth. He meant that we should see everything in the light of eternity; that we should no longer live as if this world were all that mattered; that we should set this world against the background of the larger world of eternity.

Paul is telling us to strive towards an integration in our lives between the material and the spiritual; to seek a balance in our use of the passing things of the material world by giving priority to the eternal realities of the spiritual world.

In practical terms then we won't passionately pursue power or pleasure or prestige as if they were the final goal of our lives. Instead we will use them with prudence and discretion to discover the higher values of life—values like friendship, sharing and compassion.

Also it means that we won't try to escape from reality with all its duties, tensions and stresses. On the contrary, we will bear our burdens of caring for the aged, sick and handicapped, and assume our responsibilities to eradicate hunger, injustice and oppression.

Paul enjoins us to be involved with the things of earth, but intent on things that are above; be concerned about what happens in this life, but set our hearts on spiritual realities; have a view to what is temporal, but keep our focus on what is eternal.

If we do this, then like Dr. Alvarez we won't become slaves to what is material and physical. Instead we will be free to use them in the best way possible by taking sufficient care of our own needs and ministering to the needs of others. We won't have a one-sided view of life, but will discern its spiritual dimension that sets giving above getting and serving above dominating.

Praise God for people like St. Paul who teach us how to seek the things that are above without ignoring the things that are below. Thank God for the examples of Dr. Alvarez that show us how to set our hearts on higher spiritual values without losing temporal secular values.

Nineteenth Sunday of the Year
Heb 11:1-2, 8-19

Faith in the Unseen

Robert Moffat was a Scottish missionary to South Africa. He came back to recruit helpers in his homeland and was greeted by the fury of a cold winter. At one of the churches where he was to speak only a few ladies were present to hear him, due to the cold weather. Moffat felt hopeless as he made his appeal since he realized that few women could respond to his appeal to do the rigorous work of a missionary.

But God works in mysterious ways to carry out his purposes. Although no one volunteered, a small boy assisting the organist was thrilled by Moffat's challenge. He decided that when he grew up he would follow in the footsteps of this pioneer missionary. Eventually this boy became a doctor and then spent the rest of his life ministering to the unreached tribes of South Africa. His name was David Livingstone!

This story about Robert Moffat and his influence on David Livingstone is similar to the story of Abraham and Sarah as recalled in the letter to the Hebrews: "By faith Abraham obeyed when he was called, and went forth to the place he was to receive as a heritage; he went forth, moreover, not knowing where he was going. By faith he sojourned in the promised land as in a foreign country. By faith Sarah received power to conceive though she was past the age, for she thought that the One who had made the promise was worthy of trust. As a result of this faith, there came forth from one man descendants as numerous as the stars in the sky."

Like Abraham and Sarah, missionary Robert Moffat was called to make a journey for the Lord. On that cold winter night when he looked out at his sparse audience he could not understand why he was there or how the Lord would accomplish his purpose. But he put his faith in the Lord the way Abraham and Sarah did and went out to speak anyway. As a result of this faith he influenced a small boy by the name of David Livingstone to dedicate his life to medical work on the missions.

Often the Lord calls us too in someway—to take some kind of risk, to get involved with certain people, or to do something noble. We don't know why he calls us or how we can carry out what he asks of us. But if we put our faith in the Lord, then unexpected things will happen. In surprising ways the Lord will accomplish his purpose through us.

Like Abraham, Sarah and Moffat, we may never see the final results of our faith. But that doesn't matter. If we trust in the Lord we can be confident that he will fulfill our hopes in ways we could never imagine. This is why the author of the letter to the Hebrews defines faith as the confident assurance concerning what we hope for, and the conviction about things we do not see.

For instance, parents never know how far their influence will extend through their children. However, if they remain faithful to their duties, then the Lord will bless their fidelity far beyond their greatest expectations.

When we take a chance to get involved with a stranger in need, we never know how much good we will do. However, if we put our trust in the Lord, then he will take this happiness we cause in one person and multiply it among many others.

When we follow an impulse to brighten the candle of someone's life with an act of uncalled-for kindness, we never know how many other candles we will light up. However, if we believe in the Lord, then he himself will carry our torch to dispel the darkness in other lives.

By faith Abraham, Sarah and Moffat followed the Lord's call, and as a result had their influence extended in extraordinary ways. By faith we too can have a confident assurance concerning what we hope for, and a deep conviction about things we do not see.

Twentieth Sunday of the Year
Heb 12:1-4

Perseverance

In our own era marathoner Bill Rodgers is the widely acclaimed "king of the road" among distance runners. In the 1920's Paavo Nurmi was heralded as the "flying Finn" in recognition of his exploits among distance runners.

Nurmi established himself as a legend when he competed in the Olympic Games of 1920, 1924, 1928, and won nine Gold Medals in distance races ranging from 1,500 to 10,000 meters. Truly, he was the iron man of his age.

The secret of Nurmi's success was his ability to persevere through pain and exhaustion, and to keep his eyes fixed on the finish line where he knew he would feel great satisfaction.

The perseverance Paavo Nurmi practiced every time he ran is similar to the perseverance the author of Hebrews had in mind when he wrote: "Let us lay aside every encumbrance of sin which clings to us and persevere in running the race which lies ahead; let us keep our eyes fixed on Jesus, who inspires and perfects our faith. For the sake of the joy which lay before him he endured the cross, heedless of its shame. Hence do not grow despondent or abandon the struggle."

The Hebrews addressed in this letter were recent converts to Christianity who had experienced the destruction of Jerusalem. The catastrophe left them in conditions of chaos and confusion. So the writer is trying to confirm their new and somewhat tenuous faith by encouraging them to persevere.

All of us occasionally need encouragement to persevere. In our day-to-day existence we inevitably run into times when we feel like quitting: mornings when we want to give up in the battle to even get out of bed; days when just the thought of going to work causes anguish; periods when even routine chores appear revolting.

It is easy to begin a project with joyous expectation or to make a personal commitment with enthusiasm. But as obstacles block our way and the early vision fades, it becomes more and more difficult for us to see the project through to the end or to live up to our commitment.

Many a brilliant idea for a book was born with excitement, only to be abandoned as an unfinished manuscript because the author didn't persevere. Many a marriage vow has been exchanged with ecstasy, only to be dissolved later when the couple didn't persevere.

It is not easy to be a faithful follower of Christ. We aspire to be poor in spirit, but we hesitate when we see what it will cost us. We want to be clean of heart, but we become indecisive when temptation strikes. We want to be able to suffer persecution for the cause of right, but we surrender our purpose when real trouble begins.

The author of Hebrews gives us three practical suggestions to help us persevere. We must lay aside every encumbrance of sin which clings to us. Just before a race begins, runners like Nurmi lay aside their warm-up clothes in order to move with greater freedom. In the same way we must get rid of our bad habits of sin and set aside sinful occasions in order to follow Christ with greater freedom.

We have to keep our eyes fixed on Jesus and the cloud of witnesses who surround us. When we grow weary in our struggle and want to give up, we should remember the example of Jesus and the saints who have persevered before us. Their tenacity under every trial imaginable is proof that hardship can be overcome and that perseverance is possible.

We have to have a vision, a dream, an ideal. As the author of Hebrews says, "For the sake of the joy which lay before him Jesus endured the cross, heedless of the shame." When we can anticipate the satisfaction of a work accomplished or a service rendered, we will not let difficulties discourage or deter us from our purpose. We will persevere in the pursuit of our vision, dream or ideal.

Twenty-First Sunday of the Year
Heb 12:5-13

Discipline

The television series *Bonanza* starring Lorne Greene is still a popular program even as a late-showing rerun. Part of the mystique created by the Cartwright family is due to our nostalgic yearning for traditional American values we feel are being lost today, values like close family life, loyalty, neighborliness, hard work and discipline. The Cartwrights embody these values for us, especially the happy combination of discipline and gentleness that characterizes the relationship between the father and his sons.

Discipline is one of the themes of Hebrews: "My sons, do not disdain the discipline of the Lord; for, whom the Lord loves, he disciplines; he scourges every son he receives. Endure your trials as the discipline of God, who deals with you as sons. For what son is there whom his father does not discipline? At the time it is administered, all discipline seems a cause for grief, but later it brings forth the fruit of peace to those who are trained in its school."

There are many aspects to discipline, so suppose we limit ourselves to two of them, namely, the discipline children receive from their parents, and the discipline we receive from the Lord.

Regarding the first kind of discipline, it is absolutely necessary in raising children. Just as muscles develop by straining against something, the character of a child needs to push against the personality of its parents if it is to develop. On the one hand, if he meets with no resistance, no discipline, then he arrives in the adult world without strength. On the other hand, if he has dictatorial parents and receives too much discipline, then he may be squashed and never mature.

The purpose of discipline is not to diminish the child's sense of personal worth, but to develop it; not to repress the child's energies, but to liberate them for wholesome activities; not to demand blind obedience, but intelligent cooperation.

Discipline achieves its purposes when it is changed from something received from outside oneself into something arising within oneself; when it is accepted not only on the surface of our minds, but also in the depths of our wills; when it is no longer a mechanical conformity, but a dynamic expression of our own free choice.

To achieve these purposes of discipline, parents should be reasonable, not arrogant; understanding, not condescending. Moreover, parents should control the emotions which undermine discipline—fear, anger, suspicion—and use the emotions which promote good discipline—love, patience, respect.

As regards the discipline we receive from the Lord, our attitudes are crucial. When he worked in a TB sanatorium once, Dr. Rollo May observed how patients reacted to the strict regime imposed upon them. First, there were those who gave up in the face of the demands. They refused to follow the rules and invited their own death.

Next, there were the patients who did what was required, but continually resented the fact. Most of these did not die soon, but neither did they get well.

Then there were the patients who took a realistic look at their situation and cooperated willingly. Many of these regained their physical health and almost all were enriched with a stronger personality.

Which of these three attitudes describes our own reaction when the Lord disciplines us with trials? Do we rebel and refuse to accept the trials? Do we accept them, but only grudgingly and sullenly? Or do we accept them willingly and even gladly because we realize that it is the only way to develop a strong character and find inner peace.

How blessed we are to have a Father who is all-wise and all-loving. What trust we should have when he corrects us. What peace we should experience when we willingly embrace his discipline.

Twenty-Second Sunday of the Year
Heb 12:18-24

Honor Society

The nation's highest honor society for the arts is the American Academy and Institute of Arts and Letters. At its annual meeting in New York in 1980, gold medals were awarded to playwright Edward Albee, graphic artist Peggy Bacon and novelist William Maxwell. Also honored were Architect R. Buckminster Fuller, composer Howard Hanson and sculptor Louise Nevelson, Institute members who were elevated to membership in the Academy. This honor is limited to 50 members and is for special distinction.

In the letter to the Hebrews there is another honor society described, not one located in New York, but in the heavenly Jerusalem on Mt. Zion: "You have drawn near to Mt. Zion and the city of the living God, the heavenly Jerusalem, to myriads of angels in festal gathering, to the assembly of the first-born enrolled in heaven, to God the judge of all, to the spirits of just men made perfect, to Jesus, the mediator of a new covenant."

Heaven's honor society does not admit only a select, few individuals distinguished by extraordinary careers. It admits anyone who is a "just man made perfect"—beggars and cripples, the blind and the lame, harlots and tax collectors.

When we look at the "assembly of the first-born enrolled in heaven," we see all sorts of examples to inspire us. If we are greedy and tend to hoard things, we have honor society members like John Neumann of Philadelphia and Hedwig of Poland to show us the happiness of being generous. If we are self-indulgent in matters of sex or drink, we have saints like Mary Magdalen and

Matt Talbot to show how our appetites can be controlled and produce peace in our lives.

There is no reason for us to be sad or filled with self-pity when sufferings seem to oppress us; we have the spirits of the just to strengthen us. There is no reason for us to be downcast or discouraged when our difficulties seem to defeat us; we belong to the assembly of the saints and have the noblest heroes of old to lift us up.

Everyone of us has the capacity to become a member of heaven's honor society. The assembly of saints in the heavenly Jerusalem does not consist largely of extraordinary people, but rather of ordinary people who had an extraordinary love for God and man.

When Msgr. Ronald Knox of England was asked what it takes to be a saint, he answered: "Why, you've got to be absolutely eaten up with the love of God; that's the only thing that matters."

Wearing hair shirts or having visions are not essential to sanctity. But praying to the Lord and serving our fellow man are. This we can all do—whether we have ten talents or only one talent.

We don't have to have a Ph.D. to praise and thank God for the great things he has done for us. We need only reflect on his goodness and respond with every fiber of our being. We don't have to be doctors or missionaries to minister to God's people. We need only serve the needs of the brothers and sisters who touch our lives everyday—at home or at the store, in the office or in the factory, on the street or on the bus.

Only a select few like Buckminster Fuller and Louise Nevelson are distinguished enough to enter the American Academy of Arts and Letters, but all of us have the capacity and opportunity to enter heaven's honor society. All we have to do is be consumed with love of God and of our fellow man.

Twenty-Third Sunday of the Year
Phm 9-10, 12-17

Amnesty

Near the end of the Vietnam War our country was sharply divided about the justification of the war. After the war another division arose about the question of amnesty for deserters and draft dodgers. When President Ford addressed the VFW at one of their national conventions in Chicago, he called for some form of conditional amnesty.

In their editorial the *Chicago Sun Times* said that even though President Ford's proposal won't satisfy liberal activists who insist on unconditional amnesty, nor conservative hardliners like the VFW group who want no amnesty granted, it was nevertheless the wisest course to take.

These questions of amnesty, forgiveness and reinstatement are reflected in St. Paul's letter to Philemon. While in prison Paul converted and baptized Onesimus, one of Philemon's runaway slaves. Paul asks Philemon to take Onesimus back: "Perhaps he was separated from you for a while that you might possess him forever, no longer as a slave but as more than slave, a beloved brother; and how much more than a brother, since now you will know him both as a man and in the Lord."

If only we could really feel and understand what Paul is teaching, we would be able to find better solutions not only to problems like slavery and amnesty, but also to problems like prison reform, school desegregation, divorced Catholics and ex-priests.

What are some of these teachings? First is our union with one another as brothers and sisters in Christ. When Paul baptized

309

Onesimus he identified so strongly with him that he described him as *my child, my heart, my beloved brother*. If we believe with Paul that we are all one in Christ, then we will not allow differences to come between us—differences in culture, color, economics or education.

Second, life in Christ is a power which can change people's lives. At one time Onesimus was a rebel and a thief. But now through his faith in Christ he has become a new creature and a fellow worker with Paul in prison. We must never underestimate the grace of God to transform a person. Many a bruised reed like Onesimus has been restored because the Lord refused to break it. But too often we break the bruised reed by our hostility, instead of giving some encouragement to a person who is down-and-out.

Third, Christianity strengthens us to face our responsibilities. Paul did not try to help Onesimus escape from his past and run away from it. Rather, he insisted that Onesimus face his past and rise above it by returning to his master Philemon. Our faith in Christ does not mean freedom from our responsibilities, but rather the freedom to fulfill them; not an escape from our difficulties, but rather their confrontation and conquest.

All of us are victims of mistakes in life, whether the mistakes are the ones we ourselves commit, or are the ones other people make. Paul says that we must accept the consequences of such mistakes and rise above them, perhaps like a surgeon who causes a patient to die because of a misjudgment only to go on to save hundreds of other lives; or like a businessman who loses a fortune because of a bad investment only to go on to rebuild his company.

As Christ comes in the Eucharist to make us more one with him and with each other, he also gives us the power to change our lives and to rise above our mistakes. Moreover, through us he also wants others like ex-convicts, draft-dodgers and divorcees to rise above their mistakes. Jesus says to us as Paul said to Philemon: "Welcome them as you would me."

Twenty-Fourth Sunday of the Year
1 Tm 1:12-17

Sin Remembered

Most of us know about St. Maria Goretti, the twelve year old Italian peasant girl who refused to be raped and was stabbed fourteen times. She died the next day and became a modern martyr for chastity. This was in 1902.

But few of us know about her attacker Allessandro Serenelli. He received a 30-year sentence to prison. After seven years of hostility he dreamed one night of Maria offering him a bouquet of lilies. This dream prompted him to admit his guilt and make peace with the church and with Maria's family. After twenty-seven years Allessandro Serenelli was paroled, became a Franciscan tertiary and a monastery gardener. He died in 1970.

Allessandro would always remember his sin against Maria. But after his conversion this would spur him on to reshape his life. He would always regret his past mistake. But this would only make his present gratitude for God's grace all the greater.

He could say with St. Paul: "I thank Christ Jesus our Lord who made me his servant. I was once filled with arrogance. But then I was treated mercifully and given grace in overflowing measure. Of sinners I was the worst. But now I have been given the faith and love which are in Christ Jesus. To the King of Ages be honor and glory forever. Amen."

This can be a hymn all of us can sing. In spite of the mistakes and sins of our earlier life, Jesus has lavished his love on us. There may have been times in the past when we were estranged from Jesus because we hurt the people around us, yet he forgave us and drew us closer to himself; times when we were defeated by our own drinking or gambling habits, yet he dealt mercifully with us and empowered us to begin a new life; times when we despaired because some dishonest act we had done was discovered, yet Jesus touched us with his kindness to rekindle the flame of our hope.

Like Paul and Allessandro all of us can look to the past and see the sins that caused us unhappiness, but we can also remember how God's grace lifted us up and illuminated our darkness. Such a remembering is not an unhealthy brooding over our past sins, but rather a good reason for rejoicing over God's boundless mercy. It is not a morbid preoccupation with our imperfections and weaknesses, but rather a celebration of the surpassing goodness of God.

Such remembering prevents us from getting proud over our present status; it reawakens in us a profound sense of gratitude; it urges us to serve the Lord and each other more generously; it encourages others to turn to the Lord to find the peace and joy.

When we receive the Eucharist we are reminded of our past sins: *Lord, I am not worthy that you should come under my roof.* Nevertheless, we are also reminded of the power of God's grace: *But only say the word, Lord, and I shall be healed.*

In the words of Psalm 51, we ask the Lord to continue washing us of our sins; to renew his spirit in our hearts; and to open our lips in praise of his mercy. We celebrate the Eucharist not because we were once sinners, but because we were sinners who have been saved by Jesus.

Twenty-Fifth Sunday of the Year
1 Tm 2:1-8

All Men

At one time, the *Los Angeles Times* featured a story about a seventy-four year old minister by the name of Edward L. Gilmer. His story is doubly unique. Not only was he a card-carrying member of the only hobo union in the U.S., but he was also its only official chaplain.

From 1917, until he retired, the Rev. Gilmer had pastored a floating parish in hobo jungles. His church never had any buildings—just some tin cans and a campfire—and never had any collections taken up.

Rev. Gilmer only worked enough at odd jobs to finance his hobo mission of free food and medical aid, Bible teachings and short sermons. He dedicated over fifty years of his life to serving the hobo world of boxcar riders because he understood the meaning of St. Paul's words in his letter to Timothy.

In this letter Paul stressed the universality of the gospel message of salvation: "First of all, I urge that prayers be offered for all men. God wants all men to be saved and come to know the truth. And the truth is this: Christ Jesus gave himself as a ransom for all men."

This emphasis on the universality of salvation is consoling. It is encouraging to know that God wants all of us to be saved. It doesn't matter who people are or what they have done; there is always hope for their salvation.

Men may be restless like wandering hobos, but they can find their peace and security in Jesus. Men may be lost like alcoholics and drug addicts, but they can be found through our compassion and care for them. Men may be ignorant like angry juvenile deliquents, but they can be enlightened through our patience and interest. Men may be selfish like fathers who desert their families, but they can be saved by our prayers and fasting.

It is this realization that God wants all men to be saved that compels people to dedicate their lives to serve the unwanted members of society. This is what drives people like Dr. Schweitzer to work among the sick in Africa and Rev. Gilmer to spend his life and money among the hobos in the U.S. This is what should drive us, too, to "lift up the poor from the dunghill and to seat them with princes" (Ps 113).

It is disconcerting to know that God wants all men to be saved. It is all right if God wants to be merciful and forgiving to me when I sin. But does he have to do the same for that cocky teenage rebel who damaged my car, or for that habitual drunkard next door who keeps me awake at night?

It is all right for Jesus to give himself as a ransom for me. But why should he throw his life away for that unscrupulous politician who cheats on his income tax, or for that flirtatious secretary who seduces husbands?

How dare such people come into our pews every week! What nerve they have! And yet, Paul says that we should pray for and pray with all men—not just with the respectable and nice people of society. Sometimes we get the notion that a person has to be perfect—well, at least decent—before he is allowed into church. And yet, Jesus wants *all* men to be saved!

Not all the people Jesus wants to save are nice people by our standards, and the fact that we find some sinners repulsive should not disconcert us. Rather, it should make us all the more determined to welcome them, serve them, and even embrace them if by doing so we can save them for Jesus.

Twenty-Sixth Sunday of the Year
1 Tm 6:11-16

Fight the Good Fight

A movie that had reviewers raving was *Coal Miner's Daughter*. It tells the rags-to-riches story of Loretta Lynn, the Queen of Country Music. She was born in a grim coal-mining area of Kentucky, married at age fourteen, and had four children by the time she was twenty. Her musical career started when her husband gave her a guitar as an anniversary gift and persuaded her to start singing before audiences.

To promote her first record they had to travel from one disc jockey to another. After living out of their car and eating nothing but baloney sandwiches on this tour, Loretta's song moved up on the nation's charts and earned her an appearance on the Grand Ole Opry. The coal miner's daughter emerged a star.

Loretta grew up in grinding poverty, but had true grit to reach greatness. Like St. Paul speaking out of his own experience to Timothy, Loretta Lynn can say to us: "Fight the good fight of faith. Take firm hold on the everlasting life to which you were called, when in the presence of many witnesses, you made your noble profession of faith."

There are times when a Christian has to fight like a soldier in war or like an athlete in a contest; like a person born in poverty or like someone with a handicap. There are times when we have to be bold, not timid; aggressive, not passive; daring, not hesitant. For example, there are still Christians living behind the Iron Curtain. In the midst of persecution they have to fight fiercely—not with weapons of war, but with the weapons of prayer and determination.

There are Christians suffering in hospitals with sickness and disease. To overcome their sadness and hopelessness they have to fight to keep their faith in the healing and resurrecting power of Christ. There are married couples living in a secular society. To conquer the trend to materialism and self-indulgence they have to fight to keep their Christian perspective of the superiority of what is eternal over what is temporal.

No matter who we are or in what state of life we are, there are times when we have to fight the good fight of faith. Sometimes we feel like a medical student who is depressed because he has just failed his exams. But if we are eventually going to reach our goals we have to fight against discouragement and keep alive our determination.

Sometimes we feel like giving up in our marriage or in our priesthood because everything seems futile. But if we are going to persevere in our vocation we have to fight the temptation to quit and find again the meaning or purpose of our existence.

Sometimes we suffer a severe loss because our home is burned or our business goes bankrupt. But if we are going to rebuild for the future we have to fight against despair and place our destiny in the hands of the Lord.

How encouraging it is to have gallant women like Loretta Lynn show us how to fight against the barriers of poverty to achieve success. How uplifting it is to have saints like Paul to urge us to fight off difficulties and to put our faith in the Lord Jesus Christ. How inspiring it is to see each other struggling to surmount obstacles and to take a firm hold on the glorious destiny to which we were called.

Twenty-Seventh Sunday of the Year
2 Tm 1:6-14

Enthusiasm

When Mahalia Jackson sang gospel music it was an overwhelming experience. She put so much emotional intensity into her singing that she could make listeners cry with sadness or clap with joy almost at will.

Some criticized Mahalia Jackson's rhythm and her New Orleans style of handclapping as too emotional. But Mahalia would reply: "How can you sing prayerfully of all heaven and earth and all God's wonders without using your hands? I want my hands, my feet, my whole body to speak of the glory of the Lord."

Mahalia Jackson knew what St. Paul meant when he wrote to Timothy: "Stir into a flame the gift of God bestowed on you. The Spirit God has given us is no cowardly spirit, but rather one that makes us strong, loving and wise."

Women like Mahalia Jackson and men like Paul have had a powerful influence on people because they did things with enthusiasm. When they sang or spoke they put so much of themselves into it that they created excitement among their listeners.

Indeed, Mahalia Jackson and Paul were blessed with many natural talents. But the secret of their success was their ability to stir these gifts into a flame, to stimulate the hearts of their audience.

Enthusiasm is the key to success in many areas. It is the electricity which sparks an actor into a superior performance. It is the magic which moves a musician to discover new modes of expression. It is the emotion which inspires an athlete like Magic Johnson to get fired-up over a game.

We need such enthusiasm to witness to our faith. All of us are blessed with many natural talents and with special gifts of the Holy Spirit. But unless we activate them with enthusiasm, they will remain hidden and dormant.

Until we stir into a flame the gift of our faith, we will never kindle a fire in others. We will be card-carrying Christians, but never committed; self-satisfied, but never zealous; servants, but useless servants.

Without enthusiasm no politician ever persuaded the public to vote for him, and no salesman ever convinced his clients to buy his product. This is no less true in religion. Without enthusiasm for prayer and the liturgy we will never persuade others about their value. Without enthusiasm in serving people we will never convince others about the deep satisfaction we find in religion.

Paul says that the Spirit God has given us is no cowardly spirit, but rather one that makes us strong and loving. There is no reason then for us to be timid, bored or listless. We have the Spirit of Jesus, and so we should be disciples who are daring, exciting and energetic.

Sure there will be hardships to bear and disappointments to endure. But we have the Spirit of Jesus, and so we have the strength to overcome them. Consequently, like Mahalia Jackson we can throw ourselves into his service with enthusiasm and not be afraid of failure. Like Paul we can proclaim his power with boldness and not be discouraged by rejection.

If we are enthusiastic about Jesus, then sacrifices become easy, witnessing becomes a joy, and just existing becomes real living. Moreover, our enthusiasm will be contagious, and cause others to experience the excitement of knowing Jesus and the adventure of following him.

Twenty-Eighth Sunday of the Year
2 Tm 2:8-13

No Chaining the Word

When Edward Gierek was the head of the Communist Government in Poland he made a personal visit to the U.S. to extend the foreign trade between the two nations. On the one hand, his visit brought the good news that Poland's economy was expanding and that Poland ranked tenth in world industrial output.

On the other hand, Gierek's visit was a poignant reminder that the Polish people are still under Communist control and that the Church is merely allowed to coexist with Communism. Yet, in spite of Communist interference, the Church has not only survived in Poland but actually thrived. Even under the constant threat of persecution about 80% of the Polish people are still devout Catholics.

This remarkable statistic is an instance of what St. Paul was writing about in his letter to Timothy: "This is the gospel I preach; in preaching it I suffer as a criminal, even to the point of being thrown into chains—but there is no chaining the word of God!"

Enemies of Christ can imprison his apostles, but not his truth. They can exile his teachers, but not his teachings. They can execute his disciples, but never kill his word.

All through history we have witnessed this. St. Stephen was stoned to death for proclaiming Christ, yet his words of forgiveness still ring in our ears. St. Joan of Arc was burned at the stake, yet her commitment to the cause of Christ continues to encourage us even today. St. Thomas More was beheaded for his loyalty to the doctrines of the Church, yet he survives as "A Man for All

Seasons." Alexander Solzhenitsyn was exiled from Russia for writing the truth about Communism, and now his books are spreading this truth all over the world.

If such is the power of God's word in the lives of saints, should it be less so for us? If only we have faith, there is nothing that can chain the word of God in our lives. Our past sins can't do it. Drug addiction, alcoholism, not even serious crimes can do it, because Christ can heal anybody.

Tragedies can't do it. They may test us, but if the word of God is deeply rooted in our hearts, we will survive the test. Death can't do it. It may damage—almost destroy—our faith, but if the word of God is our line of defense, it will not let death defeat us.

Sometimes we ourselves are the worst enemy of God's word in our lives. God's word may call us to curb our greed or to check our passions. But we sometimes ignore his word and go on our same old way. God's word may rebuke our hypocrisy or selfishness. But we pretend not to hear the word and carry on as usual. God's word may ask us to be more patient and forgiving, or more trusting and generous. But we drown it out with noisy distractions.

There is no chaining the word of God! Like Francis Thompson's "Hound of Heaven" it pursues us relentlessly, always speaking to us, gently inviting us. All we have to do is stop running away and let God's word enter our lives. Only then can we experience the light, peace and joy it brings.

Twenty-Ninth Sunday of the Year
2 Tm 3:14-4:2

Uses of Scripture

The movie *Patton*, starring George Scott, portrays not only the military exploits of General George Patton during World War II, but also some of the inner workings of the man's spirit. In one incident he remarks to the chaplain that he reads his Bible every night before he retires to sleep. He realized that unless he relied on divine power, all his military power would be useless.

General Patton would swagger and swear in front of his men to instill fearlessness in them, but behind the scenes he would read the Scriptures. At the battlefront he would bark orders with the utmost cockiness, but behind the lines he would search the Scriptures as the source of his confidence. Time and again when he felt weak and wanted to quit, he would turn to the Bible and find strength to go on.

St. Paul had a deep respect for the Scriptures and their different uses. He writes to Timothy: "From your infancy you have known the Scriptures, the source of wisdom which through faith in Jesus leads to salvation. All Scripture is inspired of God and is useful for teaching—for reproof, correction and training in holiness."

What we read in the Bible is none other than the word of God himself. Scripture is not a dead word fixed by static print, but a dynamic word spoken to us by a living God. It is not a word which was uttered just once in past history, but an ever-repeating word which speaks to us now about the contemporary scene.

What we hear through the Bible is not the word of a mere man like a prophet or an apostle, but the word of God himself inspiring and speaking through the man. It is not a message we can treat like a commercial on TV, but a proclamation which confronts us with a decision of faith—a decision to say "Yes" or "No" to what God is asking by way of demand or invitation.

The effects and uses of Scripture are many. Sometimes God's word calls us to repentance and healing, as when the prophet Nathan rebuked King David for his adultery and murder. At other times God's word challenges us to do something magnificent, as when Jesus invited the rich young man to sell all his possessions and follow him. Often God's word can give new life by encouraging us to go on in spite of failure, as when Jesus restored his trust in Peter after the apostle had denied him three times.

If we are sad or suffering from pain, God's word can cheer us up with the promise that the sufferings of this life can never be compared with the glory that is to be revealed in us. If we are worried or anxious, God's word can restore calm and peace with parables like the *Lilies of the Field*. If we feel lonely or abandoned, God's word can comfort us with the assurance that he would never leave us orphans but would send the Spirit to dwell with us.

Such is the efficacy of God's word in Scripture. No matter where we are or how we feel, God's word can speak to us with a message that is personal, timely and relevant. But perhaps the most startling effect of God's word is its power to change people's lives.

In the Old Testament we see how God's word made such an impact on Moses and Jeremiah that their whole lives were turned around from timid men into fiery prophets. In the New Testament we see how the words of Jesus made such a deep impression on Zacchaeus and the Samaritan woman that they were transformed from sinners into disciples. God's word can change us too, if only we open ourselves up to let its power operate in us.

Thirtieth Sunday of the Year
2 Tm 4:6-8, 16-18

Fighting and Finishing

The Texas history and legends surrounding the story of the Alamo have been set in prose, poetry, drama and film. Among the best of these is an epic poem *The Alamo* written in 1906 by Viola Riley Berry.

She writes: "Within the church like gods, they fight. Here, one by one, they fall. The altar raised for prayer and praises sweet is baptized with their blood. Ere the sun has reached his zenith, the massacre is complete. The martyrs lie, surrounded by their slain. A smile of triumph rests upon each face as though they gaze through time and space and know their sacrifice is not in vain. And while they died that glorious death, eternity looked down and laid upon each martyred brow fame's everlasting crown."

While St. Paul's words are not as poetic as Viola Riley Berry's, what he says to Timothy about his own battles could easily be repeated by those brave heroes at the Alamo: "I have fought the good fight, I have finished the race, I have kept the faith. From now on a merited crown awaits me."

The imagery Paul uses is that of the arena where athletes competed in games and races. But his imagery has become applicable to any kind of struggle—military, political, personal. Nothing could better describe the Christian life. Indeed, it is a struggle—against Satan and his agents; against our selfishness and undisciplined appetites; against sickness, poverty and injustice.

To fight the good fight and to feel a deep satisfaction with our performance, we have to train intensively, prepare thoroughly and give every last ounce of energy during the contest. In the Christian life this might mean training ourselves with penance and self-denial, preparing with prayer and Sacred Scripture, and doing our best to love and serve one another.

It is sometimes easy to begin a project or a race, but it is not always easy to finish. Not all of us have the staying-power to match our early enthusiasms. On the one hand, it makes us sad to see a famous person begin his career in glory and fame, only to end it in disgrace and shame. On the other hand, we admire people who finish their careers even more illustriously than they began them—people like Winston Churchill, Lou Gehrig and Helen Hayes.

If we were to die today and someone were to write our biography, what would the final chapter be like? Would it tell of how we quit when the going got rough, or how we persevered in the quest of our ideals in spite of the difficulties?

When Paul talks about keeping the faith, he has in mind the keeping of the rules of the Olympic Games. It was customary before the games for the competitors to take a solemn oath before the gods. They would swear that they had trained for ten months and that they would not resort to any trickery to win.

Every Sunday we renew our pledge to keep the rules of the Christian life. But do we keep these rules during the week? Do we ever take unfair advantage of someone? Do we ever do anything dishonorable or dishonest? Do we ever hurt or disappoint someone?

The merited crown mentioned by Paul refers to the laurel wreath that was awarded to the winner in the arena contests. To wear this wreath was the greatest honor an athlete could achieve, and yet in a few short days this crown would wither.

What kind of crown are we striving for? Is it the passing one of popularity, power or possessions? Or is it the one Paul strove for—the crown which never fades, the one reserved in heaven for us?

Thirty-First Sunday of the Year
2 Th 1:11-2:2

Doomsday

When the Peanuts gang went to camp one summer in Charles Schulz's comic strip, they heard a speaker say that the world was coming to an end. Peppermint Patty was worried about this. As she shared her anxieties with Charlie Brown, she told him what her friend Marcie had told to her: "The world can't end today because it's already tomorrow in Australia." Charlie Brown responded: "Maybe we should go to Australia."

Every age has its prophets of doom predicting the end of the world. St. Paul's era was no exception. Apparently some preacher had been using Paul's name to upset the Thessalonians with just such a prophecy and so Paul had written to calm their fears: "On the question of the coming of our Lord Jesus Christ and our being gathered to him, we beg you, brothers, not to be so easily agitated or terrified, whether by an oracular utterance or rumor or a letter alleged to be ours, into believing that the day of the Lord is near."

Paul is brilliant in the way he handles the situation. He knows that some of the Thessalonians will get so caught-up with this Last Day idea that they will give up doing everything just to wait for that Day to come. So he tells them not to be easily agitated or terrified. Alarm, panic and hysteria are not the mark of a true Christian. Real followers of the Lord look forward to his second coming with calmness, confidence and courage.

Nor is it the mark of a true Christian to neglect his daily duties to wait in idleness for the Day of the Lord. Real disciples are doers of his word and builders of his kingdom.

But Paul also realizes that there is some truth in the prediction that the Day of the Lord is near. In a sense the end of the world happens for us on the day of our death. However, here too the best preparation is not to worry about it or to give up our responsibilities. Instead, the best way to get ready for the Lord is to *do* our daily duties. This is why Paul says earlier: "We pray for you always that our God may make you worthy of his call, and fulfill by his power every honest intention and work of faith."

Paul's advice is so important that Fr. Caussaude even calls it the Sacrament of the Present Moment. In other words, the most perfect thing we can do at any moment is precisely what our duty is at that particular moment.

It doesn't matter whether we read the Bible or read the newspaper; attend Mass or attend a family party; receive a sacrament or receive a visitor. Whatever is our responsibility at that moment is the most perfect work of faith we can perform for the Lord.

There is the story of a saintly monk who was relaxing during the recreation period at the monastery by watching television. When another monk came rushing in with the announcement that the end of the world was at hand, this saintly monk continued to watch his program instead of rushing off to the chapel to pray. He felt that he was doing what he was supposed to be doing at that moment—relaxing and recreating in the presence of the Lord.

We shouldn't become upset then about when the end of the world will come. But we should get excited about meeting our daily commitments. We shouldn't become disturbed about when or how our death will come. But we should be dedicated to our duties of the present moment—a call to labor or to leisure, to prayer or to play. Only in this way will Jesus be glorified in us and we in him.

Thirty-Second Sunday of the Year
2 Th 2:16-3:5

Steadfast Endurance

In an article about Eleanor Roosevelt, columnist Ellen Goodman wrote: "She became a great lady, not because she was a first lady, but because she was able through enormous will to turn her pain into strength, to turn disappointment into purpose. The facts, just the facts, of her life might have defeated any of us."

What are some of these facts? As a child she wore a brace for her back, was called an ugly duckling by her mother, and became an orphan at age ten. As a woman she cared for her husband, Franklin, when he was stricken with polio and after ten years of marriage and six children saw him fall in love with another woman.

Yet, in spite of all this, she got involved in programs to help the poor, supported civil rights when it was still an unpopular cause, promoted women in government, and worked for human rights through the United Nations.

Arthur Schlesinger paid this tribute to Eleanor Roosevelt: "Her life was both ordeal and fulfillment. It combined vulnerability and stoicism, pathos and pride, frustration and accomplishment, sadness and happiness."

Eleanor lived what St. Paul hoped would happen in the lives of the Thessalonians: "May the Lord console your hearts and strengthen them for every good work and word. May the Lord direct your hearts toward the love of God and the steadfast endurance of Christ."

In this passage Paul is focusing on a twofold aspect of the Christian life: its inward and outward characteristics. The inward characteristic is an awareness of the love of God: we have a Father who created us because he loves us; he sent his Son Jesus because he loves us; he pours out his Holy Spirit into our hearts because he loves us.

This inward characteristic is a strong realization that we can never lose this love no matter how much we sin or how far we wander from the Lord. He is always rich in mercy and ready to forgive.

Furthermore, this inward characteristic is like a deep calm because we rest secure in the love of God. It is a calm far removed from all worry and anxiety because we are confident that the Lord will always "protect us in the shadow of his wings and keep us as the apple of his eye" (Psalm 17).

The outward characteristic of the Christian life is the steadfast endurance of Christ. Even though Christ was misunderstood by his listeners, attacked by the Pharisees and abandoned by his apostles, he still remained steadfast in his mission. Christ was so determined to do his Father's will of teaching, healing and serving us that he endured even death on a cross for us.

We live in an age when steadfast endurance is difficult to practice. The increase of divorces among married couples, the betrayal of public trust among government officials, and suicides as an escape from responsibility all tend to make steadfast endurance look impossible.

Still we have the example of Jesus himself. When others break, Christians should stand erect with Christ. When others collapse, we should shoulder our burdens and go on. By ourselves we cannot do it, but with the Lord to strengthen us we can face anything, cope with anything, endure anything.

Not all of us will be required to go through what Eleanor Roosevelt experienced in terms of trials and suffering. But all of us can serve one another with the same inward peace she had and with the same outward generosity she showed.

Thirty-Third Sunday of the Year
2 Th 3:7-12

Work

Based on an article in *Esquire* magazine, the movie *Urban Cowboy* recounts the tale of a typical working class male, played by John Travolta. He comes off a ranch in the rural area to the big city of Houston to work in a ship channel refinery.

His job is drab and boring, and so he bolsters his frustrated cowboy ego by means of his nightly recreations. These occur at a honky-tonk known as Gilley's, famous for its mechanical bull contests, punching bag machines and duded-up cowboys and girls doing the two-step.

The urban cowboy is typical of many workers in contemporary society who no longer find meaning and satisfaction in their jobs or professions. The reasons are many: the work itself might be very drab; the worker himself might be suffering from job burnout; the boss may be the kind who is never satisfied; fellow employees might be unsociably cliquish.

Whatever the cause, more and more we see workers just "hanging in there" till quitting time so their "real life" can begin at the nearest corner bar, club room, fitness center, disco dance hall or honky-tonks like Gilley's.

Work was a problem in St. Paul's day, too. He writes about it to the Thessalonians: "You know how we did not live lives of disorder when we were among you, nor depend on anyone for food. Rather, we worked day and night, laboring to the point of exhaustion so as not to impose on any of you. Indeed, when we were with you we used to lay down the rule that anyone who would not work should not eat."

The guideline Paul gives has been called "the golden rule of work." He was probably borrowing an old workshop slogan coined by some industrious workman to deal with lazy apprentices. If the apprentice didn't work, he was forbidden to sit down to dinner. The Jews had another proverb which says, "He who does not teach his son a trade, teaches him to steal." The Jews were firm believers in the dignity of hard work.

In his book *The Theology of Work* Fr. Chenu takes note of man's destiny to be the master of the universe. This is one of the revelations of Genesis. Each conquest man makes over matter, space and time brings him closer to his own personal fulfillment. Man is not only *homo sapiens*, but also *homo artifex*. That is, man is not only a thinker who can contemplate with his mind, but also a craftsman who must work with his hands.

Chenu also sees work as an extension of the Incarnation. By the Incarnation, Christ united our humanity with his divinity in order to redeem us. In a similar way, by our work we bring about an interaction of matter and spirit in order to transform the universe. Redemption then is not only something interior and personal to us, but also something exterior and cosmic. Our work is the Lord's instrument in creating a new earth and a new heaven.

Moreover, in Chenu's view work is an expression of our unity with one another. When we work we not only acknowledge our dependence on others, but also render a service for them. Our mutual exchange of work strengthens our social solidarity, increases our feeling of fraternity, and gives us the satisfaction of contributing something to the common good.

It doesn't matter then whether we sweep the streets or the kitchen floor, or whether we work in the mills or in the stores. What does matter is that we see the nobility and dignity of whatever we do. Work is part of our vocation to conquer the universe; it is an extension of the Incarnation; and it is an expression of our unity.

Thirty-Fourth Sunday of the Year
Col 1:12-20

What He Has Done

At the time when Gerald Ford took over the office of President from Richard Nixon, Fr. Hesburgh of Notre Dame made this comment: "We tend to look for the one man who will solve all our problems. If the American people have one overriding fault, it is the expectation that some man on a white horse is going to come along and lead us all across the Delaware. But the modern world is too complex for that. No one person can be the complete leader. We have need for all members of a community to be involved in working out the future of society."

The Feast of Christ the King suggests a similar train of thought. Christ is the King of the universe, but not the type of king who takes over and solves all our difficulties while we do nothing except say "thank you." He is the King who deserves our honor, but whom we honor most by taking responsibility for our own lives and for the needs of others.

If we are sincere and do our part, then Christ will not stand by idly. In fact, he has already done much for us. We need only review what St. Paul writes to the Colossians: "Through him we have redemption, the forgiveness of our sins. In him everything in heaven and on earth was created. In him everything continues in being. It is he who is the head of the body, the first-born of the dead, making peace through the blood of his cross."

Indeed, the Lord has already done much for us. But he wants to do still more. The seeds of his kingdom of peace and love have already been planted, but they will not reach their fruition except through, with and in us. The sun of the Lord's kingdom of light and life has already dawned on the horizon of history, but it will not reach its zenith unless we make it happen.

When we work together under the leadership of Christ, we can do great things. For example, we have made progress in resolving some of the problems dealing with racism, migrant workers and nuclear disarmament; improvements have been made regarding women's liberation, retirement benefits of senior citizens and getting new immigrants settled.

Still there is much to be done to make Christ's kingdom more visible. Famine in the Third World, pollution of our water and air, the rising rates of divorces and abortions, the energy crisis and the auto industry layoffs are problems we still have to solve.

In the face of such conditions it is easy to get discouraged and say that Christ's kingdom of peace and justice is too unrealistic, impossible to attain, and a dream that will never work. But as disciples of Christ we are never permitted to have such an attitude.

When we recite our Credo we profess our faith in the power of God to conquer all difficulties. All we have to do is make that power operative in our lives and in society.

When we pray the Our Father we express our hope in the coming of Christ's kingdom, not just at the end of time, but right now and as daily as the bread we ask for.

When we receive the Eucharist we renew our love for one another—the only convincing sign of Christ's kingdom here on earth and the foreshadowing of that kingdom in heaven.

We cannot expect our President, or even Christ, to solve all our problems. It is true that Christ has already won the victory over sin and death, but it still remains for us to claim that victory for ourselves and to make it a real thing in the world. We can't just pray for peace; we have to experience it ourselves and pass it on to others. We can't just preach justice; we have to get involved promoting it and even push for it. We can't just talk about love; we have to express it in action and practice it.

Alphabetical Listing of Homily Titles

Abraham's Faith	Page 71
Addams, Jane	59
Adoption	157
Alexander the Great	285
All Men	313
All Things	167
All Things Are Yours	65
Amazing Grace	19
Amnesty	309
Aslan The Lion	251
Baptism of the Holy Spirit	297
Bearing Lovingly	191
Becoming	149
Believing and Obeying	129
Best, The	15
Beyond All Price	35
Bicentennial Saint	101
Bite the Bullet	21
Blood	159
The Body	161
Brought Back	27
Brought Near	189
Butterflies	93
Called	55
Christ Crucified	137
Christmas with Mame	131
Circus, The	233
City Lights	259
Come	261
Coping	107
Courage	177

333

Creation's Destiny	81
Crisis	229
Death and Beyond	115
Death to Life	31
Dedication	53
Die Once	221
Discipline	305
Discrimination	203
Doomsday	325
Enriching Others	183
Enthusiasm	317
Ever Ready	41
Faisal, King	119
Faith Conquers	145
Faith in the Unseen	301
Faith and Works	205
Family Life	13
Fellowship	49
Fight the Good Fight	315
Fighting and Finishing	323
First Fruits	275
Forgiveness	147
Freedom Festival	289
Fresh Way	193
Gandhi and Paul	271
Glory of God, The	169
God's Handiwork	139
God Is Love	153
God's Word	201
Great Hope, The	43
Handing Over	265
Heaven	63

He Emptied Himself	29
He's Been There	215
He Set Me Apart	283
Honor Society	307
Hunchback, The	235
Image of the Invisible	293
Influential Books	213
In the Holy Spirit	47
Irrevocable	91
Jesus Is Lord	239
Jesus Saves	219
Joy in Suffering	295
Judgment	67
Kansas Model, The	57
Lawrence of Arabia	73
Leadership and Suffering	211
Life by the Spirit	79
Liberator	225
Light In The Lord	25
Love Impels Us	181
Love Poured Out	23
Marks of Jesus	291
Marriage and Celibacy	165
Married Love	199
Masterpiece	223
New Birth	33
New Creature, A	245
New Heavens	125
New Life	77
New Unleavened Bread	249
No Chaining the Word	319

Obedience	141
Offer Your Bodies	95
Oh God	263
One Body	269
One Bread, One Body	51
O'Neill, Eugene	85
One Step Away	243
Operation SAMM	75
Our Deepest Needs	187
Patience	7
Perseverance	303
Pioneers and Settlers	69
Power of Persuasion	61
Praying in the Spirit	83
Present Opportunities	197
Priests	217
Procrastination	3
Profiles in Scripture	5
Raised Up With Christ	143
Reaching the Goal	247
Recommendations	173
Reflection of the Father's Glory	237
Rejoice Always	127
Rejoicing	45
Renaissance Center	257
Renaissance Man	277
Restoration	241
Revitalization Corps	89
Riches	209
Richly Endowed	123
Roots	273
Scrooge	11
Seeing God	155

Show Me	151
Sills, Beverly	111
Sin Remembered	311
Something Beautiful	109
Sowing	207
Steadfast Endurance	327
Stray Sheep	37
Struck Down, Not Destroyed	175
Sudden Death	117
Superman	9
Things Above	299
Things That Really Matter	231
Thorn In The Flesh	185
Time Is Short	163
Top Priorities	135
Tramp, The	97
Transcendental Meditation	105
Unity	287
Unity In Space	103
Universality	17
Uses of Scripture	321
Values	281
Variety of Gifts	267
Victory	279
Vietnam War Vet	87
Water	133
Way of Love, The	195
We Are the Lord's	99
We Walk By Faith	179
What He Has Done	331
Winners	255
Wonder, Stevie	113
Work	329

Yes	171
You're a Good Man, Jesus Christ	253
Your Own Best Friend	39

INDEX

Abraham 71, 301
Academy and Institute of Arts and Letters 307
Addams, Jane 59
Adoption 157
Ahern, Barnabas 202
Alamo, The 323
Alcoholics Anonymous 77, 147, 189
Alexander the Great 285
Alpert, Herb 63
Alvarez, Walter 299
Amazing Grace 20
Amnesty 309
Anderson, Marian 145
Apollo-Soyuz 103
Armour, Richard 213
Aslan the Lion 251
Attucks, Crispus 35
Authors Who Have Shaped Our Lives 213

Bacharach, Burt 63
Balthasar 112
Baptism 34, 53, 77, 133, 297
Baptism of the Holy Spirit 297
Barnes, Mary 43
Basketball 51
Bayh, Marvella 177
Because He Lives 252
Becoming 149
Bellow, Saul 152
Benoit, Pierre 82
Berger, Arthur 139
Berkowitz, Bernard 39
Berry, Viola Riley 323
Beyond Boredom and Anxiety 170
Bible—*see* Scripture
Bill W. 189
Blood 35, 159
Blustein, Allen 185
Body 95, 161, 235, 241, 269
Bogart, Humphrey 177, 229
Bonanza 305
Bonnington, Chris 245
Booker, Vaughn 37
Boone, Debbie 260
Boone, Pat 79
Boswell, Charley 25
Braaten, Carl 280
Bristol, Claude 208

Brought Near 189
Brown, Charlie 99, 253, 325
Building the Human 289
Burns, George 263
Butterflies 93
Byron, William 183

Calder, Alexander 95
Caldwell, Sarah 53
Call 30, 55, 59, 266, 283, 301
Camus, Albert 206
Carney, Art 45
Carroll, James 276
Cash, Johnny 47
Cathedral 125
Caussaude, Fr. 326
Celebrate Your Existence 127
Celibacy 165
Chavez, Cesar 55, 61, 155
Chay, Juan 171
Chenu, Fr. 330
Chesterton, G.K. 42
Christenson, *Larry* 199
Christian Family, The 199
Christmas Carol, A 11
Chronicles of Narnia, The 251
Circus 233
Clarke, Wally 87
Cleaver, Eldridge 283
Coal Miner's Daughter 315
Coll, Ed 89
Colson, Charles 201, 246
Comic-Stripped American, The 139
Comito, Nick 203
Conquer 87, 107, 119, 145, 256
Conversion 19, 37, 41, 47, 55, 75, 147, 189, 249, 283, 311
Cook, Fred 75
Courage 25, 177, 229, 323
Crisis 229
Cross 138, 291, 295
Cruise Missile 179
Csikszentmihalyi, Prof. 170
Cuban refugees 17

David, Hal 63
da Vinci, Leonardo 223
Death 31, 115, 117, 177, 221, 229, 275, 280

339

DeBolt Family, The 13
Dedication 53, 89, 315
de Foucald, Charles 41
Denver, John 263
Dependence 99
Dickens, Charles 10
Difficulties 21, 25, 32, 43, 59, 71, 85, 87, 107, 111, 127, 137, 145, 175, 185, 211, 215, 229, 235, 256, 315, 327
Disasters 117, 325
Discipline 21, 248, 305
Discrimination 203
Dodd, C.H. 77
Donahue, Bridget 265
Donne, John 99
Dooley, Tom 221
Dostoevsky, Fyodor 137
Drayton, Jerome 255
Drew, Richard 159
Durwell, F.X. 32
Dutton, Joseph 19

Eareckson, Joni 31
Ehrlichman, John 67
Eight is Enough 167
Einstein, Albert 115
Emmons, Ron 175
Empire Strikes Back, The 141
Enthusiasm 317
Eron, Leonard 201
Eucharist 51, 82, 159, 265
Evely, Louis 45

Faisal, King 119
Faith 69, 71, 129, 145, 175, 179, 205, 298, 301
Falker, Clay 277
Family 13, 167, 199, 305
Fear Strikes Out 91
Fehren, Henry 38
Fellowship 49
Fiddler on the Roof 209
Fidelity 91, 199
Fight 315, 323
Fitzgerald, Edmund 117
Flesh 79
Fonteyn, Margot 199
Ford, Gerald 21, 309, 331
Forestell, Terence 116, 127
Forgiveness 37, 147, 309
Forty Martyrs 295

Fox, Robin Lane 285
Fraschalla, Linda 83
Freedom 225, 289
Freedom to Be 225
Fresh Way 193
Friendly Persuasion, The 219

Gaithers, The 252
Gandhi 151, 206, 271
Geneseo 57
Gierek, Edward 319
Gilmer, Edward 313
Gifts 84, 123, 139, 158, 188, 267, 317
Goodman, Ellen 327
Grace 19, 76, 185, 190, 312
Graduation 149
Grasso, Ella 177
Gray, Don 7
Greene, Graham 29
Gulag Archipelago, The 215

Haley, Alex 273
Haring, Bernard 148
Harper, Theodore 183
Harry and Tonto 45
Hatfield, Mark 201
Hayes, Billy 175
Health resorts 245
Hearst, Patricia 65
Heaven 63, 81, 125, 241, 307
Heikes, Glen 71
Heinlein, Robert A. 97
Hemingway, Ernest 176
Hepburn, Katherine 161
Herron, Mack 107
Hesburgh, Theodore 221, 331
Hiding Place 291
Hind's Feet on High Places 261
Hobos 97, 313
Holly, Buddy 163
Hollyday, Joyce 30
Holy Spirit 24, 27, 47, 83, 110, 112, 297, 318
Home of Our Own, A 217
Honor Society 307
Hope 6, 43, 332
Hope, Bob 157
Howe, Gordie 161
Howe, Irving 191
How To Be Your Own Best Friend 39
Human Factor, The 29

Humility 29
Hunchback of Liberty Hall, The 235
Hurnard, Hannah 261
Hurok, Sol 123
Hutton, Betty 47

I Heard the Lord Call My Name 56
If God is God 153
Incarnation 9, 11, 131, 236, 237, 293
Interpreter's Bible 87, 188
Invitation to Greatness 172

Jackson, Allen 185
Jackson, Jesse 253
Jackson, Mahalia 317
James, William 210
Jaspers, Karl 144
Jerome Biblical Commentary, The 39, 69, 75, 95, 116, 127, 196
Joan of Arc 319
Johann, Robert 212, 289
John Neumann 274, 307
John Paul II 211
Johnson, George 203
Jourard, Sidney 150
Joy 45, 112, 127, 233, 295
Joy of Being Human, The 268
Judaism 89
Judgment 67

Kazakhstan 133
Keller, Helen 155
Kennedy, Eugene 61, 268
Kennedy, John F. 5
Kiley, Richard 105
King 119, 225, 331
King, Martin Luther Jr. 214, 253
Knox, Ronald 308
Koenig, Richard 153
Kosicki, George 297
Kotulak, Ron 193

Lao-Tse 266
Laurentin, Rene 84
Lawrence of Arabia 73
Leadership 211, 225
Leisure 170
Leon-Dufour 92
Lewis, C.S. 251
Light, 25, 259
Little, Joan 67
Livingstone, David 301

Lord is My Shepherd, The 297
Lord 99, 239
Love 23, 73, 89, 97, 113, 151, 153, 155, 181, 191, 195, 199, 205, 265, 271, 285, 308
Lucas, George 141
Lynn, Janet 239
Lynn, Loretta 315
Lyonnet, Stanislaus 82

MacLeish, Archibald 153
Maly, Eugene 125
Mame 131
Marathon 255, 303
Marceau, Marcel 95
Maria Goretti 311
Marriage 165, 199
Mary, Mother of Jesus 15
Masson Wines 7
Materialism 11, 209
Maupin, Ed 105
May, Rollo 306
McIntosh, Barbara 3
McNeill, Mary 167
McNulty, Frank 172
Meaning of Man, The 236
Merton, Thomas 204, 238
Midnight Express 175
Miller, Floyd 235
Migrants, The 197
Miracle Worker, The 155
Moffat, Robert 301
Mohammad 237
Mona Lisa 223
Mooneyham, W. Stanley 205
Mouroux, Jean 236
Mother Teresa 109, 155, 182, 271
Motivation 75
Mt. Everest 247
Muggeridge, Malcolm 109, 182
Muppets 293
My Fair Lady 151

Nearing, Scott 231
New 16, 33, 77, 125, 143, 193, 241, 245, 250, 257, 277
Newman, Mildred 39
Nicholson, Jack 225
Now I See 25
Nureyev, Rudolf 95
Nurmi, Paavo 303

341

Obedience 129, 141
O'Brian, Hugh 33
O'Brien, William 297
Oh God 263
Oliver, Lucille 127
Onassis, Christina 65
O'Neill, Eugene 85
One Flew Over the Cuckoo's Nest 225
Open to the Spirit 141
Operation SAMM 75
Orsy, Ladislaus 141

Parker, Curtis 147
Passages 230
Passmore, William 127
Pasteur, Louis 115
Patience 7
Paton, Alan 195
Patten, Robert 11
Patton, George 321
Paul VI 12, 61
Paz, Nestor 23
Peifer, Claude 66
Pele 95
Pentecost 47
Perseverance 175, 247, 303, 324, 328
Persuasion 61, 109
Pierce, Hattie 207
Piersall, Jim 91
Pioneers and Settlers 69
Playboy to Priest 55
Prayer 83, 105, 128
Present Moment 3, 197, 326
Prewitt, Cheryl 27
Priests 217
Procrastination 3
Profiles in Courage 5

Queen Elizabeth II 47

Rahner, Karl 218
Ranall-el, Cecil 75
Readiness 41, 325
Redemption 81, 219, 241
Reichley, Ken 10
Rejoicing 45, 127, 233
Re-Member Me 160
Renaissance 257, 277
Resurrection 27, 31, 116, 143, 241, 251, 275, 279
Revitalization Corps 89
Reynolds, Roberta 26

Roberts, Ken 55
Rogers, Bill 303
Roosevelt, Eleanor 327
Roots 273
Rovit, Earl 176
Rudolph, Wilma 279
Ryan, Nolan 187
SALT 179
Sanskrit 4
Saraceno, Peter 83
Schlesinger, Arthur 327
Schweitzer, Albert 33, 271, 314
Scripture 5, 201, 213, 319, 321
Scrooge 11
Seduction of Joe Tynan, The 243
Seeliger, Wes 69
Self-esteem 39, 50, 139, 168, 273, 277
Selye, Hans 128
Serenelli, Allessandro 311
Seton, Elizabeth Ann 101
Shakespeare 85, 140, 224
Shalom: Peace 148
Shea, John 294
Sheehy, Gail 230
Shepherd 37, 261
Sherman, Harold 208
Shostrom, Everett 225
Sills, Beverly 111
Sin Remembered 311
Slovik, Ed 118
Social Justice 44, 61, 205
Solzhenitsyn, Alexander 49, 152, 215, 281, 320
Something Beautiful for God 109
Sowing 207
Spirit 79, 188
Stanley, David 32
Steinmetz, Charles 235
Storm, Gail 249
Strength 59, 109, 185
Stress of Life 128
St. Stephen 319
Sullivan, Ann 155
Summer, Donna 143
Superman, the Movie 9
Stewardship 183
Suffering 211, 215, 291, 295

Tagore 114
ten Boom, Corrie 291

342

Thanksgiving 128
That's Entertainment 267
Thomas, Danny 129
Thomas More 319
Thompson, Francis 320
Thomsen, Bob 189
Tigar, Clement 295
Time 3, 163, 197, 230, 325
TNT—The Power Within You 208
Tongues 84
Toward Stewardship 183
Tramp, The 97
Transformation 93, 125, 193
Travolta, John 329
Trinity 49, 157, 263
Truelock, Louis 75
Tubman, Harriet 181
Turning Point 135
Tynan, Joe 243

Ulanov, Galina 123
Unity 17, 51, 57, 103, 191, 269, 287, 309
Universality 17, 313
Unleavened Bread 249
Urban Cowboy 329
Ustinov, Peter 287

Values 136, 210, 231, 281, 292, 300
Vanier, Jean 155
Van Patten, Dick 167
Vatican Council II 184

Vawter, Bruce 117, 151
Victory 279
Vietnam War Vet 87
Violence 201
Walters, Barbara 187
Water 81, 133
Warsaw 241
Wasson, William 217
Wayne, John 177
Weakness 59, 185
Weaver, Eula 193
Weber, Nick 233
Welles, Orson 7
West, Jessamyn 219
What Do You Say to a Hungry World? 205
Will of God 102, 141, 171
Wilson, Bill 189
Winners 255
Wine 7
Wisdom 93
Wise, Joe 160
Witness 30, 41, 109, 114, 155, 174, 181, 254, 266
Woman Called Moses, A 181
Wonder, Stevie 113
Wood, Bob 265
Work 169, 329
World of Our Fathers 191
World Vision International 205
Wozniak, Bertrand 77
Wrigley Building 259
You're a Good Man, Charlie Brown 253